A PECULIAR CRUSADE

JAMES J. WEINGARTNER

A PECULIAR CRUSADE

Willis M. Everett and the Malmedy Massacre

New York University Press • *New York and London*

NEW YORK UNIVERSITY PRESS
New York and London

Library of Congress Cataloging-in-Publication Data
Weingartner, James J., 1940–
A peculiar crusade : Willis M. Everett and the Malmedy massacre /
James J. Weingartner.
  p.   cm.
Includes bibliographical references (p.   ) and index.
ISBN 0-8147-9366-5 (alk. paper)
1. Malmedy Massacre, 1944–1945. 2. Everett, Willis Mead, 1900–1960.
3. War crime trials—Germany. 4. Lawyers—United States—Biography.
5. World War, 1939–1945—Atrocities.   I. Title.
D804.G4 W39 2000
940.54'05'0949346—dc21   00-010318

New York University Press books are printed on acid-free paper,
and their binding materials are chosen for strength and durability.

Manufactured in the United States of America

10 9 8 7 6 5 4 3 2 1

Contents

	Preface	vii
1	The Everetts of Atlanta	1
2	The Internal Enemy	15
3	The World beyond Atlanta	27
4	Under the Lights	49
5	Of the Particulars and Charge, Guilty	75
6	Death by Hanging	107
7	A Troublesome Conscience	117
8	An Old-Fashioned Sense of Justice	143
9	"The Lord Has Given Me Strength to Continue"	177
10	A Michael Kohlhaas in Atlanta	198
	Epilogue	224
	Notes	229
	Index	249
	About the Author	257

All illustrations appear as a group following p. 134.

Preface

This is a book about World War II, but not in the usual sense. It is the biography of a man whose life was profoundly affected by that war, although he never experienced combat and remained in the United States throughout its duration. Nevertheless, his is a story of fortitude, self-sacrifice, and, in a strange way, comradeship rooted in the killing grounds of wartime Europe.

Willis M. Everett Jr. was the key figure in the most controversial of the postwar trials of Nazi war criminals. Without him, former Nazi SS men convicted of wholesale murder, who lived to return to their homes and families, would likely have gone to the gallows. Without him, Senator Joseph McCarthy would have been denied a means of gaining national attention. Service to Nazis and McCarthy seems to have consigned Everett to the lowest circle of the democratic Hell. Moreover, he shared the racial prejudices common to his time and place, referred to African Americans as "niggers," and was often openly anti-Semitic. Contemporary political correctness would have little difficulty vilifying Everett and might suggest a link between Everett's racial prejudices and his ferocious defense of Nazis.

But such an assumption would be badly off the mark. Everett expressed no sympathy for National Socialism. His racial biases, no surprise in someone who had grown to adulthood in early twentieth-century Georgia, were intertwined with remarkable generosity and humaneness, as well as with an unyielding and sometimes painful sense of personal responsibility and duty. He was not an intellectual and, although associated with the U.S. Army for much of a life that spanned two world wars, served as a desk soldier. Yet, he understood the moral conundrum of total war better than many of his contemporaries and believed that it was possible for SS troops of the Third Reich to have been the victims of Allied injustice. Not only did Everett believe this; he waged an extraordinary ten-year campaign to correct the situation. It was not a popular cause, but he persisted on to a quasi-victory. His "old-fashioned sense of justice and fairness," he once said, had left him no choice.

This biography is the outgrowth of a project undertaken in the 1970s. My study of the Malmedy massacre and trial, published in 1979, introduced me to Everett, an attorney from Atlanta, Georgia, who served as chief defense counsel for the former German SS men who were tried by the U.S. Army in 1946 for the murders of hundreds of American prisoners of war and Belgian civilians during the Battle of the Bulge. As the person who not only led the defense of the seventy-four defendants but subjected the investigation and trial to ten years of invective that were instrumental in the eventual release of the Germans, all of whom had been convicted and more than half of whom had been sentenced to death, Everett received considerable attention in the earlier book. But he remained in many respects an enigma. Other American lawyers fought doggedly for their former enemies in the many lesser war crimes trials, which were often obscured by the shadow of Nuremberg, but none devoted himself to the task with the passion that Everett displayed. What motivated him? Was it simply a lawyerly recognition of problematic aspects of the Army's investigation and trial of an emotionally charged case, or was Everett's pursuit of his ideal of justice for an almost universally hated enemy the result of a more complex body of impulses? Although Everett was the directing force behind challenges to the Malmedy trial, he could not have succeeded without surprisingly numerous and diverse allies. Who were they, and what motivated them? What insights into an American society "digesting" the experience of history's most devastating war might the answers to these questions provide? Evidence of continued public fascination with the controversy surrounding the Malmedy massacre and trial, in the form of frequent comments and queries from readers of the earlier book, as well as the making of a television documentary, produced in 1993, in which I participated as consultant and "talking head," convinced me that others shared my interest in answers to these questions.

Many people contributed to the making of this book. Without the cooperation of Willis M. Everett III, who made available his father's papers and shared memories of the man whom he customarily calls "Colonel Everett," it could not have been written. William Hartman, Tom Forkner, and Kiliaen Townsend contributed important insights into Everett's wartime career in domestic intelligence gathering, "Kil" adding the perspective of the subject's son-in-law. James Critchfield provided recollections of Everett as a fellow student in the army European Studies course at Columbia University, and Selma Richardson spoke movingly of Everett's support of higher education for African Americans. Thanks are due to George Goodwin, for sharing his memories of the Everett family and his seemingly boundless knowledge of Atlanta history and society. Thanks, too, to Dave McKenney, for his recollections of the "Wooglin." Valuable insights into Everett's conduct as defense counsel from opposite sides of the courtroom were provided by Burton Ellis and Benjamin Narvid for the earlier book, and they were equally important to this one. Frances A. Smith, of the Alumni Office of Washington and Lee University, generously gave of her time to locate material on Everett's student days. Joseph Halow shared his experiences of war crimes justice at Dachau. Danny Parker contributed valuable documentary materials from his own research on the Malmedy massacre. Belinda Carstens-Wickham assisted me in understanding the significance of a relevant character in German literature, and Norman Nordhauser answered questions on U.S. history. My indefatigable graduate student, Paul Brown, suggested sources of information that had not occurred to me. John Bier, John W. Gay III, Sam Hodges Jr., Bishop James Thomas, Dr. Goodman Espy, Frank Troutman, Dr. Carter Smith, Jack Spalding, Congressman Robert Stephens, William Stroud, Stephen Sanders Jr., and Charles Whiting all graciously donated time and memories.

Professional archivists are crucial to the accomplishment of the historian's craft. Amy Schmidt and Wilbert Mahoney, of the U.S. National Archives' splendid "Archives II" at College Park, Maryland, provided efficient and cheerful assistance, while the Archives' Still Picture Branch quickly located appropriate photographs. Peggy Cox, of the National Personnel Records Center in Overland, Missouri, assisted in the location of Everett's service records, while Russell Nichols and Joanne Benear, of the U.S. Army Intelligence and Security Command at Fort Meade, Maryland, facilitated my access to relevant documents. The staff of Gammon Theological Seminary in Atlanta, Georgia, graciously made available useful records.

Thanks are due to Niko Pfund, Despina Gimbel, and the editorial staff of New York University Press for making the unavoidably stressful process of evaluation and production an almost pleasant experience. A sabbatical leave granted by Southern Illinois University at

Edwardsville allowed me to complete the project much earlier than would otherwise have been possible.

Jane, my wife, has lived with this project for almost four years and contributed to its completion in critical ways. Without her insightful comments, editorial skills, and mastery of word-processing technology, this book would be much the poorer.

The Everetts of Atlanta

THE EVERETT FAMILY was not of the Old South, but, then, neither was Atlanta. Willis Mead Everett and his new bride settled there in 1888, less than fifty years after Atlanta was established as a railroad and commercial center. Everett was of old Yankee stock, with roots that extended back, on his father's side, to seventeenth-century Massachusetts and, on his mother's, to Kiliaen van Rennselaer, first patroon of Rennselaerwyck in New Holland. Timothy, his father, had commanded a company of the sixty-fourth New York Infantry during the Civil War, and it was in the midst of that terrible conflict that Willis was born, on November 18, 1863, in Randolph, New York, south of Buffalo and about twelve miles north of the border with Pennsylvania. He graduated from Chamberlain Institute and Female College in Randolph at the age of sixteen and, in 1885, received his A.B. from Allegheny College in Meadeville, Pennsylvania. While a student at Allegheny, he read law in the afternoons with Judge John H. Henderson, of the Pennsylvania Court of Appeals, although his initial postbaccalaureate employment was as professor of mathematics and German at Chamberlain. Also prior to graduation from Allegheny, he served as a passenger agent for steamboats plying Lake Chautauqua, a few miles west of Randolph, in the course of which he met his future wife, Mary Catherine Gillette, born in Schenectady but now of Atlanta, who may have been attending one of the enormously popular adult education sessions held nearby. In 1886, Everett moved to Cincinnati, where he was admitted to the Ohio bar and opened a law office with his brother, Charles. The practice does not appear to have prospered, as much of his income was earned by tutoring students in German, Latin, and mathematics. But his courtship of Mary Gillette was more successful. He visited her in Atlanta during the Christmas season of that year, and, following the death of her mother, the two were married on August 15, 1887. By then, Willis Everett had departed Cincinnati for Illinois and had opened a law office in Chicago.

He and his bride remained there little more than a year before settling permanently in Atlanta in the fall of 1888.[1]

The only direct surviving evidence to explain the motivation for the Everetts' migration south is a much later comment, in their son's hand, that notes laconically that "Chicago was too cold for Mother."[2] A winter on Lake Michigan may well have been grim for one who had become accustomed to the mild climate of Georgia, but the reasons may have extended beyond the meteorological. The Atlanta of 1888 had long since recovered from the devastation of Sherman's "visit" of 1864 and was booming. The 1880s were a pivotal period in the history of Atlanta; it was in that decade that the city emerged as the economic dynamo of the southeastern United States. Its population nearly doubled during the decade, to more than 65,000, and the volume of its commerce approximately tripled. Moreover, the commercial leaders of Atlanta energetically publicized their city's economic dynamism beyond the South and assured northerners that an enthusiastic welcome awaited them. Even Sherman had been cordially received in 1879, when recollections of the unpleasantness of fifteen years earlier had been limited to jocular references to the guest's "carelessness with matches!"[3] In short, Atlanta offered in all respects an appealing climate. Everett was admitted to the Georgia bar and opened a law office in the Judge Marshall Clark Building on Alabama Street. His general practice was a profitable one, and Everett moved easily into the growing *haute bourgeoisie* of Atlanta. The concomitants of professional success and social acceptance—a bank directorship and membership in the prestigious Atlanta Lawyers' Club—were combined with the kind of constructive community service expected of persons of "comfortable" circumstances and, in the case of the Everetts, freely given. They were both active in church affairs; Willis's dedication was eventually rewarded by his election as Moderator of the General Assembly of the Presbyterian Church, U.S. on the second ballot of its seventy-eighth convocation in Meridian, Mississippi, in 1938. Everett's successful acculturation was reflected by a benevolent paternalism toward African Americans, which was common among Atlanta's "better" families, and he provided long service as a trustee of two African American institutions, Clark University and Gammon Theological Seminary.[4]

Professional and social success was accompanied by tragedy. Between 1890 and 1900, Mary and Willis Everett produced four children, only one of whom survived beyond early adulthood. Their first-born,

Charles, died at the age of eight, and a second son, Edward, did not live to see his second birthday. Mary Louise, on the other hand, born on February 16, 1898, blossomed into a young woman of accomplishment and promise. Described as "one of the most popular and beloved young women of Atlanta," she was graduated from Washington Seminary, an elite private school for girls that numbered Margaret Mitchell, the future author of *Gone with the Wind*, among its alumnae, and prepared for a teaching career at Randolph Macon Woman's College in Lynchburg, Virginia. In May 1924, Mary Louise was completing plans to sail to China with her mother for an August wedding to Professor J. Howe, a chemist who had been a member of the faculty of nearby Washington and Lee University, where her brother had been a student, when she was killed by lightning at the family's vacation retreat on St. Simons Island. The short history of Atlanta and the success with which the Everetts had been integrated into its elite was indicated by their daughter's obituary, which identified her as "a descendant of one of Atlanta's oldest and most prominent families."[5]

Willis Mead Everett Jr. joined his parents in mourning for Mary Louise. He was two years his sister's junior and, at the time of her death, had been married for two years to the former Mary Wooldridge, an attractive young Memphis woman whose debut, at "an elaborate dancing party" with more than three hundred guests, had been described as "one of the most brilliant affairs of the season."[6] His marriage had followed preparation for a comfortable niche in Atlanta's "polite" society. The younger Everett's graduation, in 1916, from Atlanta's Peacock High School—segregated as to race, gender, and socioeconomic status (young men destined for manual occupations attended "Tech High")—had been a prelude to separation from the family home on Piedmont Avenue that summer for matriculation at Washington and Lee. The small institution, set in the wooded hills of Lexington, Virginia, was suffused by an aura of southern, elite male culture bequeathed by its namesakes and, in particular, by Robert E. Lee, who was president of then Washington College from 1865 until his death in 1870 and whose grave, located in the campus chapel, must be saluted by passing cadets of neighboring VMI. Institutional mythology records that a newly enrolled student approached Lee for a copy of the college rules. Lee supposedly replied, "We have no printed rules. We have but one rule here, and it is that every student must be a gentleman."[7]

Willis M. Everett Jr. was a gentleman, but no scholar. He entered

Washington and Lee with the intention of preparing for a career in medicine, but his academic performance fluctuated between mediocre and catastrophic, no doubt a result, in part, of his frequent absences from class. The photograph of Willis in his yearbook shows a pleasant, boyish face with broadly spaced, deep-set eyes, a wide mouth, and a somewhat angular nose framed by the slicked-down hair of the period and slightly protruding ears. Maturity would make of it a face that, in combination with his blue eyes and light brown hair, some might consider handsome. At slightly under six feet and weighing about 150 pounds, he was slender and would remain so throughout his life. It was a physique suited to the athletic field and ballroom, and he made good use of it at Washington and Lee. The summary of his college career, which accompanied the yearbook photograph, notes with gentle sarcasm that "Willis has been on the cross-country squad and also given his services to the track team, although heavy laboratory work has always interfered with his athletic ambitions." But it clearly interfered very little with his social life. Since his arrival, it was noted:

> he has been gathering friends from every part of the campus, and can now boast a host of admirers in every part of the country. . . . But it is on the dance floor and in society's vortex that the subject of this sketch is a shining light. Never absent from even the smallest hop and always glad to delight the ladies with his presence, Willis has made himself part of all such festivities here at Washington and Lee.[8]

If seriousness of purpose was not very much in evidence, it was not totally absent. It was during the spring of Everett's freshman year that the United States declared war on Germany. Everett had already enrolled in the recently established Reserve Officers' Training Corps, and he drilled under the direction of an instructor from VMI until May 1918. The remainder of the spring and part of the summer were spent at Plattsburgh, New York, where the War Department had established one of a number of officers' training camps to help provide the junior leadership needed for the mass army being deployed in Europe. He was not commissioned, probably because of his youth, and may not have completed the course. Neither his personal papers nor his military records provide much information. He returned to Washington and Lee early in the fall, served briefly as cadet captain in the campus Student Army Training Corps, and was then taken into the army as a private. He had probably been drafted, as the army had halted voluntary enlistments in August 1918. Again, the records are mute. But his service as an enlisted man was brief, limited to less than two months at the army's coast artillery school at Fort Monroe, Virginia; he was honorably discharged on November 27, 1918. In any event, his academic career was disrupted by the war, and that, along with his generally uninspired academic performance, accounts for the fact that he did not receive his A.B. degree until 1921, after he had presided over the university's Fancy Dress Ball in the company of the lovely Elizabeth Penn of Danville.[9]

A photographic portrait of Willis Everett Sr. in middle age shows the stern, bespectacled face of a man of sober character, appropriate to his standing in the legal profession and the Presbyterian Church. He could not have been pleased by his son's performance at Washington and Lee. The son's grades in the sciences were no better than average and, sometimes, considerably worse than that. A career in medicine was not a viable prospect. But his performance in the humanities and social sciences was no better, and even Bible study resulted in C's and D's. Willis Sr. may have suggested that he join him in his well-established law practice, and Willis Jr. appears to have lacked better prospects. A law school had been one of Robert E. Lee's innovations at what later became Washington and Lee, but Everett's dismal record may have precluded admission. More likely, his father decided that his son required closer paternal supervision. Conveniently, Atlanta had possessed an independent law school since 1890, which had produced a substantial number of successful local attorneys. Attendance at Atlanta Law School during the years 1922–1924, in combination with reading law in his father's office, succeeded in acquiring for the young Willis an LL.B. and admission to the Georgia bar. In the company of his young wife, he could look forward to a secure and comfortable life as a partner in the law firm of Everett and Everett.[10]

Willis M. Everett Sr. was one of Atlanta's most prominent attorneys, and the office that his son joined provided a comfortable income, if not much that could be characterized as exciting or adventurous. The younger Everett later candidly described his professional life as one that involved "abstracts and titles, estates, investments, corporation and civil law"—in short, the typical career of an attorney in general practice.[11] His father was the dominant personality within the firm and appears to have attempted to prolong a parent-child relationship with his son, perhaps because that son was the only one of four children still surviving, perhaps because he believed that his son still required parental supervision. It was a dependent relationship, reinforced by the fact that Willis Jr. and Mary lived in his parents' home on Piedmont Avenue until sometime in 1925. A letter dated January 25, 1925, Willis Jr.'s twenty-fifth birthday, and addressed to "My Dearest Boy" contained assurances of "how much I love you" and an unspecified sum of money to permit his son to "buy something you would like." The balance of the birthday missive suggests paternal concern for a son who was still struggling to attain maturity, self-discipline, and a sense of purpose. "I wish that there was something that I could do that would make you truly happy," the father wrote, and continued with the hope that his son might "accomplish the many things that I have been unable to do." What these might have been was unspecified but it appears they had a predominantly moral, rather than material or professional, character. The only worthwhile thing in life, he assured his son,

> is to help and live for others. And when you have won success, be sure that you never become a "snob." Don't feel that you are better or above others, but be true and helpful to everyone. After all, you will find the purest gold among those who are always helping someone else and are thinking but little of themselves. God bless you and keep you gentle and true to the best in life.[12]

A cynic might pass off this advice as pietism or cant; it does, in any event, contain much of the United Declaration on Christian Faith and Social Service, adopted by Everett's Presbyterian Church, in 1914.[13] The father was clearly intent upon inculcating in his heretofore somewhat sybaritic son a sense of Christian stewardship, which, even if somewhat unsophisticated, would have significant consequences.

It was probably a combination of old-fashioned patriotism, stimulated by World War I, and a desire to establish an identity independent of his father's (the elder Everett had seen no military service) that had led Willis Jr. to apply for a commission in the Officers' Reserve Corps of the U.S. Army before his admission to the bar. His application, routed through the Fourth Corps Area commander, headquartered in Atlanta, to the army's Adjutant General in Washington, D.C., is reflective of a young man unsure of himself and, perhaps, eager to conceal a less than distinguished academic career. He claimed to have been awarded a certificate on the conclusion of his two months at Plattsburgh in 1918, which, he "believed," entitled him to a commission on reaching the age of twenty-one. Whatever the case, the certificate had "since been mislaid." In describing his qualifications for a reserve commission, he noted that he possessed a knowledge of civil engineering and had, in fact, taken two terms in that discipline with "gentleman Cs." Less plausible was his claim to a "fair" speaking knowledge of Spanish, French, and German in light of his having completed introductory and intermediate courses in those languages at Washington and Lee, with grades primarily in the low passing to failing range.[14]

But his academic credentials were of little consequence. Although the National Defense Act of 1920, with the experience of World War I still fresh, had aimed to create an effective mass "citizen army" in which well-trained reserve officers were to play a key role, neither the legislative nor the executive branch of government was willing to support adequate funding for the program. After all, the United States had just fought and won "the war to end all wars," and budgetary frugality was the enthusiasm of the day. As a consequence, the U.S. Army's Officers' Reserve Corps of the interwar period was a ramshackle affair. Preparation was at best haphazard, as the army lacked the financial resources even to require periodic training for all members. In practice, reserve officers volunteered for occasional instruction as they saw fit; some enrolled in correspondence courses, while the competence of others simply evaporated, if it had ever been established.[15]

It is clear that Willis M. Everett Jr.'s appointment as a reserve officer was more a statement of his position as a member of Atlanta's "polite" society than it was a reflection of his suitability to command troops in the field. Franklin S. Chalmers, a partner in the Atlanta law firm of Chalmers and Stewart, wrote a letter in support of his candidacy to the Adjutant General. Chalmers observed that he had been "in personal contact with Mr. Everett and his family for about ten years. His father is one of the foremost members of the Atlanta Bar and Willis is now in his father's office reading law, and from my observation I am satisfied that he will in time become a worth [sic] successor of his father." The author had to admit that he had never seen Everett "on duty with troops," but he had no doubt as to his "qualities of leadership."[16] Everett's application was further buttressed by letters from the Lowry Bank and Trust Company, which assured those judging his suitability for a reserve commission that he had been "a satisfactory depositor in this institution for a long while," and from William R. Hoyt, insurance broker and tenant along with the Everett law firm in Atlanta's Connally Building, who "had never heard anything detrimental in any respect to his character" and deemed him "a high-class honorable gentleman worthy of any commission that might be conferred on him by you."[17] Following a seventy-minute oral examination before a board of reserve officers chaired by none other than "Lieutenant Colonel" Franklin S. Chalmers, Everett was commissioned a reserve second lieutenant of infantry effective May 14, 1923.[18]

Service in the army reserves would remain a feature of Willis Everett's life for thirty years, while he and his wife raised two children: a daughter, Mary Campbell, born in 1923, and a son, Willis Mead III, who followed eleven years later. The younger Everetts became prominent figures in Atlanta society in their own right, evidenced by their eventual membership in Atlanta's exclusive Piedmont Driving Club and in the fashionable First Presbyterian Church, at the corner of Peachtree and Sixteenth Streets, whose congregation included some of the city's most influential families. Although his law practice kept him busy in Everett and Everett's Connally Building office, Willis Jr. had time for his hobby of woodworking, which he pursued with a perfectionist passion; before prior to World War II, he built with his own hands a masonry addition to the elegant Spanish revival house on Rivers Road into which the family moved in 1932. He enjoyed an occasional upland hunt with one of his fine Parker shotguns. The extroversion, which had competed with his classroom performance at Washington and Lee, to the detriment of the latter, now stood him in good stead professionally and socially. He came to know a lot of people, and a lot of people liked him for his easygoing charm and gentleness. Although a nondrinker and a man who did not conceal his conventional Christian piety, he was not inclined to judge harshly those whose conduct was not as strait-laced as his own appeared to be.[19]

But he was also son, father, and husband. His own father remained an important presence in his life until the elder Everett's death in 1943. Not only were the two law partners, but the father remained for the son a model of rectitude whom he revered, perhaps feared. In some respects, Everett emulated his father in the role he assumed in regard to his own children, not spurning worldly success and the material rewards it brought but, at the same time, impressing upon them the imperative of using whatever resources accompanied their privileged positions for the benefit of those less advantageously situated. He set an example of unobtrusive noblesse oblige by frequently providing free legal services to those unable to pay for them, and followed his father in supporting with financial and professional assistance two of Atlanta's African American institutions, Clark University and Gammon Theological Seminary. He was not overbearing in his relationships with his children. His son remembers him as an "easygoing" father, who delighted in making toys for him in his woodworking shop and offering sound, practical advice on coping with life's vicissitudes. His relationship with his wife, Mary, on the other hand, appears to have been less idyllic or, at least, more complex, although this is a decidedly murky area of Everett's life. While family members recall no particular difficulties between the two, beyond tension caused by Everett's penchant for bringing multiple dinner guests home on short notice, letters written by Everett to Mary later in life, during periods of separation due primarily to military service, suggest a desperate effort to reassure his wife of his love for her and a persistent need for assurances that that love was reciprocated. Underlying this current seems to have been Everett's deep sense that he was unworthy of his wife's love, due to vaguely defined inadequacies or misdeeds. Whether this was a chronic pattern within the marriage or a phenomenon precipitated by a specific event cannot now be determined. Suspicions of her husband's infidelity clearly lurked in Mary's mind and, at one point, apparently led her to accuse him of having of an adventure with Margaret Mitchell. Everett admitted to a friendship with the author, but nothing more.[20]

Everett's career as an officer in the interwar army reserves, on the other hand, can be traced with some specificity by means of his service record. Between 1923 and 1932, he advanced from second lieutenant to captain of infantry under circumstances that confirmed the modest military value of the "organized reserves." At the end of 1925, on the basis of fifteen-day training periods in 1924 and 1925 at Fort McPherson, Georgia, and at Camp McClellan, Alabama, and with the approbation of the ever-supportive Franklin Chalmers, now working for Coca-Cola, Everett won promotion to first lieutenant. He was rated "above average," and, his promotion documents note, "he is exceptionally alert and successful in business and will develop and grow to the advantage of the reserve system."[21] And so he may have done. Additional two-week summer stints at army installations in the South, combined with enrollment in an army correspondence course on commanding an infantry company, occupied small fractions of Everett's time away from family and law practice during the mid- and late 1920s. The fractions may have been too small, as a notice in his army file registers his disenrollment from the correspondence course due to failure to make progress during 1928–1929, but the consequences were hardly severe, and he was promoted to captain of infantry early in 1930.[22]

If Everett was seeking a means of establishing an identity separate from that of his father in a way that both was challenging and reflected significant service to his country, duty as a reserve officer of infantry under the circumstances that prevailed during the twenties and thirties may have been less than psychologically satisfying. Political surveillance, on the other hand, was an alternative that meshed with the social and political outlook of a man who, although personally charitable toward those less fortunate than he, was a political and social conservative who believed in personal advancement through individual effort. His benevolence toward blacks was not inconsistent with a belief in black inferiority and support for segregation of the races. In short, he was a "good man" who was a product of his place and time and who supported the social structure that served him and his family so well. By the early 1930s, that social structure seemed in jeopardy because of the Great Depression and the widespread unrest that it engendered. Early in 1938, Everett served as host to DeLoss Walker, associate editor of the conservative *Liberty Magazine*, who visited Atlanta to speak to the city's white, business-oriented civic clubs. A newspaper photograph shows the two in smiling conversation in the context of an address in which Walker lambasted Franklin Roosevelt's New Deal. Government should not be giving people handouts, Walker emphasized, but should be teaching them self-reliance. American business was suffering under Roosevelt's policies, a result of the fact that the administration was listening to "the masses." The flaw in this approach, according to Walker, was that the masses didn't understand business. "If they did, they wouldn't be the masses. They'd be the head men, instead of working for somebody else." Unfortunately, "Mr. Ford has one vote. Mr. Ford's men have 92,000 votes. Therefore, Mr. Roosevelt listens to the men instead of Mr. Ford."[23] Everett may not have agreed with every particular in Walker's elitist diatribe, which might reasonably have been understood as an encouragement to dismantle universal suffrage, and he probably would have preferred that Walker recognize the importance of social responsibility on the part of those in possession of economic power, but he no doubt shared with the speaker a sense of anxiety in regard to the direction of social and political change in the United States. A shift in the direction of his career in the army reserves had already reflected it.

The U.S. Army, like most national armies, exercised an internal security function, in addition to that of defending the nation against foreign enemies and advancing the national interests on the battlefield. It was a function the salience of which increased early in the twentieth century as a result of the fear of German espionage and sabotage during World War I and Communist subversion following the Bolshevik revolution of November 1917. Germany went down to defeat, in 1918, but the Communist government of Russia did not, in spite of Allied (including U.S.) intervention in the Russian civil war of 1918–1920 on the side of those who were attempting to overthrow Lenin's regime. The fear that Communist leaders were working to spread their revolution to the rest of the world was not a figment of paranoid right-wing imaginations. From Lenin's perspective, revolution in Russia was only the first step in a process that would lead to the destruction of capitalism and the triumph of revolutionary socialism on a global scale. In 1919, the "Comintern," or Communist International, was organized as an association of revolutionary parties whose purpose was to achieve that objective.

Even while World War I was still in progress, U.S. military intelligence was as much concerned with an exaggerated threat of domestic radicalism as it was with neutralizing German agents. Following the end of the war, combating real and imagined leftist subversion in cooperation with patriotic civilian organizations, of which the American Legion was the chief example, appeared its primary raison d'être. It was a function with distinct racial overtones; Jews were seen as disproportionately involved in revolutionary agitation, which had blacks among its putative beneficiaries. The army's countersubversive activity declined during the 1920s, thanks to a waning of the "Red Scare," increasingly sparse government funding, and widespread outrage (particularly among labor unions) engendered by the army's spying on civilians, but it was reinvigorated by the growth of radicalism encouraged by unemployment, and its attendant misery, created by the Great Depression. A wave of strikes and demonstrations, including Communist-led hunger marches, sent a shudder through the ranks of the comfortable and the well connected. Chief-of-Staff Douglas MacArthur was initially opposed to a revival of the army's surveillance of civilian political activity, but he had changed course by the end of 1931. A policy statement, dated December 11, required all of the nine corps areas into which the army was divided to submit monthly summaries of "subversive" activities to G-2 (military intelligence), headquarters in Washington.[24]

G-2 of Fourth Corps Area, which covered the southeastern United States and was headquartered in Atlanta, expressed little concern in its first report for the danger of Communist agitation among the black population, on the grounds that "the vast majority of the Negroes are not sufficiently intelligent to grasp the Communistic doctrines."[25] But intelligence gathering clearly appealed to reserve captain and American Legionnaire Willis Everett. On October 24, 1932, he made formal application for transfer from infantry to military intelligence, noting that he had thoroughly familiarized himself with these duties and was convinced that he could render more useful service to his country in the latter capacity. He had been practicing law for eleven years and knew his way around Atlanta society. More to the point, during the previous two years he had been "actively fighting in every way, all forms of communism, socialism, passivism [sic], etc., in and around Atlanta." A month later, Everett appeared before a board of officers, which found him qualified for an appointment as captain in the Military Intelligence Reserve, an appointment that he received before the end of the year.[26]

This was duty that Everett approached with enthusiasm. His ratings on the annual two-week summer assignments to active service as an infantry officer had generally been "average" or "satisfactory"; following his transfer to intelligence, his ratings rose to "excellent" or "superior."[27] To be sure, his responsibilities were not limited to identifying subversive activity among the civilian population, nor did they always suggest high drama. During maneuvers at Fort Benning in 1935, for example, in addition to gathering and evaluating information on the "enemy" forces, he served as camp publicity officer, a function that, according to eighth Brigade commander Brigadier General R. O. van Horn, he discharged with "tact, energy, initiative and good judgment." A report in 1937 on a Major Hirai of the Imperial Japanese Army earned Everett lavish praise from the Fourth Corp's Major General George Moseley, who observed, "so often we turn to you for assistance and you always come back just one hundred percent."[28] Yet, it was as counter-radical watchdog that Everett was most valued by the Fourth Corps Area. His examination for promotion to major in November 1935 seems to have been the usual perfunctory affair, conducted by two officers who, the postexamination report noted, had known the subject "intimately" for a number of years. On that basis, they were able to observe that "he is particularly a high-type civilian [sic], well-known and prominent in Atlanta and his Americianism [sic] is unquestioned." An attachment to the report continued, "the applicant has on various occasions investigated on his own initiative individuals and organizations purportedly of an Un-American or insidious character and made reports of his findings to the civilian organizations who were interested in activities of this nature."[29] These organizations undoubtedly included the FBI, which was becoming the dominant force in matters of internal security and whose director, J. Edgar Hoover, had become an army reserve intelligence officer in 1922.[30] Franklin Roosevelt's administration had established the Civilian Conservation Corps in 1933 as a means of putting unemployed young men to work on projects such as reforestation, road building, and flood control, with hundreds of CCC camps, many of them in the South, under army control. These camps, with their hundreds of thousands of disgruntled inmates, were regarded by the army as potential breeding grounds for revolution, and corps area G-2s were instructed to include information on radical activity in the facilities as part of their monthly subversive activity reports. Everett's active duty summary of August 1938 records a summer assignment to CCC Camp F-16 at Wiggins, Mississippi, in the context of Third Army maneuvers and, while specifics concerning his responsibilities there are lacking, his attitude in regard to the camps is not likely to have been far removed from that of a fellow G-2 officer in Baltimore, who reported with concern on "the interest taken by some of our pacifists and pink (or worse) friends in the C.C.C."[31]

As Europe again made the grim transition from peace to war, Willis Everett's self-selected role as guardian of the established socioeconomic order against threats from the political left was clear. Hitler's Wehrmacht had recently completed its breathtaking conquest of France when Everett summarized his activities as a military intelligence reserve officer as having included "many talks at public gatherings" designed to discourage the spread of foreign "isms" and to thereby mold a "solid citizenry." The texts of these addresses have not survived, but it is clear that Communism, rather than Fascism, was the "ism" of chief concern. His opinions, he noted, were based on "much private investigation and reading concerning Communists and radical organizations."[32] This does not suggest that Everett was, himself, in any sense a Fascist or

Fascist sympathizer. His gentle, self-effacing humaneness, couched in a traditional Protestant belief system, was far removed from the studied brutality and essential amorality of Fascism and Nazism. It is unlikely that Everett ever made a serious study of Fascist ideology, and he probably had only a superficial understanding of Marxism. But, to him, as to many well-off members of Western capitalist societies, it appeared that Communism, with its loudly proclaimed intent to destroy capitalism and to establish a "classless," atheistic society, posed a greater threat to his status and beliefs than did Fascism, which offered itself, in part, as a defense of traditional values against the revolutionary left. Yet, it was as a consequence of the United States' approaching involvement in war with the Axis powers that Everett's heretofore essentially avocational association with army intelligence assumed more serious dimensions. Congress passed a joint resolution on August 27, 1940, empowering Roosevelt to call the reserves, as well as the National Guard, to active service for one year; in September, it introduced conscription. America was preparing for war, and Everett was directly affected. Under Special Orders No. 195, issued by Headquarters of the Fourth Corps Area on September 9, he was called to duty in the Office of the Assistant Chief of Staff, G-2, for a period of one year (which was to be extended for an additional year in June 1941).[33] Six months later, the Japanese attack on Pearl Harbor put him and millions of other Americans at the army's disposal "for the duration" and beyond.

2

The Internal Enemy

AS THE U.S. ARMY prepared frantically for its plunge into World War II, Chief of Staff General George C. Marshall remarked that its corps of reserve officers was "probably our greatest asset during the present expansion."[1] The statement might be interpreted as at least as much an index of American unpreparedness as of the quality of reserve leadership, given the neglect that Washington had visited upon the army reserves during the interwar period. For reserve officers, such as Everett, involved in domestic intelligence operations, the transition from peacetime status to an active war footing may have been relatively unproblematic. Unlike men assigned to combat branches such as infantry or artillery, reserve intelligence operatives had already engaged the "enemy" in the form of residents of the United States, most of them American citizens who appeared to the officers to be of questionable loyalty or, at least, to pose threats to the stability of U.S. society. For them, World War II would be more of the same, albeit on a greatly expanded scale.

Under an agreement between the armed forces and the FBI reached prior to the United States's entry into the war, the FBI was to have primary responsibility for investigating subversive activity among civilians, while military and naval intelligence was to exercise authority over security matters within the armed forces. In practice, however, the demarcation was not so neat. From the beginning, G-2 was authorized to deal with civilians in the Canal Zone, in Panama, and in the Philippines, as well as with those employed on military installations. Defense plants were, for a time, disputed territory between the U.S. Army and the FBI, until Roosevelt assigned responsibility for plant protection to the army shortly after Pearl Harbor, a move that lessened but did not eliminate struggles over "turf." Further complicating domestic security and intelligence rivalries was the army's top secret, elite corps of Counter Intelligence Police, renamed Counter Intelligence Corps (CIC) at the beginning of 1942 and greatly expanded in the course of the war. The CIC reported to G-2 and conducted investigations of cases of "treason, sedition, subversive activity, and disaffection," as well as combating espionage and sabotage on its behalf both in the United States and overseas. Although technically bound by the demarcation agreement between the armed forces and FBI, CIC agents were not always scrupulous in observing it.[2]

Everett's role in this domestic security and intelligence complex was an important one. For much of the war, he served as deputy to the assistant chief of staff, G-2, within the Fourth Service Command (the corps areas had been so redesignated in March 1942), while advancing in rank from lieutenant colonel, in 1942, to colonel, in 1944. Those who worked with him in the Fourth Service Command's G-2 headquarters in Atlanta's post office building are in agreement that, although Everett was formally second in command, for all practical purposes he directed the intelligence operation on the sufferance of Colonel Stacy Knopf, of the regular army, who showed relatively little interest in its day-to-day functioning.[3]

The Fourth Service Command embraced most of the southeastern United States, including all of Florida, Georgia, Alabama, South Carolina, and Tennessee and most of Kentucky and North Carolina, as well as the eastern half of Mississippi. Included in that area was a large fraction of the U.S. Army's training installations and numerous (ultimately 148) prisoner-of-war camps. By the later stages of the war, the Fourth Service Command ranked first among the nine service commands in numbers of military facilities and of prisoners of war in custody and was barely second to the Eighth Service Command, headquartered in Dallas, in overall population of army personnel, with more than three-quarters of a million.[4] Also contained in the Command were vital war production plants, the most noteworthy among them the top-secret component of the Manhattan Project at Oak Ridge in eastern Tennessee for the production of uranium 235, the fissionable core of the bomb that would be dropped on Hiroshima. Although the project had its own Intelligence and Security Division, the Fourth Service Command's operatives conducted numerous security checks on candidates for positions at Oak Ridge. Indeed, investigating the allegiance of army personnel whose loyalty was open to question constituted a major fraction of Everett's responsibilities. One such questionable case was Private von P., a young GI of aristocratic German lineage, who was placed under surveillance at Camp Croft, South Carolina, by the post intelligence officer and a CIC agent sent from Atlanta to assist him. Everett's ties to Atlanta high society may have been of value in the operation, as the young German was discovered to have been an acquaintance of a debutante who had met him during a prewar trip to Europe. The young lady volunteered her services, and a weekend furlough for the suspect was arranged, accompanied by an invitation to stay as a guest at the family residence. One Saturday evening, while the couple was taken to dinner at Atlanta's Capitol City Club by Everett and William Hartman, a CIC officer, another agent was dispatched to the home to search the GI's luggage. No incriminating items were found, and the young man was eventually pronounced a loyal member of the armed forces of the United States.[5]

But other cases had different outcomes. Private J. S. found himself dishonorably discharged from the U.S. Army and sentenced to ten years at hard labor (reduced on review to six) for having declared,

I will never fight against Germany. The German people are superior to the American people. This is a poor army and the German Army is superior. . . . I did not ask for this Goddamn uniform, I will not fight against anyone we are fighting. . . . If we go over to Germany, I would fight for Germany instead of the United States. I will try to shoot as many men in the back as possible before they get me.[6]

GIs whose "disaffection" was of a less egregious character might find themselves assigned to the 1800th Engineer General Service Battalion based at Camp Forrest, Tennessee, and operating near Lebanon, east of Nashville, nominally repairing damage caused by troops on maneuvers. This was one of a number of "special organizations" established by the War Department for "the disposition of potentially subversive personnel." It appears that, on average, ten to fifteen men per month from the Fourth Service Command were so assigned, the overall population of the camp reaching approximately five hundred by mid-1944. It is likely that, under the stress and hypersuspicion of wartime, some men were found "disaffectionate" on rather flimsy grounds. The Fourth Service Command drew information from a vast and varied network of informants, and not all of it was reliable. True, Everett's staff did not take action on a call from a woman who reported that her neighbor's dog was giving the Fascist salute (as a civilian, the dog owner was under FBI jurisdiction), but evidence that an army inductee had sung the Nazi party anthem, the "Horst Wessel Song," might have serious consequences. Everett personally reviewed these cases and was not comfortable with the likelihood that injustice, in some instances, might have been the result of an excess of caution. At one point, he ordered half a dozen CIC agents secretly inserted into the ranks of the battalion to conduct additional surveillance, and an undetermined number of men were reassigned to normal duty as a result.[7]

Not all of them were likely to have welcomed reassignment. Camp Forrest's 1800th Engineers achieved notoriety as a comfortable refuge for GIs intent upon avoiding the hazards of combat. The unit's commander, Colonel Johnson Brady, was a "likable, kindly and easy-going" officer who made few demands on his men, in part because there was little work for them to do. A report made to Everett's office noted that many "fillers" (those transferred to the camp due to suspect loyalties) had moved their families and automobiles to the nearby town and were able to enjoy both during the weekend and three-day passes that were commonly granted. Food was of a distinctly superior quality, since a number of Camp Forrest cooks had previously been employed as hotel and restaurant chefs. Many men sported Good Conduct medals, which had been awarded during service with their previous units. This was too much even for the indulgent Colonel Brady, who queried Everett on the possibility of having them revoked (it couldn't be done, Everett learned from the Fourth Service Command's judge advocate). Those so inclined seemed free to go about armed with large knives and blackjacks, reflecting lax discipline resulting in part from the fact that "cadre" assigned to supervise the potential subversives were often the incompetent or handicapped castoffs of other units. Brady lamented to Everett's nominal superior, Colonel Knopf, in May 1944 that, of five "cadremen" recently transferred to the 1800th, four had been diagnosed as psychotic or severely neurotic, one had spina bifida, and another suffered from severe respiratory problems resulting from an old case of tuberculosis. So appealing was "duty" with the 1800th Engineer General Service Battalion that suspicions were strong that at least some men had "engineered" their transfers, and it was known that fillers had written to friends at other installations offering advice on what kinds of conduct were likely to effect assignment to the unit. The camp slogan was alleged to be, "A subversive word a day keeps the foxhole away." A probable example is the letter written by an 1800th GI to his brother (with the certain knowledge that it would be read by an army intelligence agent), assessing American victory claims in the Philippines with, "I think this is another one of them bullshits." Little wonder that a request from a reporter for the *Nashville Banner* for permission to do a story on the 1800th Engineers was denied by Everett and that the unit was transferred to Camp Shelby, Mississippi, under a new commander by the end of 1944.[8]

General Sherman Miles, chief of the army's G-2, remembered the activities of German agents who had operated in the United States during World War I and was convinced of the danger that enemy agents might sabotage military installations in the present war as well, a fear that was reflected in the activities of the Fourth Service Command's G-2. But suspicions of enemy activity were seldom, if ever, confirmed. Bomber crashes during training flights led to the assignment of Tom Forkner, one of Everett's CIC agents, to twelve weeks of aircraft mechanics' school, where he learned to perform one-hundred-hour checks on U.S. Army Air Forces B-17s and B-24s. He was sent to Drew Field, in Florida, where he serviced aircraft and carefully observed the maintenance routine for evidence of sabotage. He discovered none and concluded that aircraft losses were being caused primarily by the haste with which aircrew were being trained. This conclusion was supported by his hair-raising experience accompanying a new pilot on a series of "touch-and-go" practice landings in which it was clear that the flyer was less than certain of the function of some of the plane's controls! The frequent wrecks and breakdowns of motor vehicles at the army's ninety-seven-thousand-acre infantry school at Fort Benning, Georgia, also created suspicions of sabotage and led to the employment of the versatile Forkner in the base motor pool for a month. As little evidence of enemy activity was uncovered at Benning as at Drew Field, although Forkner's detailed report led to an overhaul of vehicle maintenance procedures and contributed to a promotion for Everett![9]

Although Service Command G-2s were instructed to report on fires, explosions, and "other serious occurrences" as cases of possible sabotage, in fact there was little Axis activity to investigate in the Fourth Service Command or anywhere else in the United States. German espionage and "fifth column" operations were, in the United States, as elsewhere, largely mythological. To the extent that they did exist, they were amateurishly organized and conducted, and most German agents in the United States had been arrested by the FBI before Pearl Harbor. Like army G-2 and the CIC, the FBI investigated cases of suspected sabotage during the war, with similar results. Of more than nineteen-thousand incidents probed, none was conclusively proven to be the result of sabotage.[10]

Nevertheless, wisdom mandated caution, and Everett worked closely with "Civilian Security Education Committees," which were organized to encourage circumspection among civilians who were privy to sensitive information. Awkward slogans such as "If secrets we keep, lives saved we reap" and "Jargon of words in a cafe can cause our plans to go astray" were distributed on posters and even on cocktail napkins made for circulation to bars and restaurants. Presentation of a play about the planned American invasion of the fictitious island of "Svenston" illustrated the hazards of "loose lips," as the Germans, tipped off by seemingly innocent gossip, repulsed the amphibious assault at the cost of thousands of GIs' lives.[11] But there remained another area of concern to army intelligence: the threat of Communist subversion, radicalism, and social unrest among disaffected elements of the United States population, which had occupied so much of Everett's attention during the prewar years. The G-2 of the neighboring Third Service Command, with headquarters in Baltimore, noted, in November 1943, that, while he considered his primary responsibility to be the performance of security investigations of military personnel and defense-employed civilians, he also recognized the responsibility of army intelligence to "foresee, report, and if possible prevent," not only espionage and sabotage but sedition and racial unrest, as well. The G-2 in the Boston headquarters of the First Service Command reported intensive surveillance of "radicals" and had placed an informant on the executive committee of the Boston NAACP, while the Second Service Command's G-2 directed investigations of Communists, African Americans, pacifists, and labor groups. Racial tension became a matter of particular concern to army intelligence in the wake of the race riots of 1943, the worst of which occurred in Detroit in June. Ironically, long-standing apprehensions in regard to black unrest had resulted in the racial integration of the CIC long before the postwar elimination of segregation in the armed forces as a whole. The Sixth Service Command's G-2 had placed undercover black CIC agents in the Detroit ghetto months before the 1943 riot. The work of these men had been "of exceptionally high quality" and had produced the first warnings of the terrible upheaval to come.[12]

Everett was completely in tune with his northern colleagues. After the war, he estimated that he had dealt with "50,000 cases of Communism" in the southeastern United States.[13] This estimate undoubtedly represented a rather loose definition of what constituted "cases of Communism," although the fact that the Soviet Union operated a network of agents in the United States is beyond dispute. It is also clear that the Communist Party of the United States played some role in Soviet wartime espionage, although the extent and significance of its activity is a subject of disagreement. Information gleaned from recently opened Comintern archives in the former Soviet Union indicates keen awareness of surveillance by military intelligence and the FBI of Communist Party members in the United States, and recognition of the hazards that this produced.[14] Like his counterparts in other service commands, Everett was required by the War Department to submit monthly intelligence "summaries of subversion" and to scrutinize reading material circulating in military installations within his jurisdiction, sometimes clearing specific publications for purchase. He recalled in a postwar address to an "anti-subversive seminar" conducted by the Georgia Department of the American Legion that, after the German attack on the Soviet Union of June 1941, Communist Party members were instructed to volunteer for military service and to strive to become model soldiers, with the objective of securing duty in sensitive areas such as cryptography and assignment to officers' candidate school. Everett regaled the Legionnaires with the details of his combating not only Communist operatives but obtuse Army authorities, as well. A particularly colorful recounting of one such instance involved Everett's having blocked the efforts of the son of a "New York millionaire" to gain admission to officer-candidate school. Called upon by his commander to explain his actions to the irate father, Everett responded with a recitation of the son's "Communist activities" and the reproof that "he should be damned ashamed" to have such a son. But the father had friends in high places, and strings pulled in Washington opened the doors to OCS over Everett's objections. But Everett, it appears, could also pull strings. The father might have been laughing, "but very few can get away with laughing at me." For reasons that Everett left to the imaginations of his listeners, the young man found officer training more difficult than anticipated and "flunked out" within a few weeks. A similar example of Everett's vigilance in the face of Communist subversion and official incompetence, if not worse, was the case of another aspirant to an army commission whose mother was a Communist in California and whose brother was on the editorial staff of a Communist newspaper in the same state. With the support of a colonel in the regular army ("regulars" were often villains in Everett's worldview), the soldier of questionable loyalty entered OCS at Fort Benning and secured a commission as a second lieutenant when Everett's efforts to prevent it were nullified by direct orders from Washington. But, again, Everett had the last laugh. The freshly minted shavetail found himself assigned to a remote training facility in the desert where he could do no harm. Although the army's inspector general attempted to cover up the incident by confiscating relevant records, the effort was foiled when the Fourth Service Command's G-2 copied and retained the incriminating documents in his files, and Everett relished the prospect of someday making them public (he apparently never did).[15]

Although the Cold War naturally highlighted Everett's memories of the apparent threat from the left, he had not ignored the menace from the extreme right. American anti-Semitism was greatly stimulated by U.S. participation in World War II and was a source of considerable concern to army intelligence, although the army's own perspective was not free of a certain ambivalence.[16] In the Fourth Service Command's Security and Intelligence Division files is a report, dated June 1941, that deals with the role of subversive forces in "stirring up the Negroes." It alleges the existence of a $40,000 fund to be used for "propaganda and agitation" that was supposedly in the possession of the National Negro Congress and provided by a "Jewish Communist" named Lipschultz. Following the direct involvement of the United States in the war, however, anti-Semitic propaganda directed toward undermining the American war effort was regarded as a significant danger. The First Service Command shared with its counterparts the following scurrilous verse (to be sung to the tune of "Onward Christian Soldiers"), which was sent to the parents of a Boston-area soldier who had been killed in action:

> *Onward Yankee soldiers, fighting Jewry's war.*
> *With the flag of Stalin, marching on before.*
> *Halifax and Pepper, preach the Gospel true.*
> *And the press as you can guess is controlled*
> *by the JEW.*
>
> *Onward Lend-Lease soldiers, fighting Jewry's war,*
> *With the Cross and Sickle,*
> *Marching on before.*[17]

The Sixth Service Command's intelligence branch reported, in February 1945, on a meeting of "Constitutionalists" in Detroit, in which a certain Homer Maertz introduced a resolution that Jews be required to leave the United States within five years or be sterilized and suggested that stickers reading "Kiss a Jew and get a pack of cigarettes" be prepared; members would be urged to install these in the windows of stores such as "Sam's Cut Rate, Inc."[18]

Everett's office had already investigated an anti-Semitic as well as anti-Roosevelt "diatribe" written in a "pseudo-biblical style." Shortly before the end of the war in Europe, the Eighth Service Command intelligence division, with headquarters in Dallas, notified its Atlanta counterparts of an incident that had occurred in the rail yards of Oklahoma City. As a troop train that included a car carrying soldiers from Camp Shelby was passing through, handbills were thrown out reading: "Americans! Who is sitting behind the front line? The Jews! Who gets killed in action in France? The American soldier! Down with the Jews and the [sic] Free Masonry!"[19] Everett queried Camp Shelby's director of security and intelligence and was assured that the sergeant in command of the car had seen nothing. Later information suggested the possibility that German POWs might have been culpable, although it is clear that Americans were quite capable of the same and worse.[20]

Fear of black "sedition" by army intelligence officers in the South was, not surprisingly, intense. Agents in Jackson, Mississippi, placed a Ba'hai reading room under surveillance on the grounds that the sect contributed to unrest among the "Negro" population by preaching a doctrine of social equality. The Fourth Service Command intelligence received reports of unusual activity among black troops stationed at the port of embarkation at Charleston, South Carolina. A private had secretly organized an African American "army" within U.S. Army forces at Charleston, named himself commanding general, and appointed a corps of officers. Everett dispatched a black CIC agent to infiltrate the organization, which, although details are sketchy, he seems to have found harmless.[21] Much more common were investigations of "transportation" incidents, which often involved refusals by northern black GIs to observe the segregated seating arrangements on southern public conveyances. The army justified its interest in avoiding racial tensions on the grounds that such problems, if they were to escalate into open conflict, would be likely to disrupt war production and might require federal troops to suppress them. Remedies proposed ranged from providing "decent" places of entertainment for black GIs as alternatives to "honky-tonks" and "juke-joints," which "greatly promote misconduct on the part of these Negroes," and making available more prostitutes to the course offered in the First Service Command on "Leadership and the Negro Soldier." The latter was a series of lectures delivered by two blacks, one of them Joseph A. Douglas, a Ph.D. candidate in sociology at Harvard. The "keynote" of the course seems to have been that perceived differences between white and black troops were the result of environmental factors, an approach intended primarily for the enlightenment of Caucasian officers and that enjoyed considerable success, as the effort met with the approval of many officers who had commanded African American soldiers.[22] Everett's contribution to the ongoing debate was to urge the Army Service Forces' Director of Intelligence in Washington to consider adopting for distribution to black troops the magazine *Negro Worker*, edited by S. J. Phillips, a former professor at Tuskegee Institute. The monthly publication, Everett explained, was sold to a number of southern businesses for distribution to "Negro" employees for the purpose of promoting "harmonious labor and racial relations" and had achieved favorable results. The messages were those of Tuskegee's first president, Booker T. Washington, whose picture adorned the cover: "cast down your bucket where you are"; "good work pays"; and "cultivate industry and self-reliance." These exhortations were supplemented by illustrations of diligently laboring "Negroes" and by practical tips on subjects such as the importance of good personal hygiene and good nutrition. Everett's recommendation was made near the end of the war and appears to have had no practical consequences.[23]

    If the threat of Axis sabotage and espionage activities proved largely imaginary, World War II ended with a very modest, although physically quite real, assault upon the continental United States by Japan. Beginning in November 1944, thousands of paper balloons from which were suspended small incendiary and antipersonnel bombs were released from Japanese territory in the expectation that prevailing wind currents would carry them over the United States and Canada, where they would, it was hoped, produce forest fires, mayhem, and general consternation. Relatively few reached the United States, and damage was inconsequential, although a handful of civilians were killed by contact with the devices. Official concern was out of proportion to the actual danger, in large part because it was feared that the balloons might be used to carry bacteria or, more improbably, "agents, saboteurs, or commandos." By late March 1945, ninety-nine Japanese balloons had been recovered, some as far east as Michigan, Texas, Kansas, Iowa, and Nebraska. None is known to have reached territory under the jurisdiction of the Fourth Service Command, but public imagination was stimulated, and claims of sightings flowed into Atlanta from all parts of the southeastern United States. As intelligence chief, Everett had responsibility for investigating and evaluating these claims, requesting commanding officers of military installations within the command to report balloon sightings to his office by telephone "regardless of the hour" and organizing "balloon incident investigating teams" for in situ analysis. With the benefit of hindsight, he may have regretted this, for many man-hours were expended dashing to the scenes of alleged sightings, all of which proved to be either without substance (beyond the occasional involvement of alcohol), sightings of meteorological balloons, or the result of natural phenomena. Mrs. Francis R. of High Springs, Florida, saw something suspicious in the sky as she sunned herself on her back porch and communicated the following to the Naval Air Station in Jacksonville, which forwarded it to Everett: "Upon reading the paper this am where there were Jap Bomb Baloon [sic] over the U.S. I am convinced this was one." Investigation revealed nothing, a circumstance repeated frequently during the spring of 1945. An apparent meteor over northwest Georgia and an earth tremor in southern Tennessee near the Volunteer Ordnance Works occasioned additional apprehensions of airborne Japanese infernal devices.[24] These time-consuming and invariably futile but unavoidable investigations resulted in one of the few intemperate outbursts recorded by the normally tranquil Everett. When an army intelligence operative in Jacksonville informed him by telephone that an FBI agent had withheld information on a balloon-sighting incident for nine days, Everett exploded, "Well you tell Joe that I will cut his throat if he pulls anything like that again."[25]

Everett remained in charge of the Fourth Service Command's intelligence branch until the end of the war. That he had done his job well or, at least, to the satisfaction of his superiors was reflected in his promotion to the rank of colonel and in his ratings of "superior" in the performance of his varied duties. It had been a relatively comfortable war. He had not suffered any prolonged separation from his family and was usually sent off after breakfast to his office in Atlanta's old post office building by his wife, Mary, who saw to it that his summer khaki trousers were so heavily starched that they could "stand up and salute." Although he often remained in his office until eight or nine in the evening, he managed to maintain some involvement in the family law firm, although he and it suffered a devastating blow when, in the summer of 1943, his father was killed in a traffic accident near Jesup, Georgia, as Everett was driving him to the family retreat on St. Simons Island. He had worshipped his imposing father, and the fact that he had been driving (and he tended to drive with a "heavy foot") when his automobile struck a farmer's truck as it pulled onto the road may well have contributed to his nagging sense of unworthiness. Everett himself suffered only slight physical injuries.[26]

There had been joy, too. One Sunday morning, Everett received a phone call from the commanding general of Third Service Command requesting a personal favor. A promising attorney and good friend was interested in a career in the Counter Intelligence Corps. Might Everett have a place for him on his staff? An affirmative reply resulted in the arrival in Atlanta about a week later of the young man who would become Everett's son-in-law. Everett's receptiveness was probably grounded in more than willingness to curry favor with a Major General and enthusiasm for the bearer of excellent academic credentials (Williams College and University of Virginia Law School). Kiliaen Townsend was a van Rensselaer on his mother's side, and a bit of genealogical research revealed that he and Everett were sixth cousins. The invitation to the Everett home in which the family tree had been jointly scrutinized also resulted in Townsend's introduction to Mary Campbell Everett and the flowering of romance; the engagement that followed, in April 1945, was featured in "Cholly" Knickerbocker's New York high society column, "The Smart Set."[27] Following the Japanese surrender, "Kil" and Mary Campbell would help to hold the family law practice together, while Everett was preoccupied with other matters.

3

The World beyond Atlanta

COLONEL WILLIS EVERETT'S intelligence duties in the Fourth Service Command ended in the fall of 1945. His departure was part of a general shakeup of personnel at the conclusion of hostilities. Colonel Knopf had left by the spring of 1945, leaving Everett, for a time, as acting director of the Security and Intelligence Division, a position he had occupied de facto throughout most of the war. By war's end, Colonel Callie Palmer had been appointed permanent director, and, shortly thereafter, Major Lucius L. Deck succeeded Everett as Command G-2. Major William Hartman, the Division's Chief of Personnel Security, departed for duty in the Canal Zone.[1]

The fact that Everett had passed World War II in relative comfort and safety while millions of other Americans had been sent to sometimes remote and often unpleasant and mortally dangerous places clearly troubled him. He had "missed" experiencing combat in World War I, and he had "desperately" tried to get into World War II by applying for an overseas assignment, but to no avail. As he thought about "all those other guys in the mud and dying," he feared that he might appear "yellow" and to have dishonored his forebears, who "had always been fighters." With the end of the war, he would have preferred a return to civilian life, but his earlier efforts to secure duty outside the "Zone of the Interior" (as the army liked to refer to the continental United States) now resulted in assignment to a fourteen-week army European Studies course conducted by the Post Hostilities School at Columbia University to prepare officers for postwar responsibilities in Europe, which was not, he told Mary, what he had had in mind. But he boarded the Crescent Limited at Atlanta's Union Depot on a late October Friday and arrived at New York City's Penn Station the following morning, taking up temporary residence at the modest Hotel Paris on 97th Street while awaiting the evacuation of his dormitory by the navy personnel who were housed there. Reporting to the Morningside

Heights campus, he experienced the typical confusion of a new student, wandering from building to building and asking directions of people no better informed than he. "I even got in the museum and found a lot of old bones and rocks, but I couldn't find the Army."[2]

Although he "found" the army with the assistance of an elderly campus chaplain, Everett was not pleased with his new duty assignment. He did not tolerate separation from his family easily and almost immediately began to make plans for them to join him for the Christmas holidays. It was a rare day that did not see a letter in his small, neat hand on its way to Atlanta. Discomfort with the formal academic environment, which had been evident a quarter of a century earlier at Washington and Lee, reemerged at Columbia. The program in which he and approximately forty-five other officers were enrolled has been described by another participant as a "cram course in geopolitics"; it involved the study of European history, geography, economics, and politics. The faculty was of high quality, and included Grayson Kirk, later president of Columbia, who taught international affairs, and the brilliant refugee analyst of Nazi Germany Franz Neumann. An officer who befriended Everett remembers him as an "intelligent, quiet, reserved, serious and highly motivated officer who wanted to contribute to the postwar occupation."[3] Everett's contemporary assessment was in agreement on the quality and rigor of the curriculum; the courses were "very stimulating," he wrote his wife, and "they really throw it at you," three-hundred pages of reading one night for a single class, he complained. And Everett found material to support his conservative worldview. "Things over in Europe and China certainly look a long way from peaceful—Russia in Iran, Bulgaria, Rumania, Greece, Hungary, Poland, . . . Manchuria. . . . Well, I could go on and on, and why do we have to put up with such a bunch? As you see, I haven't changed much . . . [but] I have more ammunition to fire now."[4]

But he often questioned his own capacity to respond adequately to the academic challenge. He worked very hard, sometimes until 3:00 A.M. and read the *New York Times* "cover to cover" for international news but, typically, was filled with self-doubt. He feared that he was too old for serious study, that the work was "all very deep and maybe too complex," that he read too slowly, and that he was, perhaps, "dumber than most people," marveling that other officers seemed able to "run around" New York and still get by. On December 5, he took a quiz on French history and lamented that he "knew nothing." The following day found him studying furiously for a geography exam and "miserably ashamed" of his performance. The more he studied, the less he seemed to know, a judgment apparently confirmed by an exam a few days later, which, "as usual," he doubted that he had passed. The lean, athletic frame, which had served him so well in track and field at Washington and Lee, rebelled at the demands of the fencing classes in which he enrolled for "light exercise." "I'll be plenty sore tomorrow," he moaned after the first session with Professor Sentelli, his instructor. He smoked heavily the cigarettes gotten during regular expeditions to the Governor's Island PX and slept little, often getting by on a few hours a night, because of both the heavy academic demands and psychological turmoil.[5]

Everett's burdens were intensified by worries about the health of his law practice, which had already suffered as a result of his wartime duties in army intelligence. He attempted to keep in touch with some of his clients by mail and looked to his daughter, Mary Campbell, and to his secretary, "Miss Sophie" Belfor, to maintain some semblance of continuity, but this was a clearly unsatisfactory arrangement. "Kil," his new attorney son-in-law, was still in the army, and, in any event, Everett doubted that he had much interest in keeping the family law practice alive. Reduced income from the firm might well account for his interest in selling off some of the family's property on St. Simons Island. And he fretted about his family. He was concerned about his son, now about to turn eleven; he eagerly devoured news of young Willis's football exploits and experiments with his chemistry set and delighted in receiving examples of his artistic efforts. "Those were swell drawings of the Roman soldier," he wrote in a letter shortly after his arrival.[6] His marriage was clearly under some stress. Letters to Mary are rich in fanciful expressions of love for her ("higher than the Empire State Building" and "I love you . . . one trillion times more than I did 23 or 24 years ago"), but combined with depression rooted in a sense of failure or inadequacy as a husband. This was nothing new, but the rift seems to have been intensified by separation. For her part, Mary clearly suspected him of taking advantage of his sojourn in New York for romantic adventures, and Everett was at pains to reassure her. He was too busy and too old for such things, he wrote, and he missed her desperately. But, at the same time, he questioned his wife's devotion to him. Over the twenty-four-year course of their marriage, "the wind from the North Pole" had blown pretty hard, sometimes; "Have you forgotten how to love me?" he asked on December 11, and, in a poignant letter the following month, he expressed regret over having been "so much trouble" to her in spite of his efforts to do right. "Maybe someday I'll change and be as you want." He planned avidly for his family's trip to New York for the Christmas holidays. His wife and son would take the train from Atlanta (he urged that she reserve Pullman space so that they could get plenty of rest), while Mary Campbell and Kil would travel by automobile. He worried about expenses and confided to Mary that he would pay for his daughter's and son-in-law's meals only if they ate with the family, as he was not about to finance dinners at the Stork Club or similar places where you can "get stuck." But Mary was slow to make train reservations, in spite of Everett's frequent prodding, and the reunion between the two may not have been an entirely happy one, as he later expressed regret that the visit had not been "much fun" for her and apologized for having been "so no count [sic] and tired and worn out. . . ."[7]

The demands of his wartime duties had made church attendance—an important part of his life since childhood—difficult for Everett, and he had "missed," he said, regular Sunday morning devotions. While in New York, he derived satisfaction from sampling the variety of opportunities for worship that the city offered. Not surprisingly, this was usually accomplished in Presbyterian churches, but Everett was capable of a degree of ecumenism, as his visits to Greek Orthodox and Roman Catholic services indicate (he had been studying these denominations at Columbia, he explained somewhat apologetically to Mary). The more liberal atmosphere in some Gotham churches was not always comfortable. He was distressed to find "two black negroes" in the choir of "Fosdick's church" (Riverside Church, presided over by the prominent liberal theologian Harry Emerson Fosdick), who, he said, "spoiled the service, as I see no use in putting them in choir when [the] congregation was all white." But he tolerated it and returned, pronouncing Fosdick's sermon of November 11, which dealt with the spiritual condition of the postwar world, "magnificent" and promising to try to obtain a copy for Mary. The First Presbyterian Church, at Fifth Avenue and 12th Street, on the other hand, proved a disappointment. The sermon delivered the following week by Paul Moody, son of Dwight Moody, "one of the greatest Bible students the world ever knew," was "very poor" and the congregation not at all friendly.[8]

His racial prejudices were in evidence at Columbia, too. Everett was dismayed to discover that he was sharing the bathroom on his floor in John Jay Hall with a "Negro," apparently a civilian student at the university. He seems to have explored the possibility of having the black student moved to other quarters but found that "the school said he could not be moved." He immediately set about finding another room for himself, writing to Mary that he could not "stomach the toilet business." The affair made him uneasy, and he conceded that he was perhaps being "foolish" about the matter but asserted that he was too old to change. In any event, he seems to have found a sympathetic ear at Columbia in Grayson Kirk, who assured Everett that his request was not unreasonable. The "problem" appears to have been solved by reassigning him to a room in a house on West 117th Street occupied by Lieutenant Colonel Manter, the school's commandant. It was typical of the paternalistic variety of racism common among well-off Southern whites to demonstrate solicitude for the blacks who were, at the same time, to be kept "in their places," and to this Everett was not an exception. He wrote to his legal secretary, "Miss Sophie" Belfor, to make sure that there was work during the winter months for Emmet and Royal, the two black farm hands and handymen who normally cared for Everett's farm near Conyers, southeast of Atlanta. Under no circumstances did he want them to "go hungry," and employment would have to be found for them either on the farm or "out at the house." Less sympathy was shown for "Miss Sophie" herself. Hired by Everett's late father, Sophie Belfor seemed to the son to be less than responsive to his own wishes. He believed that she was taking advantage of his absence from the offices of Everett and Everett to operate a real estate business on the side although, Everett fumed, he was paying her a fair salary. This, he was convinced, was contributing to the decline of his law practice. His suspicions of Belfor seem to have been enhanced by the fact that she was Jewish and associating with that "claptrap crowd (Jewish) and now real-estate Monguls [sic]." He vowed to deal with the problem "in short order" upon his return home.[9]

Final examinations for the European Studies course were held at the end of January 1946, and, in spite of Everett's frequent gloomy assessments of his academic performance and his occasionally expressed fear that he might "flunk out," he passed with respectable grades, primarily C's, with his best performance a B-plus, in "Geography of Europe," and his lowest grades two C-minuses, in "French Government" and in the "Economic Problems of Contemporary Germany." What this represented in terms of actual academic achievement is not clear, as there had been rumors that many officers were failing examinations but being given passing grades nonetheless. As the end of the course approached, he expressed doubt that he would actually be sent to Europe and may have hoped for assignment to Washington. Other officers, he had earlier noted, were much better qualified for duty in Europe than he, having been born there or having had some significant prior European experience that he lacked. But, on January 29, he was issued "movement orders" for shipment to Europe, to take place after a thirty-day leave beginning on February 2, the formal termination date of the course. That schedule permitted Everett to return to Atlanta, to reconnect briefly with his law practice (Sophie Belfor may have been dismissed at this point), and to enjoy some much-needed relaxation with his family, while deciding how best to use his 175-pound baggage allowance. February passed quickly, and, on March 8, Everett reported to Fort Jackson, North Carolina, for "processing," including the required typhus and influenza inoculations. He then and awaited transportation to the port of embarkation at Brooklyn, New York.[10]

Prior to his departure from Columbia University, Everett had committed himself to a "Category #2" obligation, entailing active duty for an additional eighteen months. Attached to this was an understanding that the army would arrange for his family to join him as soon as he had received a permanent assignment. He therefore arrived in Le Havre on March 22 after an eight-day voyage in the expectation that separation from his wife and his son would be brief.[11]

It was Everett's first visit to Europe, and the Europe he saw was one devastated and dazed by sixty-four months of the most destructive war in history, concluded less than a year earlier. Close to forty million Europeans (including citizens of the partly non-European Soviet Union) had lost their lives as a direct or indirect consequence of the war, including six million Jews murdered because they were Jews. Physical destruction was vast and unprecedented, with many millions of human beings barely surviving under conditions of appalling misery.

Everett represented a nation whose wartime experiences had been, in many important respects, unique. The United States had entered the war early in the third year of the conflict and had suffered casualties that, although significant, were the lightest of those for any of the major participants (the deaths of Americans attributable to the war had been about 1 percent of those suffered by the Soviet Union and between 7 and 8 percent of those sustained by Germany, although only slightly fewer than those experienced by the United Kingdom). Foreign armies had not invaded the continental territory of the United States, nor had enemy air forces bombed American cities and factories. The United States emerged from World War II with a nuclear monopoly, most of the world's industrial productivity, and the realization that a return to the isolationism of the interwar years was neither feasible nor desirable.

Everett's own emergence from isolation came in the course of a trip via Red Cross bus from Le Havre to Paris. The journey was almost immediately interrupted by the effects of water in the gasoline supply, which necessitated an unscheduled stop to drain the offending fluid from the carburetor. While halted, the bus was struck (deliberately, Everett was convinced) by a streetcar, knocking the British driver to the pavement. "If I ever felt like punching anyone," raged the normally gentle Everett, "it was this [streetcar] operator. The Red Cross man [an American] said that all Frenchmen as a rule were just like that. No wonder the American GI hates the French. . . ." But he found the farm fields through which the once again mobile bus passed on its route eastward "very, very beautiful. . . . Hills steeper than ours on the farm were rounded off. . . . Well, it really made you want to own one of them." The towns wore a different aspect: "the Allied Air Force and artillery had simply blasted all the downtown business and residence [sic] areas off the map."[12]

Paris had survived the war largely unscathed, and Everett marveled at the beauty of the architecture and the general cleanliness of the city but was horrified by the profusion of streetwalkers. "McComas said he took a walk and he had so many propositions he didn't know what to do. The streets seem to be full of those kind [sic] of Ladies (?). . . . What will happen to the world?" His expressions of outrage were probably intended to reassure the ever suspicious Mary and were accompanied by undoubtedly sincere expressions of enthusiasm at the prospect of his wife's soon being able to share the surviving fascinations of Europe with him. But there was little opportunity to be delighted or offended by Paris. Three days after his arrival in the French capital, Everett and his cohort of Columbia-trained officers boarded a night train for Frankfurt am Main and the headquarters of USFET (United States Forces, European Theater).[13]

As the train rolled into Frankfurt on the morning of March 27, Everett was stunned by the scenes of devastation that greeted him, even though the war in Europe had been over for almost eleven months. He had been told, he said, that half of the city had been destroyed, but it looked worse. As he and Lieutenant Colonel Athanason and another officer walked through the central city after having found quarters in the Carlton Hotel, Everett noted that the only military target in sight was the railroad station, but houses, apartments, and churches lay in ruins. As they walked to and along the river before returning to their hotel, they "caught" from time to time a "terrible odor," the consequence, they were told, of thousands of corpses still buried beneath the rubble. Everett was being introduced to the results of the total war the great powers had waged but the effects of which the United States had been largely spared. He might have reflected ironically on the contrast between the desolation wrought by Allied air power and the "threat" of Japanese balloons that had occupied so much of his attention in the late months of the war.[14]

Although dispatched to Europe as an agent of the nation best equipped to bring order out of chaos, Everett found that his introduction to USFET's bureaucracy was not an auspicious one. When he and his fellow officers reported to the IG Farben building, which had been requisitioned by USFET for most of its offices (it looked a lot like the Pentagon, he thought), he discovered that the colonel in charge of making duty assignments had been expecting only half of them but had, in fact, jobs for none! "He had us fill out a bunch of papers and leave [them] with him. He said for us to look around and find us a job. Well, that's what I thought. A lot of work at Columbia thrown away. . . . The whole USFET looks like the most disorganized outfit I ever saw." An exploratory visit with a G-2 colonel at USFET headquarters sharpened Everett's negative assessment. "I have never seen a worse organized or [more] inefficient office. . . . There is not an officer doing 1/10 of a day's honest work." Other newly arrived officers were equally dismayed. Colonel Glavin, assigned to USFET's public relations office, immediately recommended a cut in staff from thirty-eight officers to four, and "agrees that the whole matter is terrible." Everett's progressive alienation from the U.S. Army in Germany had begun.[15]

His scathing initial criticisms of the USFET bureaucracy were rooted in part in his desire to be reunited with his family. Everett knew that until he received a duty assignment he could not make application for the transportation of his wife and son to Europe. In apparent confirmation of the U.S. Army's legendary penchant for assigning personnel

to duties remote from their qualifications, some graduates of the aca-
demically rigorous Columbia University course began to scatter, seemingly at random. Everett's friend Athanason found himself posted to
truck maintenance, while a Colonel Lathrop who, in addition to having
studied at Columbia, had been an instructor of French at West Point,
was appointed a post exchange officer. Everett's orders were less eccentric. On March 29, he was ordered to report the following morning to
the office of the theater judge advocate.[16]

March 30, 1946, was a Saturday, and most of the staff of the Judge
Advocate's office had gone for the weekend. But the officer in charge,
a fellow Atlantan by the name of Allen, informed Everett that he had
been assigned to work involving the trial of German war criminals.
Particulars were to be gotten from Colonel Claude B. Mickelwaite, in
command of the War Crimes Branch, which was headquartered in the
former Deutsche Bank building in Wiesbaden, the ancient watering
resort about twenty-five miles west of Frankfurt. The drive took
about an hour, and Everett was flattered to learn from Mickelwaite
that he might be named law member (that officer on a military court
with formal legal training) or trial judge advocate (prosecutor) in an
important case. "Well, I know very little about the exact work now,"
he wrote Mary, "but I can work hard and I'll do my best," this in spite
of some disappointment at not having been given the kind of responsibility for which his studies at Columbia had prepared him. More
than adequate consolation was the fact that now, with a definite assignment in hand, Everett was able to initiate the process that he
hoped would soon result in reunion with his family. He assumed that
Wiesbaden would become his (and their) home, and the prospect
suited him, for Wiesbaden had not been "all blasted up" like Frankfurt, and "we should have pretty fair accommodations." He delighted
in describing the amenities offered by the Rose Hotel, where he was
billeted—a dining room reserved for full colonels and their guests,
"grand" food served by well-trained, elderly German waiters, and
bathtubs that dispensed four kinds of mineral water. In short, he and
his wife could look forward to re-creating some semblance of their
comfortable lives in Atlanta, and he indulged his sense of social
"place" by contracting with a German jeweler to make heraldic rings
for himself and for members of his family.[17]

But he was also oppressed by the suffering around him. Strolling
through the ruins of Frankfurt after church services on the balmy

Sunday following his conversation with Mickelwaite, Everett was disturbed and depressed by

> Germans [who] would look at you until you got almost to them and then drop their eyes, but once in a while they would scornfully stare at you. . . . All so solemn—no laughter among either old or young. They didn't have a chance under Hitler and now they have no chance. . . . They brought it on themselves or, should we say, Hitler fooled them into it. I will really be glad to leave Frankfurt with all its devastation, dismal monuments to the futility of war, and its stench of human bodies by the thousands. . . .

He was saddened by the appearance of malnourished German children, especially their legs, exposed to the early spring sun—"so slender, . . . so 'pipe-stem.'" And the churches, so important in Everett's own life as symbols of a stable and moral universe: "The Churches are terrible spectacles. I have seen no less than 7 ghost-like skeletons whose interiors were gutted by flame or shell," and "I think the Germans are probably more incensed over the destruction of their churches than anything else. They say they do not destroy churches. I don't know the answer, but certainly none here are standing." The comments inspired by a Sunday afternoon walk suggest the emergence of an interpretive framework through which Everett responded to the catastrophe that Nazi Germany had unleashed. The German people were, to be sure, "responsible," but as the largely helpless instruments of their criminal leadership; it was their present and tangible misery that occupied his attention, rather than abstract and somewhat remote questions of their historical guilt. The victors, moreover, were not above moral reproach.[18]

Beyond whatever excesses Everett believed U.S. forces might have committed in their drive to victory, he often expressed disgust at the conduct of U.S. Army personnel in postwar Germany. Again, some of this was probably intended for the benefit of his wife, but there is little doubt that it was also a reflection of his own strict code of personal morality. While noting that German girls seemed clean, "but nothing worth writing home about," Everett also observed that many other American men stationed in Germany were less critical. He estimated that 25 percent of U.S. Army officers, many of them married, had made "living arrangements" with German women, while others were simply "running around some," a practice that later entered Everett's vocabulary as the phrase to *"Fräulein* around." "I hope," he wrote Mary, "that I get run over or shot or some other horrible death before I start such activities." When sexual license was combined with rampant black marketeering and the administrative inefficiency he had observed at USFET headquarters, it is little wonder that Everett approached his new war crimes assignment primed to detect further evidence of army corruption.[19]

On April 2, he was flattered to learn from Mickelwaite that he was to be assigned to "some big Belgian case," the "biggest case," in fact, currently on the army's docket, and one of which the army was determined to make a "big show." But the mills of the War Crimes Branch ground slowly, and Everett was left to fill his time by reading what he could find on war crimes trial procedure and attempting to substitute pipe smoking for his heavy consumption of Chesterfields. His growing sympathy for the German people whom he encountered was much in evidence. He conversed with two of the English-speaking waiters who served him in the Rose Hotel's dining room and learned that one had a son who had fought in the East and was a prisoner in the Soviet Union (sure to elicit Everett's compassion) and the other a daughter whose husband had been killed, leaving fatherless a three-year-old child. Both had gardens but were unable to obtain seed. Everett undertook to rectify the situation by requesting that Mary send off a shoebox filled with packets of seed for distribution to the two hotel employees and other needy Germans. And German girls seem to have risen in his estimation. They are "100 percent nicer behaved than the French. I haven't talked to any," he hastened to assure his wife, "but at least you don't get stopped 10 times in a block!"[20]

Monday, April 8, found Everett on a six and a half hour trip in a Jeep without brakes, operated by a "typical Army driver . . . looking like he was going to run over someone or something every 100 feet," traveling on cratered roads from Wiesbaden via Heidelberg to the War Crimes Branch office in Ludwigsburg, to which he was to be assigned for thirty days. In part his assignment was to observe the trials of one or more "flyers' cases," involving the prosecution of Germans for the murder of downed American airmen. His impressions were mixed. Although he initially judged one trial a "travesty of justice" because the judges allowed the admission "of every kind of evidence imaginable," he ultimately confessed to being favorably impressed by the "very fair" trials being conducted at Ludwigsburg. The hotel in which he was lodged, on the other hand, was primitive, with no heat or hot water; the bath was across the hall, and the toilet downstairs. But he had little time to learn or to suffer. Two days after his arrival, he received orders from Wiesbaden to proceed to Schwäbisch Hall, where there was, he wrote, a "concentration camp" of German prisoners (it was, in fact, a German prison being used as an annex to the Seventh Army's Central Suspect and Witness Enclosure), there to assume responsibility for the defense of "60–70" Germans who would be charged with having committed the "Malmedy massacre."[21]

Everett had heard of the "massacre"; indeed, few Americans had not. It had occurred during the bleak days of December 1944, when Hitler had shattered optimistic Allied assessments of Germany's ability to conduct major offensive operations by launching a massive attack against lightly held American positions in the Ardennes. The German objective was to capture the major Allied supply port of Antwerp and split Anglo-American forces in northwestern Europe, thereby seriously disrupting, if not permanently disabling, the eastward drive that had begun in Normandy six months earlier. The German offensive, initially code named "Watch on the Rhine" and later called "Autumn Mist" but commonly known to Americans as the "Battle of the Bulge," was a dismal failure that did not come close to achieving its objectives, but U.S. losses were heavy, totaling some eighty-one-thousand casualties, of which about nineteen-thousand were fatal.[22]

The vast majority of these deaths occurred in battle, as American forces fell back in the face of the German onslaught, desperately held on to their positions, or, later, counterattacked to erase the "bulge" created by the enemy advance. Americans grieved over sons, husbands, brothers, sweethearts, and friends "killed in action"; but reports of the Malmedy massacre produced fury. Early on the afternoon of December 17, 1944, the second day of the offensive, German mechanized troops spearheading the attack had captured roughly one hundred men of Battery B of the 285th Field Artillery Observation Battalion, a lightly armed technical unit whose function was to locate enemy artillery and to transmit their positions to U.S. gunners for counterbattery fire. Accounts by survivors indicated that the Germans had assembled their prisoners in a field at a crossroads south of Malmedy, then opened fire with machine guns, subsequently walking among the prostrate forms giving the coup de grace to those who still seemed alive. Morality and American public opinion demanded that the perpetrators be apprehended and brought to justice. This was the army's "biggest case," of which Mickelwaite had spoken to Everett a week earlier.[23]

Everett had become part of a complex undertaking. The United States's war crimes trial program was rooted in the "Moscow Declaration" of November 1, 1943, in which the Allies had declared their intention to apprehend and punish those responsible for Axis and, in particular, German wartime atrocities. That resolve eventually involved the United States in a three-tiered system of war crimes justice in Germany. By far the best-known component of this system was the International Military Tribunal sitting in Nuremberg, in which twenty-two German leaders and a number of organizations were tried before a panel of judges drawn from France, the Soviet Union, the United Kingdom, and the United States. This trial had begun in November 1945 and was still in progress when Everett arrived in Schwäbisch Hall. A series of twelve subsequent trials of lesser Nazi leaders at Nuremberg before American civilian judges would begin in 1946, following the adjournment of the International Military Tribunal. These courts would pass judgment on an additional 185 German defendants before ceasing operation in 1949. By far the largest number of defendants, 1,672, would be tried in 489 proceedings conducted between 1945 and 1948 before courts established by the U.S. Army. These trials constituted the third tier. The trial of the "flyers' cases," one of which Everett had observed at Ludwigsburg, and the Malmedy massacre trial were among them.[24]

Near panic replaced Everett's earlier enthusiasm. He had anticipated serving as the law member of a court, which would have entailed ruling on procedural issues, or as chief prosecutor, which might well have seemed a relatively simple matter, given the overwhelming burden of Nazi guilt, and he had been led to expect a significant period of time to prepare himself for trial responsibilities. Now, he confronted the prospect of organizing and conducting the defense in a mass trial in the space of a month. Doubt was piled upon anxiety. He knew no criminal law. The defense lacked a "decent lawyer." He questioned his ability to remember the names of the defendants, much less to defend them. In any event, he clearly found the prospect of aiding Germans to offer "excuses" for murdering American soldiers "in cold blood" highly distasteful.[25]

The Malmedy trial was scheduled to begin on May 16 at the former Nazi concentration camp at Dachau, a suburb of Munich. Dachau would be the site of most of the war crimes trials conducted by the U.S.

Army in Germany. It offered ample facilities for the housing of German prisoners and witnesses and adequate, although dreary, accommodations for the trials themselves. The symbolism of prosecuting German war criminals at Dachau was strikingly apt. *Konzentrationslager* Dachau had been established by *Reichsführer-SS* Heinrich Himmler in March 1933 as the first of the concentration camps operated by the SS and the model on which the empire of death that was the camp system would be based. Dachau was a particularly appropriate venue for the trial of the Malmedy defendants, for all had been members of the Waffen-SS, or armed SS. These had been Hitler's "political soldiers," who had been at the forefront of Nazi Germany's ideologically motivated drive for a racially "pure" and German-dominated Europe. Dachau had also been the scene of an incident that demonstrated the hatred the SS had generated in the minds of Americans. The concentration camp had been liberated on April 29, 1945 by troops of the U.S. Forty-fifth Infantry Division. Infuriated by the discovery of thirty-nine boxcars filled with the corpses of thousands of prisoners, the GIs massacred SS men whom they captured in the camp, perhaps as many as five-hundred.[26]

Everett proceeded to Schwäbisch Hall and then to Dachau. He was not favorably disposed toward the defendants. According to the evidence he had seen, he wrote to his family, "these 'clients' of ours were really some terrible murderers and probably the hangman's rope would be mild punishment for them." But he was determined to give them a full-blooded defense, although, he added, "what that is now is beyond my knowledge. I can only hope that God will lead the court to a real sense of justice and His Will will be done." By the middle of April he had three offices and desks and one German secretary and had been joined by a young Chicago attorney, Lieutenant Wilbert J. Wahler. Beyond that, however, "no car, no equipment, no nothing." He met for the first time his opposite number, Lieutenant Colonel Burton F. Ellis, who had been named Trial Judge Advocate, or chief prosecutor for the Malmedy case, late in February. Like Everett, he had been a peacetime civilian lawyer whose career as a corporate tax attorney had been as remote from the practice of criminal law as Everett's. But Ellis's experience with the U.S. war crimes trial program in general and the Malmedy case in particular was far more extensive than Everett's. He had been assigned to the War Crimes Branch in April 1945 and had been involved in the investigation of German atrocities ever since, having taken charge of the Malmedy case in February 1946, although he had been associated with its investigation since November. Everett's opinion of Ellis appears to have peaked at haughty disdain. At first meeting, he found his opponent "a nice boy" but someone with whom he wouldn't want to live, "as he has no chin and wears a mustache in addition." Ellis had no intention of sharing quarters with Everett, and the two set out to locate housing near the camp for their respective staffs. Everett disliked the experience. Ellis's conduct, he thought, was "intolerable" ("as I had expected from his chin"), while the process of requisitioning accommodations (two houses for each) clearly troubled him. German families were forced to vacate their homes and allowed to take with them only personal clothing, while leaving all else behind. "It really is a tough break." The houses selected were on the road to the camp, and if Everett ever reflected on what the residents might have witnessed while the Dachau concentration camp had been under its original management, he did not record it.[27]

Everett was scrambling to organize some semblance of a defense for men for whom, initially, he had little sympathy. He was acquainted with an Atlanta attorney who had been involved with war crimes trials in Japan, and he asked Mary to seek his advice (nothing seems to have come of this), while the War Crimes Branch promised much but delivered little—no telephones by April 16, and he and his growing staff of defense attorneys were "sweating blood" with the opening of the trial a month away. He had "met" his clients for the first time on the evening of April 11 in the prison at Schwäbisch Hall in an event that had been arranged by Ellis. Most of the defendants were brought hooded into a room in groups of ten and, after the removal of the hoods, were read the charges against them. Everett and three other members of the defense staff, Lieutenant Colonel John Dwinell, Captain Benjamin Narvid, and Lieutenant Wahler, were introduced by Ellis in "flowery" terms as the best legal talent the United States had to offer, after which the defendants were required to sign a sheet acknowledging the service of charges. They were then made to bow at the waist to Ellis, after which they were led away. Some prisoners did not bend deeply enough and were ordered by German-speaking members of Ellis's staff to repeat the gesture. Although Everett did not comment on the event in one of his frequent letters to his family, he later recalled it as a bizarre phenomenon and evidence of the unwholesome character of the Malmedy investigation and trial.[28]

He was aware that some of the defendants had made sworn statements during the investigatory phase that amounted to confessions of murders committed during the Battle of the Bulge. Everett's initial efforts to secure these crucial documents before the trial began were rebuffed by Ellis with the support of Colonel Mickelwaite, but a compromise brokered by Colonel Corbin, judge advocate of the Third Army, whose commander had court-appointing authority in the case, released most of the confessions to the defense on April 20, along with two badly needed Jeeps. But an important turn in the pretrial development of the case, and a fundamental shift in Everett's own perspective on it, occurred shortly after the transfer of the suspects from Schwäbisch Hall to Dachau. By then, the defense team had secured interpreters, as well as the invaluable services of Herbert J. Strong, a German-born Jewish attorney who had emigrated to the United States after the Nazi takeover of the Reich and had volunteered as a civilian for war crimes duty after the war. When assigned by Mickelwaite to assist in the defense of the Malmedy accused, Strong had accumulated experience in a variety of army war crimes proceedings, including one of the "flyers' cases" and the trial of the staff of Mauthausen concentration camp.[29] On April 23, Everett and his staff of lawyers, interpreters, and stenographers proceeded to the prisoner holding area and, divided into several teams, interviewed the defendants. What they heard would later become a source of intense controversy and a subject of considerable confusion on the part of Everett as well as others. But, with the experience of the day fresh in mind, Everett wrote to his family:

> The heat is on as far as work is concerned . . . the boys got all steamed up about the underhanded methods employed by Col. Ellis and his gang of Nazi method boys. Several defendants today said they thought they had had a trial . . . a Col. sat on the Court and his defense counsel rushed the proceedings through and he was to be hanged the next day so he might as well write up a confession and clear some of his other fellows seeing he would be hanged. The another kind of court had black curtains. . . . The Lt. Col. sat as judge at a black-draped table which had a white cross on it and the only light was two candles on either end. He was tried and witnesses brought in and he was sentenced to death, but he would have to write down in his own handwriting a complete confession. Then the beatings and hang-man's rope, black hoods, eye gougers which they claimed would be used on

them unless they confessed. Not a one yet wrote out his statement but each stated that the prosecution dictated their statements and they said it made no difference anyway as they would die the next day. So on and on it goes with each one of the defendants. The story of each must have some truth because they have each been in solitary confinement. I can't make up my mind what to do about it yet and will continue the interrogations for [the] next few days. All of the above is for the family only, as I am afraid the case will really smell bad and if newspapers pick up this stuff you will really see the headlines. I for one do not want to be responsible for informing the American public about the atrosities [sic] the Americans perpetrated. One of their investigators shot a man (who I don't know as yet) while he was trying to get a confession out of him.[30]

Jochen Peiper, the former commander of the offending SS battle group and the central defendant, presented to Everett a written summary of allegations of mistreatment by U.S. Army investigators that had been reported to him by other accused. Former *SS-Unterscharführer* (sergeant) Anton Motzheim claimed to have been beaten for nearly an hour in Schwäbisch Hall in an effort by army personnel to extract a statement that would incriminate Peiper or former *SS-Sturmbannführer* (major) Josef Diefenthal, one of Peiper's battalion commanders, and was allegedly confronted with other prisoners whose swollen faces made them unrecognizable. Another defendant claimed also to have been beaten and to have had a rope placed around his neck preparatory, he was led to believe, to hanging; similar treatment was alleged by another German prisoner. Peiper himself claimed to have received a note, passed to him in Schwäbisch Hall (in the middle of February, as best he could remember), describing the suicide of Arvid Freimuth, who had been heard to cry from his cell prior to having hanged himself, "One drew a perjury from me. I cannot go on living." Peiper's memorandum alleged a total of at least seven beatings during interrogations in addition to that of Freimuth, whose body was claimed to have shown evidence of battery.[31]

While Everett was disturbed by allegations of misconduct on the part of army investigators, he was also alarmed by the prospect of having those accusations reach the outside world. But justice and the interests of a defense in disarray clearly required that the matter be pursued. Everett and his colleagues prepared a questionnaire designed to elicit further personal information on each prisoner and on alleged investigatory misconduct, and they had copies distributed to all of the defendants. The questionnaires were collected the next morning and the results analyzed. The questionnaires contained claims, Everett much later recalled, of "beating, mock trial, death cell incarceration, and about 15 or 20 similar brutalities by the prosecution." The question of what to do with this information was a difficult one. If Everett were to bring the matter to the attention of the War Crimes Branch, the result would be to forewarn the prosecution and to provide Ellis and his staff with time and opportunity to develop a defense prior to the start of the trial. Nevertheless, Everett and his colleagues agreed to reveal the allegations to Colonel Corbin.[32]

Corbin immediately phoned Colonel Mickelwaite, the deputy theater judge advocate for war crimes in Wiesbaden, with information of Everett's disturbing allegations, and Mickelwaite dispatched Lieutenant Colonel Edwin Carpenter to Dachau to investigate. Carpenter received the completed questionnaires from Everett and, with the assistance of an interpreter, interviewed the defendants—between twenty-five and thirty, he later remembered—who had alleged irregularities by army investigators. Unfortunately, Mickelwaite did not require Carpenter to compile a formal written report of his findings, but he recalled three years later that Everett, as well as the defendants, had emphasized the use of mock trials rather than incidents of physical brutality, although four prisoners had claimed to have been struck on their way to or from interrogation sessions. Carpenter was certain, however, that no defendant had alleged that a confession had been extracted from him by physical force.[33]

Carpenter returned to Wiesbaden and reported his findings on April 28 to Mickelwaite and to Lieutenant Colonel Clio E. Straight, soon to succeed Mickelwaite as deputy theater judge advocate for war crimes. Carpenter advised them that he had uncovered no plausible evidence that any of the confessions had been secured under duress. Everett and Ellis had also been summoned to Wiesbaden, and, in a subsequent meeting, Everett was required to repeat the allegations in the presence of, he later recalled, a "smirking" chief prosecutor. Ellis was directed to return to Dachau to question his staff on the offenses alleged and was assured that the allegations of improprieties were groundless, although the denials appear to have applied only to allegations of physical violence, and not to the use of psychological stratagems.[34]

Everett may have hoped that the unwholesome odor beginning to emanate from the prosecution case might derail it or, at least, postpone the opening of the trial. If so, he was disappointed. Mickelwaite concluded that the most expeditious means of determining the accuracy of the defendants' confessions and, in particular, whether or not they had been voluntary, was to offer them to the scrutiny of an army court in the framework of the trial, already scheduled to begin in mid-May.[35]

In the little more than two weeks remaining, Everett and his team of six army attorneys struggled to assemble a credible defense, an effort that was complicated by the fact that the defendants were permitted under army regulations to engage civilian German attorneys to supplement appointed counsel. This was done with the assistance of Herbert Strong, who combed Munich for suitable candidates. The consequence was a group of six additional lawyers to whom American trial procedure was literally "foreign," and, although at least one of the attorneys was fluent in English, most were not. Everett later recalled the difficulty of attempting to prepare the case in the absence of a law library, which necessitated the dispatch of Frank Walters, a civilian attorney assigned to the defense staff, to exploit the bibliographical resources of USFET in Frankfurt. A "minor" detail (but one of crucial significance to the German attorneys), was the need to secure for the Germans army ration tickets, one of many administrative matters that distracted the hard-pressed Everett.[36]

But Everett's attention was most disrupted by matters personal, rather than official. Separation from his family had tormented him at Columbia and was vastly more burdensome now. Army mail service in Europe was slow and the opportunities for regular phone conversations almost nonexistent. Everett had been assured that, by committing himself to active duty until June 30, 1947, he had guaranteed the prompt conveyance of Mary and young Willis to Germany, and Mickelwaite had promised to do what he could to expedite the reunion. On April 27, 1946, in the midst of the crisis unleashed by the initial claims of duress surrounding the confessions, Everett received a phone call from the War Crimes Branch in Wiesbaden with discouraging news. The families of officers who had agreed to active duty until mid-1947, designated "Category #2," were no longer eligible for transportation to Europe; that privilege was now limited to the dependents of officers in "Category #1," those committed to an indefinite term of service. To make matters worse, the opportunity to make such an indefinite commitment, he was informed, was no longer available. Everett was furious, and Mickel-waite agreed to dispatch an officer to Frankfurt to plead his case. His success was limited to securing for Everett permission to alter his commitment to Category #1, which he did the following day, but with the realization that he was placing in jeopardy a law office that, as he noted to Mary, had not been closed since 1886. Even so, Everett was not to see his family until the fall, and his sense of having been bamboozled further perforated the already tattered esteem in which he held the U.S. Army.[37]

Everett's revelations of the German defendants' claims of investigative misconduct had resulted in "shaking loose" copies of most of the confessions for examination by defense counsel. Ellis had initially been unwilling to provide more than summaries to Everett, but Colonel Corbin had threatened to allow the defense an additional six months to prepare its case unless the confessions were made available. But Ellis's enforced cooperation was at first counterbalanced by resistance from the defendants. This was later to be explained as natural suspicion on the part of men who had been tricked and subjected to abuse by other men wearing the same uniforms. Everett's contemporary account provides a somewhat murkier picture. Writing to his family late on the evening of April 30, he noted that

> We had 4 young kids (18 & 19 yrs.) back for reinterrogation as it looked very suspicious that they were all lying. . . . but by my strategy we were able to break one and then all admitted that they were not telling the truth in some details. Tomorrow night I am going to get all of them up and have Colonel Peiper . . . there so as to try to force and persuade them each to tell us the whole truth. The case is bad enough to have to defend without having to have our defendants lie to us. Don't think for a minute that these 74 people are not a real responsibility and a bad one.[38]

Unfortunately for the historian, Everett did not explain the matter further. What were the defendants lying about? The contents of their confessions? Their claims of duress? The latter is strongly suggested by an entry in Colonel Ellis's diary for April 30. It reads, "Colonel Everett said today that Sprenger, Neve, Hoffman, J., and Jaekel (four of the defendants) admit fabrication of story of beating. . . ."[39] This statement, of course, did not rule out the possibility that others had been beaten but indicated the existence of a degree of skepticism on Everett's part with regard to prisoners' allegations of physical abuse that would later disappear. In any event Everett, with the assistance of Strong and Lieutenant Colonel John Dwinell, succeeded in convincing Peiper of the sincerity of the defense effort and of the necessity for cooperation by the defendants. On the evening of May 1, Peiper delivered a "fine appeal" to the assembled defendants, impressing upon them the need to tell the truth if they were to be helped.[40]

With little time left to prepare the defense of more than seventy men, a mood approaching despair seems to have settled over Everett and the rest of the defense team. Defendants who had earlier been sullenly resistant now deluged defense lawyers with their versions of events in the Ardennes seventeen months earlier, descriptions usually quite different from the narratives contained in their written confessions and containing the names of witnesses alleged to be able to support them. But it proved impossible to interview all of the defendants before the trial began, much less to locate and question the many hundreds of suggested witnesses. With the opening of the trial a week away, Everett returned to his room in a requisitioned house on Dachau's Stockmannstrasse late in the afternoon and collapsed into bed with a headache and no appetite for dinner. A hot bath "to draw the blood from my old head" eased the headache but did not facilitate sleep, and Everett lay the entire night in escapist thought about his family back in Atlanta. The stress under which he was working was reflected in a despondent and partially incoherent letter he wrote on May 12.

> . . . it was impossible to counsel or [sic] any of the prisoners. Some papers over here so Capt. Narvid [a member of the defense team] said [he] had chosen my short opening to print in full rather than the inciting and blood dripping speach [sic] of the prosecution. I am not particuarily [sic] proud of it, but if the Court would analyze it a bit they might do well to adhere to it rather than put on a mock trial. Simply go out and shoot all 74, which might be best to do anyway and not sham a trial under American system. Anyway, we will see what the next week brings. If no better, I'll have to take over all the cross-examination and work myself. Maybe the Lord wants it this way, but I

doubt it. I don't think He wants done unfairly [*sic*] and vengeance and malice and hatred are written all over the record.

Everett closed the letter to his family with "I do so hope we can close that coming over deal very soon, or I'll be on the boat coming back."[41]

4

Under the Lights

THE TRIAL THAT began on May 16, 1946, was officially designated *U.S. vs. Valentin Bersin, et al.*, the twenty-five-year-old former tank commander's name appearing first on the alphabetically arranged list of defendants on the charge sheet. Neither Everett nor Ellis had had experience in criminal court procedure in the United States, but that was not as disadvantageous as it might appear, for the trial procedure employed by military government courts of the U.S. Army was different in important respects from that which an American lawyer would have experienced in a civilian court in the United States. In outward appearance the court was similar to a U.S. Army court martial. Evidence would be heard and judgment rendered by a panel of officers appointed for that purpose by higher authority, in the case of the Malmedy trial by Headquarters, U.S. Third Army. One officer, the "law member," was to be in possession of formal legal training; he would have responsibility for interpreting the law and for rendering procedural decisions. In effect, therefore, the officers detailed to hear a case served both as judge and jury, in a manner not dissimilar to continental European practice.[1]

Some procedural elements lent to the Dachau courts a summary character. A two-thirds majority of the presiding panel of officers was sufficient for both conviction and sentencing, including the imposition of the death penalty. This stood in contrast to court martial practice, which required unanimity in the application of capital punishment. Secrecy surrounded the numerical division of the judges in arriving at verdicts and in imposing sentences, as well as the reasoning behind their decisions; this, too, was a feature of continental procedure. Likely to be most alien to American attorneys were the rules of evidence. In effect, there were none in the Dachau courts. Hearsay and opinion, in most cases excluded from normal United States courts (including courts martial), were admissible, as well as all else that might, in the minds of the judges, have a bearing on matters before the court. These rules were adopted in large part to reduce the likelihood that defendants guilty of horrendous crimes would escape justice on legal "technicalities" and did not necessarily preclude fair trials, but adopting procedures for the trials of enemy personnel that were expressly rejected in the trials of U.S. citizens ("Hearsay is not evidence," says the *Manual for Courts Martial, U.S. Army*) enhanced the trials' vulnerability to later censure.[2]

Eight officers had been appointed to hear the case. Highest in rank and the president of the court was Brigadier General Josiah T. Dalbey, then serving with the Third Infantry Division. The remaining members of the judicial panel were full colonels, most of infantry or field artillery. Colonel Abraham H. Rosenfeld, the law member, was the dominant figure on the bench. In addition to the judicial power he wielded, he had impressive, perhaps intimidating, credentials. A graduate of Yale Law School, Rosenfeld, like Everett, had combined the peacetime practice of law with service as an officer in the Army Reserves, but he had gained considerable courtroom experience before being called to active duty in 1940. While serving at Fort Dix, New Jersey, he had acted as either prosecutor or defense counsel in approximately two hundred cases tried by court martial. Unlike Everett (and Ellis), he had acquired battle experience as commander of a combat team in North Africa; although brief, this phase of his career entitled him to wear the Combat Infantry Badge over the left breast pocket of his tunic. Everett may have encountered Rosenfeld's name while still in Atlanta. One of the many publications in the files of the Fourth Service Command's Security and Intelligence Division files is a pamphlet, entitled *Hitler's Typhoid Marys*, that refutes the common anti-Semitic charge that Jews shirked military service. In it, Rosenfeld is cited as having led the first American unit to land at Algiers. When the unit was dissolved after about a month, Rosenfeld was assigned to a variety of administrative and judicial duties for the remainder of the war before being sent to Dachau in March 1946 for service in the trial of the former masters of Mauthausen concentration camp, where approximately forty thousand human beings had died.[3]

The first Nuremberg trial excited controversy, in part because of the novelty of the offenses with which the defendants were charged. Never before, for example, had national leaders been tried by an international court for conspiracy, "crimes against peace," or any other offense. Most of the Dachau trials, on the other hand, were conducted for alleged violations of the well-established "laws and usages of war." Although the

Malmedy massacre gave its name to the trial in popular parlance and was the central event that had precipitated both outrage and investigatory zeal on the part of the U.S. Army, it was only one of a complex of related offenses specified in the official charge sheet. The seventy-four defendants, according to the prosecution,

> did . . . at, or in the vicinity of Malmedy, Honsfeld, Büllingen, Ligneauville, Stoumont, La Gleize, Cheneux, Petit Thier, Trois Ponts, Stavelot, Wanne and Lutre-Bois, all in Belgium, at sundry times between 16 December 1944 and 13 January 1945, willfully, deliberately, and wrongfully permit, encourage, aid, abet, and participate in the killings, shooting, ill treatment, abuse and torture of members of the Armed Forces of the United States of America, then at war with the then German Reich, who were then and there surrendered and unarmed prisoners of war in the custody of the then German Reich, the exact names and numbers of such persons being unknown but aggregating several hundred, and of unarmed allied civilian nationals, the exact names and numbers of such persons being unknown.[4]

Crimes of this character were infractions of Article 2 of the Geneva Convention Relative to the Treatment of Prisoners of War, signed in 1929, which mandated the humane treatment of captured enemy combatants, and Hague Convention (IV) Respecting the Laws and Customs of War on Land, Annex to the Convention, whose Article 46 requires military forces in occupation of enemy territory to respect "Family honour and rights, the lives of persons, and private property. . . ."[5]

General Dalbey called the court to order under the glare of photographers' floodlights (much of the trial would be filmed) at 10:00 A.M., May 16, 1946, a Thursday. Judges and prosecution and defense staffs, as well as stenographers and interpreters were introduced and the charges read by Lieutenant Colonel Ellis. There followed a challenge by Lieutenant Wahler for the defense to the jurisdiction of the court on the grounds that, inasmuch as some of the defendants were accused of murdering Belgian citizens, they should be tried by Belgian, not U.S., authorities. The grounds for this legal ploy lay in the Moscow Declaration of November 1, 1943, which called for the return of war criminals to the countries where their crimes had been committed for trial. The prosecution, prepared for this largely pro forma maneuver, countered with the argument that the defendants were charged with infractions against international law, not the laws of Belgium, and that all "civilized" states had a legitimate interest in their trial and punishment. Belgium, in any event, had raised no objections. The challenge had been raised and rejected in other cases, and Rosenfeld's denial of the motion could have surprised no one. A similar fate befell motions by two of the German counsel, Drs. Leiling and Rau, which challenged the court on the grounds that it was seeking to act as judge in its own case and that the trial was in violation of the Geneva Convention of 1929, which required that prisoners of war be tried according to the standards applied to the soldiers of the captor state. Dalbey then ordered each defendant to state his name, nationality (not all were German), legal residence, and branch and length of military service. Each was assigned a number corresponding to his position on the alphabetical list of the accused. That number, stenciled on a white placard approximately six inches square, would be worn suspended around the neck by each defendant for purposes of easy identification for the duration of the trial.[6]

The defendants' dock, with its seventy-four occupants, represented a significant characteristic of the Malmedy trial and a major problem for Everett and his team. *U.S. vs. Valentin Bersin, et al.*, was a mass trial, a condition that offered advantages to the U.S. Army, which lacked the resources, particularly personnel, to try war crimes suspects individually (almost all U.S. trials involved multiple defendants), and to a prosecution that could plausibly frame its case as involving some measure of collusion or common design on the part of the perpetrators. Not only were mass trials schematically appropriate for crimes of this nature, but evidence brought against one defendant would tend, perhaps properly, to rub off on all. But the defense's realization of the difficulties that such a trial structure would present was reflected in a motion offered by deputy counsel Captain Benjamin Narvid. His motion appeared to be a modest and reasonable one. In place of a single trial, he requested two separate trials for two distinct sets of defendants, one for those whose alleged offenses consisted of issuing illegal orders and another for men accused of having carried them out. If such a severance was not granted, Narvid pointed out, the defense arguments of many individual defendants would tend to be antagonistic, as subordinates attempted, as they surely would, to claim superior orders as a mitigating circumstance.[7]

Ellis's chief deputy, Captain Raphael Shumacker, responded with a carefully prepared counterargument that introduced the conceptual framework within which the prosecution team was to present its case. It was appropriate for all defendants to be tried jointly, he argued, in that all had been members of a criminal conspiracy:

> If it be true, as alleged in the charge, that the named accused acted together in this shooting and killing of prisoners of war, each accused became a cog-wheel in a monstrous slaughter machine. Now each such cog-wheel or group of cog-wheels comes into court and demands severance as a matter of right because their teeth mesh less smoothly when they drip with blood then when oiled with prospects of victory. . . . They demand, we submit, retail justice for wholesale slaughter.[8]

In less dramatic prose, Shumacker pointed out that the division between the givers and the executors of orders was not as clear-cut as the defense had suggested. Some defendants had both received criminal orders from superiors and transmitted them to subordinates. Again, Rosenfeld sided with the prosecution, citing as precedents the recently completed Dachau and Mauthausen Concentration Camp cases (Rosenfeld, it will be recalled, had participated in the latter) in which forty and sixty-one defendants, respectively, had been tried. Yet another defense motion offered by Wahler requesting greater specificity in the charges met a similar fate. The denial of that motion brought the first day of the trial to an end on a note less than encouraging to the defense.[9]

In his letter home that evening, Everett shared with Mary and with young Willis his reaction to the day's events. Both Dalbey and Ellis had been palpably nervous. The general, in fact, had shown genuine fright, his hands trembling as he read from the trial documents before him. Everett confessed only to having been bothered by the lights deployed by the movie cameramen, both U.S Army Signal Corps and German. There must have been at least one hundred of them, he complained, and "We were almost baked." A strong antipathy, clearly sharpened by anti-Semitism, had already emerged on the part of Everett toward the law member, Colonel Rosenfeld, due to rulings that Everett regarded as hurtful to the defense. German defense counsel had been distressed by the court's seemingly arbitrary decision not to allow them to wear their traditional robes (this had been permitted at Nuremberg, where, unlike at Dachau, all the defense counsel were German). Herbert Strong, Everett's German-Jewish deputy counsel, had protested but had been told that if the German lawyers didn't like the decision, they could simply stay away. But, to Everett's satisfaction, Rosenfeld, the "Jew legal member" who had "gloated" throughout the Mauthausen trial, had been overruled by Dalbey on the issue of the immediate translation into German of the several motions offered by the defense in the opening phase of the trial.[10]

With the preliminary sparring over, the trial began in earnest the following morning. Through defense counsel, the defendants all entered pleas of "not guilty" to the charges against them. The prosecution began its presentation with a slashing opening statement in which it stressed the ostensibly conspiratorial aspects of the offenses and, of course, the criminal taking of American and Belgian lives. Adolf Hitler stood at the apex of the conspiracy that the prosecution now proceeded to outline. At a conference before the opening of the offensive, Hitler had ordered his commanders to break enemy resistance by terror. One of those commanders, Hitler's former bodyguard *SS-Oberstgruppenführer* (General) Josef "Sepp" Dietrich, who led the key Sixth Panzer Army, lent greater specificity to the *Führer's* wishes by urging his subordinates to remember the victims of Allied bombings of German cities and to shoot prisoners of war in the imminent offensive, at least when combat conditions "required" it. That order, the prosecution argued, was passed down through corps and divisional levels and ultimately to the battalions, companies, and platoons that made up *Kampfgruppe* Peiper, the mechanized battlegroup, commanded by the dashing *SS-Obersturmbannführer* (lieutenant colonel) Jochen Peiper, that was to spearhead the attack. Commanders of these units transmitted the murderous intent of the order with varying degrees of bloodthirstiness, but all members of the battlegroup were made aware that the legal protection of the lives of enemy prisoners of war and civilians mandated by the Hague and the Geneva Conventions were to be ignored.

Criminal carnage was the result. Ellis and his staff were prepared to prove the murders of from "538 to 749" prisoners of war and "over 90" Belgian civilians while intimating that, in fact, the numbers slaughtered had been even greater. In addition to seventy-two American prisoners killed at the Baugnez crossroads (the Malmedy massacre proper), the prosecution alleged that SS troops of *Kampfgruppe* Peiper had murdered from twenty-eight to forty prisoners in six incidents at Honsfeld, sixty-two to ninety prisoners and at least nine Belgian noncombatants in thirteen incidents at Büllingen, forty-eight to fifty-nine POWs at Ligneauville, eight prisoners and at least seventy-three Belgians in and around Stavelot, at least six civilians in three incidents at Wanne, at least one civilian at Lutre Bois, forty-one to fifty-one prisoners of war in two incidents at Trois Ponts, 104 to 109 prisoners and at least one Belgian civilian in twenty-four separate incidents at Stoumont, 175 to 311 prisoners and at least three Belgian civilians at La Gleize, and, finally, a single starved and frostbitten American prisoner at Petit Thier.[11]

Noteworthy in the prosecution's opening statement were aspects of imprecision in what Ellis and his team claimed to be able to prove. They spoke in loose numerical terms of the victims alleged to have been killed by the defendants and were not always able to make their totals jibe. The problem was more than arithmetic. For murders other than those at the crossroads on December 17, 1944, the evidence beyond the sworn written statements of SS prisoners and a few Belgian civilians was sparse, and some of it was confused and contradictory. During the trial it would be supplemented by the testimony of prosecution witnesses, but this testimony would suffer from similar flaws. The prosecutors recognized the evidentiary problems in their case and conceded that it was "practically an impossibility to present to the Court the evidence on this mass of murders in a chronological sequence and in an understandable manner. . . ." Nevertheless, the case that began to unfold on May 17 was powerful and compelling.[12]

But, first, in an unusual gesture of indulgence and over Ellis's vigorous objection, the court permitted Everett to make an emotional and somewhat awkward statement:

May it please the Court, the Defense Counsels [sic] in this case were duly appointed by the Third Army and are a part of our American jurisprudence system. Our Government has said each defendant or accused shall be represented and assured of a fair trial. We, as Defense Counsels, will serve these 74 defendants in a dignified manner and with our utmost zeal. We will attempt to interpose no objection or conduct useless interrogation for the sake of delay. We must of necessity seek out and call the Court's attention to any evidence which tends to be unreliable or which shows prejudice or malice. Also the Defense Counsels are charged under our American system of trials to cast aside any personal feelings that we may have, and guarantee the immutable rights of the individual under our Constitution to these defendants by throwing around each the cloak of "America's fair trial." May the proceedings of this trial rise above any spirit of victor or vanquished as

well as any popular passion or frenzy to retaliate for our fallen comrades. Let it be said at the conclusion of this trial that the mighty Army
of the United States, even in the afterglow of victory and during our
enemy occupation, have not destroyed the right of the fair trial which
further demonstrates our spirit of Democracy. . . . [W]e have full confidence that each of you will abandon during this trial any spirit motivated by prejudice, hatred or vengeance . . . the war crimes as charged
by the prosecution are generally against American soldiers and a few
Belgium [sic] civilians. There is no "common design" as in concentration camp cases nor is there any premeditated murderous extermina-
tion plans over a long period of years. This is entirely a heat of battle
case, a desperate counteroffensive by our beaten enemy. . . .[13]

The points made by Everett in his slow, deliberate drawl are significant for an understanding of his later conduct. He did not deny that
war crimes had been committed by German troops during the Battle of
the Bulge, but he characterized them as "heat of battle" offenses. In
other words, they were the products not of a unique Nazi conspiracy of
evil, as were the concentration camps, but of the universal stresses of
battle, which often produce savage responses in combatants. The defendants, moreover, were entitled to a "fair trial," "fair" as understood
in the context of a domestic criminal court in the United States. And,
while he admonished the army judges to put aside their prejudices,
Everett was not always capable of doing so himself.

The prosecution in the presentation of its case consumed three
weeks (with half-day sessions on Saturdays). Suspended from the
courtroom wall was a 1:100,000 scale map depicting the road and to-
pography over which *Kampfgruppe* Peiper had fought during that fren-
zied December seventeen months earlier. And there was much testimony. Some veterans of *Kampfgruppe* Peiper who had not been charged
with war crimes but reserved as prosecution witnesses were called to
the stand to corroborate the contents of the crucial sworn statements.
An important witness was the blond and baby-faced Kurt Kramm, former *SS-Untersturmführer* (second lieutenant) and adjutant on the staff of
SS-Sturmbannführer (major) Werner Poetschke's First Battalion of the
First SS Panzer Regiment. Kramm's appearance for the prosecution
elicited the German equivalent of a "Bronx cheer" from the defendants,
resulting in an admonition from General Dalbey against "demonstrations" by the accused. Kramm's testimony, at least partially in English,

suggested that the defendants had been incited to violate the laws of war. In exercises prior to the offensive, he alleged, Peiper had said that the "rules" previously observed by German troops fighting in the West should no longer be respected and that, henceforth, Peiper's troops would be expected to fight as they had in Russia, where the rules of war in regard to prisoners and civilians had generally been ignored. But, as far as specific orders were concerned, Kramm was vague. An objection by Herbert Strong to testimony by the witness as to what had transpired at a preattack conference of *Kampfgruppe* Peiper's company command- ers at which he had not been present was overruled by Rosenfeld on the grounds that hearsay evidence was admissible. Strong lost again when he attempted to cross-examine Kramm on aspects of earlier statements made to army investigators at Schwäbisch Hall. Prosecution objections were sustained on the grounds that the matter had not been raised dur- ing the witness's direct testimony, a narrow ruling in light of the fact that Kramm had been questioned by Ellis on a statement he had made shortly after his capture. Everett's frustration and his lack of familiarity with trial procedure was evident in his effort to clarify the limits of cross-examination and the circumstances under which he would be permitted to attack the credibility of witnesses. Rosenfeld replied brusquely and without elaboration that cross-examination might occur only "according to the rules and regulations of cross-examination" and that the credibility of witnesses was to be attacked "in the prescribed manner."[14]

Testimony by successive prosecution witnesses reinforced that part of the prosecution case that alleged the transmission of criminal orders. A former SS man testified that his company commander had incited his troops with the observation that the impending offensive offered an op- portunity to avenge German women and children killed in Allied air raids and that "there wouldn't be any prisoners of war . . . and there wouldn't be any mercy shown to Belgian civilians, either."[15] With minor variations, the same story was told by several other witnesses. But the defense was able to deliver some significant counterstrokes. Johann Budik, a former private in the Sixth Company, First SS Panzer Regi- ment, testified that either his company commander or his platoon leader (he was not sure which) had declared prior to the attack that "prisoners will not be taken." But a German member of the defense team, Dr. Otto Leiling, elicited in his cross-examination that the witness did not regard the statement as applying to him because he did not consider it an order. The prosecution felt obliged to clarify the potentially damaging testimony but may have regretted doing so.

CAPTAIN SHUMACKER: What was it to be considered as?
WITNESS: That was to say that the infantry following us was to take the prisoners and not we.[16]

When a later witness testified that he had understood the "no prisoners" statement in the same sense, Shumacker moved to strike the testimony on the grounds that, as a conclusion by the witness rather than a factual statement, it was not proper evidence. But, in this instance, the very loose evidentiary rules that had damaged the defense worked to its advantage. Rosenfeld overruled the prosecution on the familiar grounds that the court would assign to the evidence its appropriate weight. The defense exploited that rare success by eliciting from the witness the statement that not only had he interpreted "no prisoners" in a benign manner but so had the entire company.[17]

The prosecution had warned the court of the possibility of hostile witnesses, but they were in the minority. Prosecution witness and former *SS-Sturmmann* (private first class) Fritz Geiberger testified that his platoon leader had given a blanket order requiring the shooting of prisoners of war, and other witnesses shared similar recollections, although the fact that some could seemingly remember nothing else about their commanders' preattack directives stimulated skepticism among Everett's team.[18] The testimony of witnesses was interspersed with the reading of written sworn statements secured earlier by army investigators, primarily at Schwäbisch Hall. These, in general, were more detailed than the oral testimony of prosecution witnesses but, in their overall import, no less ambiguous. They ranged from a flat denial by the former commander of the Sixth Panzer Army, Sepp Dietrich, that orders issued to his army directed the shooting of prisoners of war ("Whoever claims anything of the sort is speaking the [sic] untruth") to what might be termed a prescription for the selective and discretionary killing of prisoners—prisoners were to be shot "where local combat conditions required it," according to one of Peiper's sworn statements—to avowals such as that of former *SS-Unterstürmfuhrer* and defendant Hans Hennecke, who averred that his company commander had said "to give no quarter and to take no prisoners."[19]

The emotional high point of the prosecution case was reached with the testimony of survivors of the alleged SS atrocities. Virgil P. Lary, then a student at the University of Kentucky, appeared before the court on the morning of May 21 to recount his experiences at the Baugnez crossroads. Early on the afternoon of December 17, 1944, Lary, then first lieutenant, Battery B, 285th Field Artillery Observation Battalion, was traveling in the lead Jeep of a convoy of some thirty vehicles. Approximately "one thousand meters" south of the crossroads, the convoy came under heavy fire from the high ground due east. The picture that he painted was one of the confusion and terror of sudden combat.

Q: After you were fired on, what did you do?

A: I discussed with Captain Mills, who was in the leading jeep and who was in charge of the convoy, what would be best: to continue en route, to attempt to turn around, or to abandon the vehicles and get into the ditch.

Q: What did you do?

A: The firing became so intense that we decided to get into the ditch, stopping the convoy.

Q: After you got into the ditch, what did you do?

A: We continued to lie in the ditch while the artillery and small arms fire came into the convoy.

Q: Was anyone in the ditch with you?

A: Yes. Captain Mills and Corporal Lester, driver of the vehicle.

Q: Can you describe what happened after you were in the ditch?

A: I spoke to Captain Mills and said, "Do you think a patrol has broken through or is it too heavy for a patrol?" and he said, "The fire is too intense."

Q: Then what happened?

A: At this time I spoke to Captain Mills and said, "Let's crawl up this ditch and attempt to make a stand for it besides [sic] that small house which we just passed."

Q: What did Captain Mills say?

A: He said, "All right."

Q: Then what did you do?

A: We crawled up the ditch for approximately 100 meters in the direction of the house, north.

Q: Did you take refuge in the house?

A: We did not.

Q: What did you do?

A: At this time I was almost opposite the house. I started to cross the road in the direction of the house. At this time I noticed almost upon me a German tank.

Q: How did you know that it was a German tank?

A: I saw the black crosses on the side.

Q: What did you do after you saw the German tank?

A: As the personnel had their heads out of the tank, I dropped down to the ground and pretended to be dead.

Q: Then what happened?

A: The tank passed me without incident.

After another narrow escape, Lary succeeded in reaching the house, in front of which he found fifteen to twenty American soldiers standing with raised hands. He then claimed to have tried to organize these men for further resistance but was reluctantly dissuaded by Corporal Carl Daub.

A: . . . Corporal Daub stated, "look up the road, Lary," and this I did and saw an entire column of armored vehicles approaching in our direction. At this time I stated, "It will be necessary for us to surrender to these people."

Q: Did you surrender?

A: At this time, no.

Q: What did you do?

A: I crossed back over the road and spoke to Captain Mills.

Q: Where was Captain Mills at that time?

A: He was still lying in the ditch.

Q: What did you say to Captain Mills?

A: I said, "Captain Mills, are you hit?" and there was no answer. I repeated the question . . . and he said, "No, go away or they will come back and kill me."

Q: Did you have further conversation with him at that time?

A: I did.

Q: What was it?

A: I said, "Captain, come out of the ditch. These people have gone." This he did and joined our group across the road.

After making an effort to conceal his rank, Lary and his comrades awaited the approaching Germans with raised hands. An SS trooper in the lead tank motioned them to begin marching to the rear, that is, back toward the crossroads.

A: At the time we started to move back in the direction we had come or in the direction north to the crossroads. Approximately six or seven vehicles back in this column, a German stated the following as his vehicle passed us traveling south, "It's a long way to Tipperary, boys." No one in our group responded or made comment and we continued to march to the rear.

Q: Did any other German say anything further to you?

A: Yes. A German on foot came to our group and stated, "Stop, stop, I want drivers for these vehicles." We passed on and paid no attention to this man and continued to walk north in the direction of the crossroads.

Lary then described taking his place in an adjacent field along with other prisoners.

Q: Did you observe what the Germans were doing on the road?

A: At this time the half-track vehicle, mounting a cannon, was brought up and faced—or the attempt was made to face it— in the direction of our group. For some reason unknown to me, this cannon was ordered off, and it proceeded off down the road.

Q: Then what happened?

A: At this time two vehicles drove up and parked on our flanks, approximately 30 yards apart. At this time I saw a German in one of these vehicles place a machine gun over the side of the vehicle.

Q: What else did you notice on the road?

A: At this time another vehicle drove up and stopped in the center of these two.

Q: Do you know what type of vehicle this was?

A: I do not recall, but I saw only one-half of a man standing in this vehicle.

Q: What else did you observe?

A: I saw the man take a pistol and aim it in the direction of our group.

Q: Did he aim the pistol more than once?

A: He did, in the following manner: his hand on his hip. Three times.

Q: Then what happened?

A: He then fired two shots into our group. At the first shot a man to my right front, approximately here (indicating), with his hands up in this manner, went down like this.

PROSECUTION: Let the record show the witness indicated that the man shot had his arms extended over his head and fell sideways to the left.

At the prosecution's invitation, Lary identified one of the defendants, a twenty-three-year-old Rumanian, Georg Fleps, as the man who had fired the pistol.

Q: Now, what happened after these two shots were fired?

A: At this time, I heard two machine guns open up on the group. The firing seemed to become more intense. Those of us that were not killed originally fell to the ground. I fell with my face in the mud, my feet pointed toward the road.

Q: How long did the machine guns fire at the group?

A: For approximately three minutes.

Q: Did you hear any noises after the firing ceased?

A: I did. I heard the agonized screams from the American wounded.

Q: Did you hear anything else?

A: I heard single shots which sounded or seemed like they came from pistols.

Q: Did you see any German come into the field?

A: I did not. My face was in the mud.

Q: Did you hear any firing in the field?

A: I did. I heard those shots that sounded like pistol shots.

Q: After the pistol shots, did the moaning and groaning cease?

A: Yes, completely.

Q: Did you hear the Germans say anything during the shootings?

A: Only laughter.

Q: Did any vehicles pass along the road while you were lying in the field?

A: Yes.

Q: Did you hear any noises from these vehicles?

A: Yes, I heard laughter and more machine gun fire.

Lary concluded his testimony by describing his escape from the field and his success, although he was slightly wounded, in reaching American forces in Malmedy.[20]

Lary's testimony, despite its self-serving aspects, was compelling. In general terms and in many specifics, it agreed with sworn statements describing the crossroads incident that the prosecution would soon introduce into evidence, and the witness's description of laughing Waffen-SS troops finishing off wounded GIs heightened animosity toward those sitting in the dock. Other survivors gave accounts of the brief engagement and the subsequent shooting of American prisoners that were essentially identical to that offered by Lary. Samuel Dobyns, however, a former private first class in the 575th Ambulance Company, Ninety-ninth Infantry Division, who had been swept into *Kampfgruppe* Peiper's bag of prisoners earlier in the day, presented some interesting nuances. As the Germans assembled the prisoners in the field, Dobyns found himself in the front row, within a few feet of the road.

A: One German soldier stands up in the tank, he takes his pistol and points it at the crowd and waves it around two or three times (indicating) and drops it to his side. Then he raises his pistol again and waves it around again two or three times and then some American prisoner who was laying [sic] in the field, I don't know who he was, hollered, "Stand fast!" The next time he pulls the pistol and takes deliberate aim and fires. I see a man center ways [sic] of the front flank go down.

Q: What did you do then?

A: After the first shot was fired, I broke ranks and run [sic] around to the rear of the column.

Q: During that time did you hear any more shooting?

A: Yes. I heard one more report from the pistol.

Q: Then what did you do?

A: I run [*sic*] 15 or 20 feet to my rear and hit the ground in about one inch of water where the snow melted.

Q: Why did you hit the ground?

A: Because the two machine guns or maybe more started firing on us.[21]

That the defense recognized the potential value of Dobyn's testimony to its case was revealed by Lieutenant Wahler's cross-examination of the witness.

Q: Do you know if any other American soldiers broke ranks with you at the same time?

A: As far as I could see, none in the front ranks had broke [*sic*], but when I got to the rear, I had heard the 2nd report from the pistol then all from the rear columns began to break ranks and disperse and hit the ground.

Q: . . . Now when did the machine gun fire commence?

A: Immediately after the second report from the pistol.[22]

Dobyn's testimony supported Everett's contention that the murders had been not the premeditated products of a conspiracy or common design but, rather, spontaneous "heat of battle" offenses. The crossroads incident had been, perhaps, no more than a tragic error. A trigger-happy young German had fired his pistol in nervous response to a shout from one of the prisoners that he could not understand. The prisoners had panicked and begun to scatter, which had precipitated the devastating response from the German machine guns. Testimony from some of the prosecution witnesses was not inconsistent with this scenario. An enlisted man who had served with the Seventh Company of the First SS Panzer Regiment told the court that his tank had reached the crossroads on the afternoon of December 17 and had halted behind "two or three" other German vehicles. Battalion commander Poetschke was heard to order the German crews not to park their vehicles too close to one another in light of the ever present danger of Allied air attack. The witness was watching the American prisoners in the field and observed a sudden burst of machine gun fire from the vehicles ahead of him. The commander of the witness's tank then commenced firing with the machine gun mounted atop the turret. No evidence of premeditation was presented, although the witness testified that he had not seen any effort on the part of the prisoners to escape.[23]

In spite of the defense's occasional minor successes, Everett was pessimistic as the trial neared the end of its first week. The long-awaited assignment to him of a four-door Opel sedan complete with Hans, a German driver, relieved him of "a month of terrible jumping up and down in a jeep" but was more than offset by evidence of tension within the defense team and the overall development of the case. Everett's long-smoldering anger had been ignited by Frank Walter's decision to absent himself from court in order to have his car repaired.

> I really told off my Mr. Walters. I don't believe I have been so frank to anyone in my life but he is absolutely no good at all. . . . He is white haired and about 55 or 60. Selfish, self-centered, inconsiderate of others, incompetent, and a few other attributes all wrapped up together. . . . Oh well, it is just one thing after another like that with this whole staff.

By May 23, Everett conceded that there existed a state of mutual disaffection. "I think everyone is thoroughly mad with everyone else . . . too many lawyers and especially these American civilians."[24]

The appearance in court of the survivors of the crossroads massacre was rough going for the defense.

> The sympathy of the court is so much with them we do practically no cross-examination. As a matter of fact, on most witnesses we do very little because the Law Member is so hostile to any defense that we have rough sledding.

> They have turned the courtroom into a pure mockery . . . a Hollywood in Germany under the infamy [sic] of purported American Justice or Jurisprudence.

> The prosecution seems to be trying the case in the press and movies rather than on a dignified court basis. Our gang is getting harder and harder to hold in line.

While the crossroads shootings were the prime focus, many other alleged atrocities were included in the prosecution case. Ambiguity, often inherent in the confused and brutal interactions of combat, was evident in many of these "satellite" incidents. On the afternoon of May 28, the prosecution entered into evidence a series of depositions that were relevant to incidents that had occurred in Honsfeld on the morning of December 17. These depositions had been taken from American soldiers of the 612th Tank Destroyer Battalion during the previous year. T/5 Charles L. Morris described the murder of members of two tank destroyer platoons who attempted to surrender to the crew of a German tank. The tank's commander, speaking in English, ordered them to approach his vehicle, whereupon he shot them down with his machine pistol. Sergeant John M. Dluski succeeded in surrendering to Waffen-SS troops in Honsfeld and fell in with a column of approximately 250 American prisoners who were marching to the rear. He witnessed the cold-blooded murder of a member of his battalion when a crewman of a German tank that was passing the column shot T/5 "Johnie" Stegle between the eyes with an American .45 automatic. Two other depositions described the killing of Americans who attempted to surrender in Honsfeld but also described the successful surrender of others. In confronting evidence such as this, the defense was at a disadvantage, since cross-examining the sources of the information was impossible. Lieutenant Colonel Dwinell moved to strike the depositions on the grounds that they contained nothing to link the incidents described to specific defendants or units in the present trial, but he was overruled by Rosenfeld on the previously well-established and most liberal evidentiary rule.[25] But even when the defense had the opportunity for cross-examination, it did not always use it effectively. The prosecution, for example, elicited the following testimony from the gunner in a Panther tank in the Panzer Regiment's first Company:

Q: What did you observe as you entered Büllingen?
A: I saw Americans come out of a house about 100 meters ahead of us.
Q: How many were there?
A: Eight to ten.
Q: How were they holding their hands?
A: They were holding their hands above their heads.
Q: What firearms did they carry?
A: They were not bearing any arms.

Q: Were any of the group carrying any objects?

A: One of them was waving a piece of white cloth.

Q: . . . At the time these American soldiers came out of the house, did you see company commander *Obersturmführer* [first lieutenant] Kremser?

A: Yes.

Q: Where was he?

A: He was standing in the turret of his vehicle.

Q: What did he do?

A: He motioned to the American soldiers.

Q: Show the court how he motioned.

A: (Indicating)

LIEUTENANT COLONEL CRAWFORD: Let the record show the witness extends his right arm and brings it back to his right shoulder.

Q: What did the American soldiers do?

A: They then ran toward his car.

Q: What happened then?

A: When they were about ten meters away from his vehicle, Kremser's vehicle opened fire with machine guns upon them.

Q: How many bursts were fired?

A: I couldn't observe any fire. I would say there were about 50 rounds.

Q: What did the Americans do?

A: They fell forwards towards the front and remained lying there.

Q: After they fell did the firing cease?

A: No, they continued firing.

Q: Did you see these Americans after the firing ceased?

A: We continued to drive on right after that. I couldn't see them.[26]

The witness had described events that strongly suggested the commission of a war crime, but his testimony contained several obvious gaps. He had testified that he had seen GIs run toward Kremser's tank with the clear intention of surrendering, that the tank had fired a burst of machine gun fire, and that the Americans had fallen forward. But had they been hit? Had the Germans actually been firing at them, rather than at some other target? In light of the witness's testimony that the tanks's machine guns had continued firing after the GIs had fallen, that possibility might have been worth exploring by the defense in cross-examination. Instead, Herbert Strong limited himself to examining the witness on his field of view from the tank:

Q: Did you have opportunity from the place where you were sitting to observe what you told us just before?
A: Yes.
Q: Isn't it a fact that you have only a very small slit through which you can see, that you have practically no observation possibility whatsoever?
A: That slit, that is not a slit. It's some optical arrangement.[27]

The extreme caution exhibited by the defense probably reflected Everett's earlier expressed conclusion that the judges and, in particular, the law member were biased in favor of the prosecution and that aggressive cross-examination of prosecution witnesses would simply sharpen the court's hostility. On the previous day, he had complained sarcastically about the "unprejudiced" law member and General Dalbey, the court president, "with rope around his shoulder."[28] The two, moreover, had recently aggravated Everett's own prejudices, both moralistic and ethnic, within the broader framework of his growing sense of alienation from a military government he regarded as ethically defective. On Sunday, May 26, he had written to his family that he had gone to chapel that morning with another officer.

We both went in—only 8 people there. The Capt.[ain]—Chaplain was even worse. No program and he said they might have to make [it] at another time because of having to preach somewhere else. Well, I don't know what I'll do, but something will work out. . . . The boys say that they had quite a time at the Club last night. Show with girls with few clothes, etc. Said Prosecution and Defense joined forces and had a big table together and everybody had plenty of drinks. I haven't been there for a couple of weeks but I don't think I have missed much. Most of the Court went away for the weekend. The General and the Jew Law Member and the red-headed ex-Red Cross gal who I first thought pretty decent but anyway I was wrong again.[29]

Ironically, and with a double perversity, Everett's anti-Semitism may have threatened the harmony of a defense whose unity was already strained. Everett noted that Rosenfeld had approached him with a request that he attempt to restrain Captain Narvid and Herbert Strong, whose conduct was "annoying" the court, an event sure to be interpreted by Everett as further evidence of the law member's ethnically determined bias. Strong, understandably, was indignant at being muzzled, and the chief defense counsel, while sympathetic, could not forbear to couch his commiseration in anti-Jewish terms. The interests of the defendants had to take precedence over the feelings of one civilian lawyer, Everett noted, although he felt sorry for "the nosey-talking-arguing Jew."[30]

Everett's discordant defense team was required to combat charges other than the murders of U.S. prisoners of war. The prosecution had also alleged that members of *Kampfgruppe* Peiper had slaughtered a substantial number of Belgian civilians, most in and around Stavelot. Witnesses, both German and Belgian, offered appalling testimony. Two former enlisted men of the First SS Panzer Division's Reconnaissance Battalion testified to having witnessed their platoon leader shoot two adult male civilians under a railroad overpass on December 19. Achille Andre and Henri Delcourt related a horrific story of having been forced into an eight-by-twelve foot shed along with nineteen other men. German soldiers had fired two belts of machine gun ammunition into the tightly packed mass, after which several Germans had finished off with pistol shots those who showed signs of life. Straw had then been piled on the bodies and set ablaze. Remarkably, eight persons, including the witnesses, had survived to tell the tale. The testimony, although it failed to name specific defendants or even units (the defense, in vain, moved to strike it on these grounds), was nevertheless damaging in that it served to enhance the murderous aura that surrounded *Kampfgruppe* Peiper and, hence, all of the defendants.[31]

Madame Regina Gregoire of Stavelot related to the court her experiences of Waffen-SS brutality. On December 19, she, her two children, and twenty-six other townspeople had sought refuge from the combat raging around them in the basement of a house on the outskirts of town. Shortly before 9:00 P.M., two grenades were thrown into the crowded basement, which, amazingly, killed no one. Germans then ordered the civilians out of the basement. Madame Gregoire, who spoke German,

attempted to reason with a soldier who insisted that he and his comrades had been shot at from the same basement, an accusation that Gregoire vigorously denied. Her efforts unavailing, two SS troopers then
opened fire on the civilians, although Gregoire and her children were
spared, perhaps because of her command of German. In the course of
the following four days, she, her children, and other civilians were de-
cently treated by the Germans and directed by them to places of safety.
Under cross-examination by Dr. Leiling, Mme. Gregoire admitted that
she did not know whether or not there might have been other people in
the upper reaches of the house in whose basement she and other townspeople had sought refuge. This raised the possibility that the shooting
of the civilians had been in savage reprisal for shots fired at the Germans by other civilians in the house. In any event, heavy fighting was
in progress, and, she noted, "there was some shooting everywhere."[32]
Antoine Colinet, an innkeeper and factory worker from Stavelot, told
an equally harrowing tale of brutal SS conduct toward civilians. He, his
wife, his infant child, and another couple and their children were fired
upon by a German tank crewman while they were crossing a street
within a few yards of four parked German tanks. Two of the adults were
killed and two wounded.[33]

In reacting to those and other incidents involving the killing of
civilians, the defense could do little but suggest, as Leiling had done in
his cross-examination of Mme. Gregoire, that the killings were in response to guerrilla activity, but this was difficult to demonstrate in specific cases. The defense won a minor victory, however, in its cross-examination of Jean Elias, an electrician from Trois Ponts, who testified to
having discovered the bodies of fifteen civilians whom he knew near
the village. He added proudly that he had later accompanied American
troops in the recapture of Aisemont. Leiling cross-examined:

Q: Were you wearing the American uniform at that time?
A: Yes.
Q: Where did you get the American uniform?
LIEUTENANT COLONEL CRAWFORD (PROSECUTION): May it
   please the Court, I do not think there is any materiality to
   this question at all.
PRESIDENT: Objection overruled.
THE WITNESS: I got it from the Maquis.
Q: What is the Maquis?

A: It is the Army of the resistance.

Q: It is composed of Belgian civilians, is it not?

A: Yes.[34]

Elias's testimony, while hardly justifying the murder of civilians, seemed to inch it away from arbitrary slaughter by placing it in the context of the irregular warfare that had stimulated atrocities from at least the days of Napoleon's army in Spain.

Yet, it was not the testimony of a relative handful of German and Belgian witnesses that constituted the core of the prosecution case but, rather, the mass of sworn statements that the army investigators had gathered between December 1945 and April 1946. Testimony given by prosecution witnesses was often vague as to the nature of ostensible criminal acts or indefinite as to the individuals responsible for the crimes. Many of the nearly one hundred sworn statements, on the other hand, associated specific SS men with crimes that were described in exhaustive detail. If the statements were accepted by the court as literal truth or even close approximations thereof, the case against the defendants was sealed.

The sworn statements had been the primary focus of attention for Everett and his colleagues since they began the preparation of the defense case, both because of the statements' highly damaging contents if accepted at face value and because of the startling allegations by some of the defendants concerning the circumstances under which the statements had been executed. Everett's decision to bring the allegations to the attention of the War Crimes Branch had alerted the prosecution staff to the likelihood that the defense would attempt to discredit this key evidence by suggesting that at least some of the statements had been secured under duress. Hence, Ellis, in his opening statement, had recalled the extreme difficulty experienced by the investigative staff in extracting information from the suspects and had asserted that, therefore, "all the legitimate tricks, ruses and stratagems known to investigators were employed. Among other artifices used were stool-pigeons, witnesses who were not bonafide and ceremonies." Punctiliously, as each sworn statement was introduced into evidence, the prosecution asked the investigator who had elicited the statement whether duress in any form, including "threats," "promises," or "harsh, cruel or inhuman treatment," had been employed. These questions were invariably answered in the negative. Promptly offered as a prosecution exhibit in order to preclude a later sensational revelation by Everett was a black cloth hood similar to those that the suspects at Schwäbisch Hall had been required to wear while being conducted from their cells to the interrogation room and back in order to prevent them from learning the identities of other prisoners and to render them more tractable.[35]

The initial strategy of Everett and his staff was to attempt to exclude the extremely damaging sworn statements from evidence, but not on grounds of duress. Dwinell had objected to the prosecution's introduction of the first statement as a contravention of the rules laid down for the conduct of military government trials. In a concession to continental procedure, the U.S. Army's *Technical Manual for Legal and Prison Officers* barred the sworn testimony of defendants. The purpose of this prohibition was not to deprive the accused of the benefits of testifying under oath but to spare him the conflict of choosing between perjury and self-incrimination. Whether or not this was intended to apply to pretrial statements, as Dwinell suggested, the enjoining of sworn testimony in rebuttal of sworn statements did, in principle, place the defendants at a disadvantage. Rosenfeld had not addressed the merits of the argument but had simply cited the court's openness to all evidence that had a bearing on the case.[36]

It was therefore incumbent upon Everett and his team to discredit the statements on which the prosecution case largely hinged. In its cross-examinations of prosecution witnesses, the defense sought to implant in the minds of the army judges the suspicion that many of the sworn statements were less the confessions of guilt-laden war criminals than the fabrications of desperate and vengeful investigators. Under defense questioning, investigators steadfastly denied having employed physically coercive methods but did admit having used intensive methods of interrogation upon some German prisoners. Of particular interest was the questioning of Arvid Freimuth, a suspect who was not present in the defendants' dock, for he had hanged himself in his cell in Schwäbisch Hall in March 1946, a fact that did not deter the prosecution from introducing as evidence a statement allegedly made by the deceased, although a significant portion of it did not bear Freimuth's signature. In the document, Freimuth appeared to have admitted to having shot American prisoners or Belgian civilians on three occasions during the December 1944 offensive, once near Stavelot and twice in or in the vicinity of La Gleize. Lieutenant William Perl, the most active of the pretrial investigators, was cross-examined on June 6, 1946, in regard to the circumstances surrounding the interrogation of Freimuth and admitted that it was "possible" that he had threatened to turn Freimuth over to Belgian authorities, who, presumably, might be less restrained in their treatment of SS prisoners than the U.S. Army. This could hardly be characterized as a flagrant case of duress, although it did call into question the truthfulness of the blanket denial that "threats," "promises," or "harsh, cruel or inhuman treatment" had been employed.[37]

Dwinell cross-examined Joseph Kirschbaum, another of the investigators, in regard to a "mock trial" (or "*schnell* procedure," as the investigators preferred to call these stratagems) in which he had participated:

Q: At that *schnell* procedure, who else was present besides yourself?

A: There was Lt. Perl, myself and several other persons whose names I don't remember at present.

Q: Did each person have a part to play in the supposed trial?

A: Yes, Lt. Perl played a part and I played a part.

Q: What part did Lt. Perl play?

A: For myself, I played the part of the good guy and Lt. Perl played the part of the bad guy. . . .

Q: During that procedure you have referred to, did Lt. Perl have many conversations with [the defendant] in your presence?

A: All I know is that I was keeping the bad fellow away.

Q: How long did this procedure take?

A: Anywhere from, I would say, 10 to 25 minutes or less.

Q: Do you know whether Lt. Perl had a conversation with [the defendant] after the procedure had concluded?

A: You are referring to the *schnell* procedure? Well, after the *schnell* procedure, I was the fellow who spoke to [the defendant] and no one else. . . .

Q: I believe you stated on direct examination that no promises were made to [the defendant]. Now isn't it a fact that you promised [the defendant] that if he would make a statement he would only get six months or possibly one year as a result of that statement?

A: I personally never made such a promise to him.

Q: Do you know whether anyone else made such a statement
or promise . . . ?
A: I never heard of it.[38]

But "mock trials" and the interrogation of a suicidal suspect were
not necessarily typical of the means by which the sworn statements had
been secured. In some cases, statements had been gotten in the course
of one or two brief and straightforward interrogation sessions, although
the testimony of investigators revealed that, in many cases, the sworn
statements were not in the words of the prisoners who had made them.
The investigators had often drafted statements on the basis of notes
they had taken during interrogations and had then offered these to the
prisoners for signature, although the court had been assured that each
former SS man had been invited to first make whatever textual changes
he deemed necessary, a point on which the memories of investigators
and prisoners sometimes differed.[39]

Everett and his staff had been able to make only tentative thrusts
against the prosecution case. They had pried open some cracks in it, but
the volume of evidence against their defendants was enormous. In
order to make breaches of those cracks, they would have to produce a
substantial body of evidence to contradict that presented by the prosecution and to accent the dubious character of some of the sworn statements. As the prosecution closed its presentation, on Friday, June 7, the
court demonstrated a greater degree of magnanimity than Everett was
later inclined to recall. In response to a request by the German defense
attorneys for a recess of five days, the court adjourned until Monday,
June 17, providing Everett and his colleagues with a precious ten days
to accomplish the seemingly impossible.[40]

5

Of the Particulars and Charge, Guilty

EVERETT'S PSYCHIC ENERGY continued to be divided between organizing a credible defense for the seventy-four Malmedy accused and expediting the transportation of his wife and son to Europe, the frustrations produced by both accounting for his growing sense of alienation from the U.S. Army. His admiration for Germans and things German and his tendency to exclude from consciousness what some Germans had done and many others had condoned during the grim period between 1933 and 1945 was much in evidence. Nowhere in the many letters written in the weeks and months during which he was occupied in Dachau is there a reference to the purpose that the camp had served prior to its capture by American forces little more than a year earlier. He seems to have dealt with the riddle of the culture capable of producing both Dachau and Beethoven by simply repressing the former in preference to the latter. In the midst of the prosecution phase of the trial, he wrote enthusiastically to his family of a night in a Munich whose ruins could not dim the glory of German art:

> Last night, I went to Beethoven Symphony #9. It was beautifully conducted. I never saw any more masterful handling of an orchestra and chorus. The contralto and baratone [sic] were simply magnificent. It started at 6 o'clock and lasted for 2 hours.

> We all (Col. Dwinell, Mr. Strong, Mr. Walters, Capt. Narvid & wife and myself) were guests of Dr. Pfister, who is atty. on our case and also atty. for Opera Company. Then at about 8:45 or 9:00 P.M. we went to Dr. Pfister's house. He had an elderly Bavarian minister there and quite a number of people. . . . His wife had long flowing hair like you, Mary Campbell, except black. They have a 3-year-old daughter who is just as pretty as can be. Dr. and Mrs. Pfister have been married for 10 years. Both are very attractive, as well as Dr. and Mrs. Leiling. . . .[1]

Keeping company with refined and physically attractive German families like the Pfisters and Leilings was, however, inadequate compensation for the prolonged separation from his own wife and children and for the society of other Americans in Germany, most of whom he tended to judge harshly. Everett wrote his son on June 3 that, if the family could not be reunited soon in Europe, he would find a way to return to the United States, a point he reinforced the next day in a letter to his daughter and son-in-law: "I will probably be on my way back in September. . . . Sure wish I had Kil over here. He is so much better than almost all my attys. Boy, only two of them could even make a living in the U.S. I sure will be glad to get out of the inefficiency and rottenness of the ETO."[2]

The events of June 7, however, raised Everett's spirits. Not only did the court grant the defense a ten-day recess, but also he received a phone call from Wiesbaden with the welcome news that Mary and his son had been placed on the list of dependants to be shipped to Europe on or about August 1. Typically, his jubilation was tinged with guilt. "I don't know how I forced it at this end because I have only been here a couple of months and others have been here 1–2 & 3 years, thus giving them rightfully the preference."[3] He had, in fact, secured the assistance of friends and associates, including the politically well-connected Atlanta attorney Elbert P. Tuttle, later to be an Eisenhower appointee to the federal bench, in advancing the date of his reunion with Mary and young Willis. He continued to be oppressed by the burden of organizing a probably futile defense with a staff in which he had little confidence, although his opinion of the panel of officers hearing the case, including Rosenfeld, seems to have risen in the euphoria of the moment:

I have so very much to do tonight and I am already worn out. The prosecution have "rested their case," and I secured a delay until Monday a week. We sure need this time and it means night and day work for us. . . . I have some plans, but every time I turn around these various lawyers I have start trouble. Today, the court just raised the very devil with this old civilian white-haired worthless lawyer. I have kept his mouth shut most of the time but today he got loose and after court, I appoligized [sic] for him to the Court. They said forget it, that they knew what a problem I am having. All the members of the Court have been so nice to me as well as others. Anyway, maybe I'll live through the trial. I hope so anyway.[4]

In the days that followed, Everett, Dwinell, Sutton, Narvid, and Wahler worked furiously to prepare a coherent defense. Everett recognized his limitations as a strategist in criminal law and depended heavily on Dwinell, a New York attorney with extensive courtroom experience, for procedural advice. Lieutenant Wahler, a stenographer, and an interpreter were dispatched by air to Belgium to question witnesses at the scenes of atrocities alleged in the prosecution case, while other witnesses within easier reach of the defense team were questioned in Dachau. "The boys have lots of work," Everett noted, "and I hope the Defense puts on a smooth show."[5] A major distraction intervened on June 11. Everett was visited by Colonel Corbin, Third Army Judge Advocate, to whom Everett had reported the initial allegations of duress in the interrogation of German suspects back in April. Corbin suggested a stroll in the balmy late spring weather and related that Lieutenant Colonel Clio Straight, who had succeeded Colonel Claude Mickelwaite as deputy theater judge advocate for war crimes the previous month, had visited him in Dachau. According to Corbin, Everett was to be named chief administrative officer of a consolidated army war crimes trial program in Dachau following the Malmedy proceedings. Everett expressed dismay in his letter home:

> There will be 4 courts running all the time and I understand they have over 2000 cases pending. . . . What headaches there are here—worthless lawyers, civilians and Army, the hundreds of problems like temperamental court reporters, German interpreters, fraueleins. Fighting over typewriters, mail, weekend trips, automobile and transportation problems, getting witnesses, etc., etc. Endless inefficiency and loafing.

But he was pleased, too.

> Well, why all this I don't know, but at any rate they think it is quite something. I guess God knows best and I have little choice since I am in the Army. . . . I have had the respect of all the males and females here, which is more than most all the rest have.[6]

The incident invites questions. If Straight wanted Everett for the position, why didn't he convey that information himself, rather than delegate the responsibility to Corbin? That question occurred to Everett, although he brushed it aside with the perhaps naive speculation that Straight and Colonel Howard Bresee, who had accompanied him, had simply been "too busy." But if Straight and Bresee had wanted to see Everett in regard to an important assignment, as Corbin indicated they had, it is difficult to imagine business that would have prevented a short personal interview or even a phone call. Might Straight have wanted to suggest to Everett the possibility of a future reward in return for conduct that would not embarrass the U.S. Army in the most sensitive of its war crimes trials, while providing for himself the protection of deniability by conveying the offer through a third party? If so, his timing, less than a week prior to the opening of the defense phase of the trial, was appropriate.

The matter was apparently not raised again. If "good behavior" on Everett's part had been an implicit prerequisite, it is not difficult to understand why.

Brigadier General William K. Harrison had sent a remarkable letter at the end of May 1946 to the office of the adjutant general in Washington. At the time of the events addressed by the trial, Harrison had been assistant commander of the U.S. Thirtieth Infantry Division, one of *Kampfgruppe* Peiper's primary antagonists during the offensive of December 1944. Harrison noted that American troops under his command had recaptured La Gleize on December 24, 1944, and had found no evidence of the murders of the 175 to 311 U.S. prisoners of war that the prosecution alleged had occurred there. Major Harold D. McCown, commander of the division's Second Battalion, 119th Infantry Regiment, was in possession of additional information and could be reached at Fort Benning. Harrison bluntly declared his belief that the alleged La Gleize murders were "figments of the imagination" and requested that his letter be forwarded to Dachau "in order that no injustice be done."[7] In fact, the written record of McCown's experiences was in the possession of Third Army's Historical Division and was made available to Everett, while the author was flown to Europe, arriving in Dachau on June 14. Everett recorded that his "star witness" had been "given instructions" at Wiesbaden, by which he clearly meant to imply that the War Crimes Branch had attempted to influence McCown's future testimony. Everett seems to have instinctively liked McCown, not least because he was a fellow Southerner, and liked him still better when he confided that he was infuriated each time he read newspaper accounts of the trial and the "lies" that they contained. Everett was delighted to enhance the indignation of someone whom he believed capable of turning the case around and came away from their meeting satisfied that he had gotten McCown thoroughly "steamed up." Everett went to bed that night thanking God for having sent the young Louisiana State University graduate to the assistance of his defendants, and his excitement prevented sleep until 3:30 A.M.[8]

Court reconvened at 8:30 on the morning of Monday, June 17. The testimony that McCown was prepared to give, although of great potential value to the defense, was not likely to be sufficient to neutralize the cumulative effect of the mass of sworn statements that the prosecution had introduced into evidence. Everett undoubtedly knew that his motion to dismiss charges on the grounds that the prosecution had failed to prove a prima facie case would be denied, but it provided the defense an opportunity to remind the court of the problematical aspects of the primary component of the prosecution case. Dwinell recalled introductory language used by the prosecution that indicated its own doubts regarding the persuasiveness of the evidence and followed with a review of the incredible detail of many of the sworn statements and the vagueness in crucial areas of others.[9] Wahler embarrassed himself by including in his argument an allusion to McCown's experiences in La Gleize, evidence that had not yet been presented, as the prosecution was quick to point out, and followed that gaffe with an irrelevant reminder that under domestic criminal law confessions, even if evidently voluntary, are insufficient to prove the corpus delicti without corroborating evidence. Ellis had no difficulty countering the defense initiative with a citation of the very different rules of evidence under which the Dachau court was operating, and, in any event, Rosenfeld's decision to allow the trial to proceed was a foregone conclusion.[10]

Everett followed with another motion as unlikely to be sympathetically received by the court as the first, but useful in impressing upon the officers occupying the bench how far war crimes trial procedure diverged both from international law and the statutes that governed U.S. Army courts martial. Crucial to this argument was the fact that the defendants, although in custody of the U.S. Army, were not, technically, prisoners of war. They had officially lost that status on April 11, 1946, when criminal charges had been served upon them, altering their status to that of "civilian internee." The then deputy theater judge advocate, Colonel Claude Mickelwaite, had requested this legal transmogrification "in order to preclude the possibility of legal complications with respect to the trial of the case. . . ."[11] What Mickelwaite had meant by that cryptic statement was revealed by Everett's team in a powerful attack not simply on the character of the sworn statements but also on the army's system of war crimes justice. As prisoners of war prior to their release from that status in April, the defense argued, the defendants had been under the protection of the Geneva Convention of 1929, which forbade the coercive treatment that, the defense contended, had been employed to extract the sworn statements. Under Article 45 of the Convention, moreover, prisoners of war were to be "subject to the laws, regulations and orders in force in the armies of the detaining powers." Accordingly, while the defendants were prisoners of war, U.S. laws of courts martial were controlling, and these laws would not have admitted confessions as evidence against defendants other than the deponents. Under the same laws, confessions made by an inferior to a superior officer were generally held to be inadmissible, because of the difficulty of excluding elements of duress.

> The alleged confessions or statements of these accused are absolutely void and not admissible in evidence in this case. The laws of our nation provide that a man should have only one wife at a time, and any subsequent marriage without appropriate divorce decrees render[s] the second marriage void. The contracts of minors are void unless subsequent ratification [sic] after they reach their majority. The contracting of a party to commit a crime is void. Certain prerequisites are necessary to make a note negotiable, such as date due, a sum certain to be paid, etc., and without those elements they are void. As previously outlined, International Law laid down certain safeguards for treatment of prisoners of war, and any confession or statement extracted in violation thereof is not admissible in a court martial or any subsequent trial under a code set up by Military Government. If a confession from a prisoner of war is born in a surrounding of hope of release or benefit, or fear of punishment or injury, inspired by one in authority, it is void in its inception and not admissible in any tribunal of justice.
>
> Could anyone, by artifice, conjure up the theory that the Military Government Rules and Ordinances are superior to the solemn agreements of International Law as stated in the Geneva Convention of 1929? Is this court willing to assume the responsibility of admitting these void confessions? . . . It is not believed that the Court will put itself in the anomalous position of accepting statements into evidence which were elicited from prisoners of war in contravention of the Geneva Convention and therefore a violation of the Rules of Land

Warfare on the one hand and turn squarely around and mete out punishment for other acts which they deem violations of the same laws. To do so would be highly inconsistent and subject the Court and all American Military Tribunals to just criticism.[12]

Not to be outdone in resourceful argument, the prosecution responded with a startling rationalization. The Malmedy defendants had never been under the protection of the Geneva Convention of 1929 because they had never been prisoners of war! They had become war criminals at the moment of having committed their atrocious acts and had therefore forfeited the honorable status of prisoner of war and the safeguards that, under international law, accompanied that status. Ellis reiterated that the defendants had not been under duress when they gave their sworn statements but maintained that even if they had, the statements would retain their validity as evidence, according to the regulations that governed the trials of "certain" war criminals:

> To admit a confession of the accused, it need not be shown such confession was voluntarily made and the Court may exclude it as worthless or admit it and give it such weight as in its opinion it may deserve after considering the facts and circumstances of its execution.[13]

Ellis's counterthrust was disturbing and could only have reinforced Everett's growing conviction that "Dachau justice" was an oxymoron. If the defendants were already for legal purposes criminals, then were not the proceedings at Dachau merely a charade? And the existence of a trial regulation, which seemed to absolve prosecutors of the need to demonstrate the voluntary character of confessions, might appear to condone and therefore encourage the employment of duress. To permit the bench time to ponder the merits of defense and prosecution arguments, Dalbey adjourned the court. After twenty-five minutes, Colonel Rosenfeld announced to the reassembled company without explanation that the defense motion to withdraw the sworn statements was denied.[14] But Everett could now hope to have created a more sympathetic audience for the evidence he and the defense team were about to present. The prosecution had painted a picture of a demonic orgy of murder, which had been unleashed upon GIs and Belgian civilians by none other than the twentieth century's arch-fiend, Adolf Hitler, and had thereby implied a moral equivalence between the Malmedy massacre (and other atrocities committed by *Kampfgruppe* Peiper) and the hell of the death camps and the Holocaust. This the defense undertook to dismantle, and Everett hoped that his job would be facilitated by the fact that the bench was occupied by active line officers who understood the grim and universal realities of waging modern mechanized war.

> Again and again it must be emphasized that these accused are members of a spearhead fighting desperately under the worst battle conditions. Each of you must bear in mind that this was an armored unit advancing rapidly into enemy territory and being totally cut off from supplies and reinforcements. The practical difficulty of armored units taking prisoners is well recognized, as they are tightly organized and have absolutely no men to spare for evacuation of prisoners of war. The Prosecution has developed their case without taking these factors into consideration and have very deftly emphasized "no prisoners of war will be taken." We believe the evidence will show why no prisoners could be taken in this rapidly advancing column and we believe the Court has already recognized that "motioning of prisoners of war to the rear" was necessary. We believe the evidence will further show under these difficult and trying battle conditions that a vast distinction exists between an armored spearhead movement in combat and a quiet sector on a battlefield. Prisoners can be taken in these slower and comparatively quiet sectors, but not so under the conditions of warfare we are here considering. There will develop ample proof that once this swift moving armored column was stopped, that every consideration was shown all captives. No greater injustice could possibly be done than to compare this case with the concentration camp murder cases. We believe the evidence has shown and will further show that the breaking of ranks and dispersing of prisoners of war was the primary factor of most of the deaths at Malmedy. We believe the evidence will show that violations of land warfare are rare in this case and when the true combat situation has been shown to this Court, two words can accurately describe the over-all picture—"intense combat."[15]

This was an ambiguous summary of the bloody events of December 1944, in which the likelihood that some illegal killings had been committed was implicitly conceded but attributed to the exigencies of the moment and simple confusion rather than to criminal conspiracy. At worst, Everett hoped, his defendants would be found guilty of manslaughter and spared the death penalty.

Multiple German witnesses testified to the absence of formal directives to murder prisoners of war. Hitler's former adjutant General Gerhard Engel, whose Twelfth *Volksgrenadier* Division had been assigned the task of punching a hole in American lines through which Peiper was to begin his dash for the Meuse, had been present at the preattack conference attended by Sepp Dietrich and other top officers of the Sixth Panzer Army; he denied that anything Hitler had said could be interpreted as orders to kill prisoners of war or civilians. Fritz Kraemer, Dietrich's former chief of staff and the first of the defendants to testify, denied that orders distributed by the Sixth Panzer Army had contained directives to engage in illegal killings but admitted that tactical orders had referred to the possibility of resistance by Belgian guerrillas and that such resistance, when encountered, was to be broken "at all costs." Far from having killed its prisoners, Kraemer testified, Dietrich's army had taken captive between five and seven thousand American soldiers during the offensive, although orders had specified that the collection of prisoners was not to be the responsibility of fast-moving German forward elements. He had first learned of the possibility that American prisoners of war had been shot at the Baugnez crossroads when his G-2 reported to him on December 20 or 21 that such a claim was being broadcast on *Soldatensender Calais,* a German-language British shortwave propaganda station. Kraemer testified that he had queried subordinate units for information regarding the alleged incidents but had received only professions of ignorance.[16]

The testimony of additional German defense witnesses, not surprisingly, was in overall agreement with that of the two former generals. But professions of innocence by accused war criminals and sympathetic testimony by their former comrades were probably of little value in the defense's efforts to neutralize the damning sworn statements and the testimony of some prosecution witnesses. Everett had attempted to interview some of the former SS men who had testified against their comrades, apparently because he hoped to uncover further evidence of duress or illicit inducements, but Ellis had succeeded in blocking the effort while accusing the defense of intimidation of its own by placing some witnesses in the same room with defendants. But their testimony was only the prelude to the playing of the ace in the defense's hand, the witness for whom he had thanked God several days earlier, Lieutenant

Colonel Harold D. McCown. Everett attempted to while away the evening of June 19 by taking McCown to a floorshow at a Munich nightclub. The show was "fair," but Everett had too much on his mind to enjoy it. He knew that his best chance to unhinge the prosecution case would sit in the witness chair the next morning.[17]

Visually, "Hal" McCown, wavy-haired and with a clean-cut, boyish face, could have come from the easel of Norman Rockwell. His military record was impeccable. An officer in the regular army since July 1940, he had entered combat in Normandy in June 1944 as operations officer of the 199th Infantry Regiment, serving in that capacity until November, when he had received command of the regiment's Second Battalion. In articulate sentences uttered in a soft southern accent that no doubt enhanced their appeal to Everett, McCown described the entry of the 119th into combat east of Werbomont on December 18, 1944, under orders to intercept Peiper's armored spearhead. While fighting over rough terrain between Stoumont and La Gleize on the afternoon of December 21, McCown was captured, along with his operations sergeant and a radioman. The three were disarmed and searched by four SS men and marched immediately to Peiper's command post. Peiper, according to McCown, attempted to interrogate the American officer but learned nothing other than McCown's name, rank, and serial number. Later that day, McCown was taken to a building in La Gleize whose large cellar held 135 American prisoners of war, the bulk of whom were members of his own regiment's Third Battalion, captured two days earlier in Stoumont. He was able to ascertain that the Americans were being well treated, complaining only of poor-quality food and that watches and rings had been taken from them. The value of McCown's testimony was immediately evident, as it served to soften the demonic image of *Kampfgruppe* Peiper that had been elaborately constructed by the prosecution, and Everett and his team skillfully built upon it.

Q: Did you learn of any infractions of the Geneva rules?

A: I believe the two that I have mentioned [thefts and poor food] are infractions of the Geneva rules, but inasmuch as we are guilty of the same, I found no—

PROSECUTION: If the court please, I object to that part of the answer.

A: I found no serious infractions.

PROSECUTION: I move to strike that part of the answer and the court be instructed to disregard it, referring to treatment by Americans.

PRESIDENT: The objection is sustained and that portion of the witness's statement as regards the actions of Americans will be stricken from the record and disregarded by the court.[18]

Nevertheless, the words had been spoken, and Everett could legitimately hope that the officers occupying the bench had been reminded that American soldiers had not always been punctilious in their adherence to the laws of war.

Far more significant than evidence of what GIs might have done was testimony as to what the German defendants had not done. In its opening statement, the prosecution had asserted that "one hundred seventy-five to three hundred eleven" American prisoners and "at least" three Belgian civilians had been murdered by men of *Kampfgruppe* Peiper in La Gleize between December 18 and December 23, including a large group allegedly shot on the eighteenth along the cemetery wall of the only church in the village. La Gleize was a tiny place of fifty or sixty houses, and, although McCown could not claim to have seen every street and corner, he had moved about the village and passed the church under German guard during his four-day captivity but had seen no dead American soldiers or Belgian civilians except for the body of a captured lieutenant who had been killed by shrapnel from U.S. artillery fire. On the other hand, in one of the five conversations that McCown had had with Peiper, the commander of the German battle group had informed him that nine American prisoners assigned by their captors to labor details had been shot and killed while attempting to escape to nearby American positions. Thus, nine prisoners had been killed, although perhaps legitimately, without McCown's having observed evidence of it.[19]

McCown made no secret of having been favorably impressed by Peiper and by other members of the *Kampfgruppe* whom he had encountered. In the report written after his escape from his German captors, he wrote of Peiper, "I have met few men who impressed me in as short a space of time as did this German officer" and described the discipline and humanity of the enemy soldiers he had seen. His testimony before the court was somewhat more restrained but strongly favorable to Peiper and his men. McCown told of having been summoned to Peiper's command post on the evening of December 22, 1944, and having conversed until the predawn hours, during which time Peiper expounded the Nazi *Weltanschauung* and assessed Germany's prospects in the war. In the bitter atmosphere of the Dachau courtroom, the revelation of a protracted and cordial conversation between the American major (as McCown was then) and the *SS-Obersturmbannführer* carried with it a scent of unwholesomeness that may have limited the favorable impact of McCown's testimony and certainly angered Colonel Rosenfeld, who later declared McCown and Peiper to have been "entirely too friendly."[20] Further damage may have been done when Everett permitted McCown to recount another conversation in which Peiper had complained that U.S. forces were firing on his armored vehicles with an antitank gun emplaced on the ledge of a chateau outside La Gleize that the *Kampfgruppe* had earlier used as a hospital. He was reluctant to order his gunners to fire on the building, he told McCown, out of concern for the German and American wounded who might still be there. McCown assured Peiper that it was American policy to evacuate wounded in such a situation "and that he could be reasonably sure that there were no casualties in the castle." Everett, no doubt, hoped that such testimony would serve the purpose of humanizing Peiper in the eyes of the officers judging the case, but it may have had the effect of impeaching McCown as an officer willing to share information of military value with an enemy commander.[21]

McCown went on to describe yet another meeting with Peiper the following night in the presence of the recently captured Captain Chrisenger of the 803rd Tank Destroyer Battalion. Peiper had received orders that day from divisional headquarters to attempt a breakout from La Gleize, now encircled by American forces and under heavy artillery bombardment. It was at this meeting that Peiper proposed a plan according to which all American prisoners in La Gleize, then numbering about 150, would be set free, with the exception of McCown, who would accompany the retreating Germans and, Peiper hoped, later be exchanged under a flag of truce for German medical personnel and wounded, whom the *Kampfgruppe* would be forced to leave behind. Chrisenger's function was to apprise the commander of the 119th Infantry Regiment of the proposed arrangement when it entered La Gleize. Although stressing the unlikelihood that American forces would honor such an agreement, McCown joined Peiper in signing a document that contained the terms.[22]

McCown described how he had marched out of La Gleize with the German column shortly after midnight on December 24. A day later, he succeeded in escaping from his captors and making contact with an outpost of the 82nd Airborne Division. But, in describing *Kampfgruppe* Peiper's escape from encirclement, McCown was again able to attest to the Germans' high level of competence and humane treatment of their bag of prisoners, now reduced to a single major of the U.S. Army.[23]

Under cross-examination, McCown could not be shaken from his straightforward account, although the prosecution was able to elicit from him the admission that he had not seen all of La Gleize during his captivity; therefore, by implication, some evidence of foul play might have eluded him. McCown also conceded that he had witnessed "minor" infractions of the Geneva Convention other than those he had earlier described, such as the use of prisoners to carry artillery ammunition in a zone of combat, but, again, he candidly noted to the annoyance of the prosecution that these were offenses of which the U.S. Army was also guilty.[24]

For all of its problematical aspects, McCown's testimony should have raised substantial doubt in the minds of the judging officers of the credibility of those elements of the prosecution case that dealt with the murders of American prisoners in La Gleize and, more generally, of the reliability of the sworn statements, which constituted the sole evidence for the alleged crimes. But Everett was both furious and disconsolate over the events of June 20 in the courtroom at Dachau and informed his family in one of two letters written that day that he had been unable to eat dinner because of his disgust with the day's proceedings, which appear to have crystallized his conviction that the Malmedy court, as it was constituted, was incapable of producing justice for his clients. He railed against the fact that McCown had been prevented from testifying to American violations of the laws of war, some of which went far beyond what he had been able to suggest during his testimony. McCown had personal knowledge, Everett wrote, of the murders of "hundreds" of German prisoners after they had surrendered, and while it is not evident that Everett had intended his star witness to testify to American atrocities that were comparable to those with which the German defendants had been charged, he was convinced that he had been betrayed by Ellis in the matter of testimony on comparative respect for international law. McCown had been prevented from giving evidence on

"minor" American infractions but had then been cross-examined by
Ellis on comparable German offenses he had observed while in captivity but had not mentioned during his direct testimony, in violation of an
agreement that Everett believed he had had with his opposite number.
This, Everett was convinced, had been a treacherous stratagem designed to discredit McCown. But reasoned indignation gave way to vis-
ceral fury when Everett addressed himself to the conduct of Colonel
Rosenfeld. At one point in his cross-examination by the prosecution on
his experiences in La Gleize, McCown had apparently directed his response to the questioner standing to his right, rather than to the officers
sitting on the bench directly before him. Everett recalled that "the Jew
law member" yelled at McCown to face the court in "a louder voice
than I would yell at a nigger." The official trial transcript does not, of
course, reveal the volume or tone of voice in which "Will you please
face the Court in making your reply" was uttered, but it does indicate
that the request was made by the president of the court, General Josiah
Dalbey, and not by Rosenfeld. The discrepancy may be the result of a
court reporter's error or of Everett's faulty memory, its fallibility perhaps the subconscious result of anti-Semitism. In any event, a leitmotiv
of Everett's assessment of the trial—that it had been fatally flawed by
Jewish vengefulness—was being established. The impact of the day's
events, perhaps enhanced by the suspicion that McCown's testimony
had not had the effect that he had hoped and the depressing effect of
sixteen consecutive days of rain, had moved Everett to consider resign-
ing rather than be a party to what he feared might result in "legalized
murder." But the impulse passed quickly. "Please excuse this letter and
forget it when you receive it," he instructed Mary, as "it all will have
blown over some way externally [although] not inside for me."[25]

He might have felt relief at a narrow escape, had he known of it.
Shortly after McCown's departure, Ellis came into possession of the
summary of an interrogation of Peiper by Captain Leroy Vogel of U.S.
military intelligence dated September 15, 1945. If Peiper spoke the
truth during the interrogation and if Vogel had recorded it accurately,
McCown's interaction with Peiper had been more cordial than the
American officer's testimony had indicated. McCown had allegedly
provided Peiper with an evaluation of the U.S. Thirtieth Division's
artillery fire falling on La Gleize, which had facilitated the Germans'
escape. He had, moreover, indicated sympathy for the German war
against the Soviet Union and had jokingly volunteered his services

against the Russians, in return for which Peiper might reciprocate by coming to the United States to help him hang Jews! The alleged exchange, if not a malicious fabrication by Peiper, may have been nothing more than an ill-considered effort by McCown to ingratiate himself with his captor for the benefit of other GIs held prisoner in La Gleize, but it would have been, at the very least, a grave embarrassment for the defense if Ellis had had the opportunity to cross-examine the star defense witness on the matter.[26]

A few minor witnesses followed McCown to the witness stand. The defense then called Jochen Peiper, clearly the central defendant in the trial and a man whose personality made him stand out decisively from the mass of the accused. In spite of his uniform, now stripped of insignia and decorations, Peiper scarcely appeared the defeated enemy and prisoner, with his carefully slicked-back hair and his attitude of controlled yet unmistakable disdain for the events that he had seen unfolding in the Dachau courtroom over the preceding weeks. Testifying in his own behalf, Peiper had the unenviable task of refuting major portions of his earlier sworn statements. But he had given his testimony careful thought and needed little guidance or prompting from the defense team, as he spoke in colorful terms of his experiences at the hands of American pretrial investigators. Peiper had, in fact, prepared notes on the investigation procedure and was given permission to refer to them while on the witness stand.[27]

He testified to having spent five weeks of solitary imprisonment in a dark cell at Zuffenhausen without opportunity for physical exercise before having been questioned by Lieutenant William Perl. Peiper suggested that the depressed psychological condition that resulted from this treatment had made him vulnerable to Perl's interrogation tactics, which included flattery combined with efforts to impress him with the hopelessness of his situation and suggestions that the fate of his comrades depended upon his conduct. Peiper asserted that Perl had informed him that among the American prisoners killed at the crossroads had been the sons of a senator and a business tycoon, whose influence had created a public demand for Peiper's head that was so powerful that not even the president of the United States could save him. Peiper's military career had been a brilliant one, Perl supposedly had conceded, but the days of glory were forever gone. The United States could not permit high-ranking SS officers such as he to ever regain their freedom. His life, therefore, could have only one conceivable purpose: to minimize the sufferings of his comrades by assuming personal guilt for the murders attributed to *Kampfgruppe* Peiper. Peiper testified that he thereupon declared his willingness to sign anything set before him if, by so doing, he could secure freedom for his men.[28]

This encounter between Perl and Peiper could only have taken place prior to December 1945, when the Malmedy suspects had been transferred to Schwäbisch Hall. Oddly, Perl did not take advantage of Peiper's declared willingness to cooperate until March 1946, when Peiper executed his sworn statements, one of which was of a routine informational nature, while two were of material consequence to the Malmedy case. On March 21, Peiper testified, Perl confronted him with two young officers, one his former adjutant, who declared that *Kampfgruppe* Peiper had received an order that encouraged terrorism and the killing of prisoners. Initially, Peiper had denied the existence of such an order. But, in the face of repeated assertions to the contrary and assurances by Perl that Dietrich, Priess (former commander of the First SS Panzer Corps), and Kraemer had already admitted "everything," Peiper told the court, he permitted Perl to dictate a statement that contained the fateful admissions. Even then, Peiper claimed, he had been unwilling to sign the statement before carefully reading it but had been denied the opportunity by Perl, who had demanded Peiper's immediate signature and, having received it, had hurried off with the precious document. An English translation was later shown to him, which he rejected as being untruthful but was not permitted to revise. Peiper testified that his second material statement, that of March 26, had been made under circumstances similar to those under which he had made the statement of March 21. It was in this second statement that Peiper had confessed to having permitted the shooting of POWs in La Gleize and elsewhere. But the "confession" had, he claimed, again been the product of psychological debilitation and depression, produced by the false assertions of former comrades.[29]

If Peiper's sworn statements were untrue and the products of a form of psychic exhaustion that had rendered him vulnerable to Perl's blandishments, how had he conducted himself during the Ardennes offensive? Peiper testified that he had been ordered to fight "fanatically" but that this had held no sinister connotations. His troops were simply expected to commit themselves unreservedly in a spirit of self-sacrifice to the winning of the battle. To be sure, Peiper had expected and ordered that men and material be employed ruthlessly and that the

Kampfgruppe preserve forward momentum at all costs, but prisoners of war were to be simply disarmed and left standing where captured or directed to the rear, in either case to become the responsibility of German units following his own.[30]

Yet, Peiper's direct testimony for the defense was not totally exculpatory. While denying having issued orders that required or permitted the killing of prisoners, as had been alleged in many of the sworn statements, he admitted having observed to Perl that such orders were unnecessary, as it was "obvious" to experienced commanders that prisoners sometimes had to be shot "when local conditions of combat should require it." And, although denying immediate responsibility for the killing of prisoners, he did admit to having knowledge of it. On December 18, 1944, outside Trois Ponts, he testified, he had been informed by *SS-Sturmbannführer* Hein von Westernhagen, the commander of the *Kampfgruppe's* battalion of heavy King Tiger tanks, that there had been a "mix-up" in the vicinity of Ligneauville and that a rather large number of prisoners of war had been killed; he maintained, however, that he knew no details.[31]

Peiper's testimony in his own defense occupied the whole of the court's June 21 session. Everett was not sanguine about the day's events, and, indeed, Peiper had made some concessions that were clearly damaging to the defense case. In refuting the prosecution charge that U.S. prisoners of war had been murdered in La Gleize, for example, he had suggested that sworn statements to that effect might have been the result of confusion. A firing squad had been organized, he explained, but for the purpose of executing a German discovered removing the SS runes from his uniform collar, an act assumed to be preparatory to desertion. Killing a comrade on suspicion of planning to desert might well have suggested an attitude toward human life consistent with the killing of prisoners and civilians, and the judges might have been forced to ponder why a prospective deserter would have been intent on dissociating himself from the Waffen SS. Resignation was again on Everett's mind, as he raised that evening the possibility of paying from his own pocket the costs of the eagerly anticipated reunion with his family so that, if he decided to "skip out," he could not be accused of defrauding the Army.[32]

On Saturday, June 22, the prosecution had its opportunity to question the chief defendant, and Ellis subjected Peiper to a fierce cross-examination. The chief prosecutor focused on Peiper's claim that he had been subjected to inhumane conditions of imprisonment prior to having made his sworn statements. Ellis skirted the question of what Peiper had described as dungeonlike confinement at Zuffenhausen. He elicited the admission from Peiper, however, that his cell in Schwäbisch Hall, where he had spent three months before making the three depositions that had been introduced as prosecution evidence, had been comfortably furnished. But the defendant responded defiantly when Ellis suggested that his sworn statements had been candid admissions of truth that Peiper was now trying to disavow in an effort to avoid the gallows:

> Q: Well, you wouldn't have signed them if they weren't true, would you?
> A: I already explained yesterday why I signed them, which was the situation when I signed them.
> Q: Well, you told me . . . that you believed in the sanctity of an oath.
> A: Yes
> Q: Do you mean to tell me now that you don't believe in the sanctity of an oath?
> A: I believe in the sanctity of an oath if it's taken under fair conditions, but not if an oath is taken under false conditions and under pretext of false facts and under pressure.

Ellis was acidly persistent and Peiper disdainfully defiant:

> Q: In other words, anything that would be damaging would be untrue and anything that was not damaging would be true, is that the situation?
> A: I already said before that I personally do not care at all what could do me harm or what was not damaging to me.[33]

Peiper was, in fact, remarkably candid on matters clearly damaging to his defense, a circumstance that must have filled Everett with personal admiration but professional despair. Under cross-examination on the duties he had performed while adjutant to the *Reichsführer-SS*, he admitted to having accompanied Himmler to a demonstration that involved the gassing of human subjects. And, while denying that he had ordered the killing of prisoners of war at La Gleize, Peiper declared that he would have shot those prisoners if his troops had been forced to fight to the finish in the village, "since I thought that it was impossible that all of us would die here and the next day a hundred and fifty Americans would get new weapons and fight against the German Army. I could not take the responsibility for that toward my commanders."[34] As Everett undoubtedly realized, the same rationale could have been used to justify the killing of prisoners of war whom an onrushing battlegroup could spare neither time nor manpower to guard. Peiper's candor and experience in the grim business of combat again surfaced as Ellis, reacting to one of many denials of the prosecution's allegation that the men of the *Kampfgruppe* had been ordered to shoot prisoners, queried sarcastically:

Q: Now were all your men so undisciplined that they killed prisoners of war without orders?

A: During combat sometimes there are situations about which one cannot talk on the green table.

Q: Now, Peiper, I asked you if your men were so undisciplined that they killed prisoners of war without orders. Can you answer that question without talking about green tables?

A: That doesn't have anything to do with discipline.

Q: Well, I'll ask the question again. Were your men so undisciplined that they would kill prisoners of war without orders? Can you answer that "yes" or "no"?

A: No, this question doesn't have anything to do with discipline, and for this reason, I cannot answer it with "yes" or "no."

Q: Well, were your men so ill-trained in the rules of the Geneva Convention that they killed prisoners of war without orders?

A: . . . During combat there are desperate situations, the answer[s] to which [are] given out very fast . . . and which do not have anything to do with education and teaching.[35]

Everett might have hoped that Peiper's frank assessment of the tension between the laws of war and the often overwhelming stresses of combat would sound a sympathetic chord with the experienced line officers on the bench. But Ellis ended the day's cross-examination on a strong note, demonstrating several discrepancies between Peiper's testimony under direct examination by the defense and statements he had made to U.S. Army investigators in the summer of 1945, concerning which there were no allegations of duress. Moreover, at that time his memory of the events of December 1944 had presumably been fresher than it was at the time of the trial, almost a year later, as Peiper was forced to concede. Most damaging was Ellis's introduction of the fact that in August 1945, Peiper had told army interrogators that his men had held "about 200 or 250" American prisoners in La Gleize, which, if true, left unaccounted for a sizable number beyond the 150 released by the Germans. Peiper could only respond, somewhat lamely, that as commander of the *Kampfgruppe*, his mind had been on matters other than prisoners of war and that he had never known with any precision how many prisoners his troops had taken, a statement that harmonized poorly with the numerical specificity with which the defendant had spoken of prisoners of war in his direct defense testimony.[36]

At the end of the day's proceedings, Everett proclaimed himself "pretty well whipped down," in spite of the fact that he thought that Peiper had had the better of the exchange with Ellis. That part of Everett's depression was due simply to difficulty in coping with the normal adversarial atmosphere of an American criminal proceeding is suggested by his somewhat naive complaint that the prosecution seemed always inclined to "slur" the efforts of the defense and that the "sneering" manner in which Ellis had cross-examined Peiper must have prejudiced the court. What effect Ellis's courtroom style had had on Colonel Rosenfeld was, at best, ambiguous, as the law member, according to Everett, had fallen asleep three times.[37]

Everett's admiration for Peiper's intrepidity on the battlefield and under prosecution had progressively intensified since their initial meeting in April. But Ellis had not been immune to the German's qualities, either, as was revealed with embarrassing clarity as Peiper was about to leave the witness stand the following Monday, June 24. The witness asked for permission to make a final statement to the court. With a laconic "Go ahead," General Dalbey assented, and Peiper began:

> Early in May, here, I had a personal conversation with Lt. Colonel Ellis. This conversation occurred on a personal, human plane . . . and in that connection I asked Colonel Ellis whether he, personally, really believed all of the things [of which] I am accused of here.

Ellis was on his feet, clearly flustered:

> If the court please, I object to that, that it is irrelevant whether I believe
> what is going on here or whether I don't believe what is going on here.
> I don't believe that has any bearing on the case here.

The objection, while technically correct, was intriguing, and Dalbey
permitted Peiper to continue:

> I had told him that—Colonel Ellis would surely know that all my tes-
> timony resulted only from my attitude, that I wanted to save my men.
> . . . Lt. Colonel Ellis said, "I admire you, and I hardly know another sol-
> dier who I estimate as highly as I do you, but you are sacrificing your-
> self [for] an ideal that no longer exists. The men whom you today think
> you have to cover up for are bums and criminals. I'll prove that to you
> in the course of the trial. We are now parting as friends, and when we
> see each other again before [the] Court [we will be] as enemies, and I'll
> have to paint you in the worst bloody colors, but you'll understand
> that I will only be doing my duty."[38]

Everett's pleasure was matched by Ellis's embarrassment and the
chief prosecutor moved that the remarks be stricken from the record.
The motion was denied by Colonel Rosenfeld, with the by now thoroughly familiar qualification that the court would attach to the matter
"the value it deems necessary." While a point of high drama in the trial,
Peiper's revelation could be of little substantive significance. The chief
prosecutor had, it appeared, expressed a degree of admiration for the
defendant that made for strange listening by those who recalled the
prosecution's opening statement, but Ellis's remarks had indicated not
a belief in Peiper's innocence of war crimes but, at most, an inclination
to believe that he had been willing to assume responsibility, in some
cases, for the crimes of others.[39]

It is clear, at any rate, that the defense team derived little encouragement from Ellis's discomfiture. By the end of the day, all but Everett
had concluded that the defense should rest its case, largely in the belief
that guilty verdicts were a foregone conclusion and that further efforts
were hopeless. Everett was of a different mind. He argued that if the defense rested now, the result would be not only seventy-four guilty verdicts but seventy-four death sentences as well, whereas their continued

exertions might soften the hearts of members of the court in regard to at least a few of "these kids." Everett's opinion prevailed, and, on the following day, the testimony of defense witnesses resumed.[40]

In the course of the next several days, the defense called to the stand former SS men who offered testimony that contradicted the major accusations brought against the Malmedy defendants: that they had received and transmitted orders to murder prisoners of war and civilians and had consistently done so. Some of the testimony was believable. A former *SS-Rottenführer* (corporal) of the Seventh Company, First SS Panzer Regiment, spoke simply of prisoners he had taken in Büllingen on December 17 and near La Gleize on the night of December 20–21, 1944. In the first instance, the witness's company commander had ordered him to send prisoners to the rear in the direction of Honsfeld; in the second incident, he had been ordered to escort a prisoner to the regimental command post. Other examples of defense testimony were more difficult to accept at face value. A noncommissioned officer of the Ninth Panzer Pioneer Company solemnly assured the court that his company commander, one of the defendants, had instructed his troops to treat prisoners of war as they, themselves, would want to be treated if captured. An order based on the "Golden Rule" issued by an officer of the Waffen-SS, indeed, any combat officer at that stage of a brutal war, strains the limits of credibility. Witnesses sometimes contradicted one another. One young ex-SS trooper testified that his company commander had issued verbal preattack orders that no prisoners were to be taken, a directive that listeners had interpreted to mean that surrendered Americans were to be swept up by units following *Kampfgruppe* Peiper. Another former member of the same company, however, testified that the commander had said nothing about the disposition of prisoners of war.[41]

Other witnesses sought to reinforce the defense assertion that pretrial confessions had been secured under duress. One testified that he had been struck in the face and thrown to the floor of the interrogation cell at Schwäbisch Hall while he had been a suspect. Not content with that level of intimidation, he claimed, American interrogators had also threatened him with hanging and indicated that his parents, then living in Polish-controlled territory, would suffer harm unless the witness swore to a statement that accused his company commander of ordering the shooting of prisoners of war and confessed that he, himself, had shot captured Americans in La Gleize. Curiously, the witness had not made the statement demanded of him at Schwäbisch Hall but testified that he had executed a false statement later in Dachau, "under the impression of Schwäbisch Hall because I was afraid."[42] In a similar vein, the ex-commander of the Third Panzer Pioneer Company testified that he had been frightened into signing statements that attested to the existence of orders to kill prisoners by threats of hanging and by beatings, the latter allegedly administered by Lieutenant William Perl. His credibility suffered when Captain Shumacker of the prosecution called attention to the respective physiques of the two men. The former SS officer, a powerfully built man more than six feet tall, towered over the short and pudgy American.[43]

But a far more serious problem manifested itself as a consequence of the fact that, in the continuation of the defense presentation, defendants in addition to Peiper insisted on testifying. The accused, motivated by the desire for self-preservation, offered testimony that minimized or refuted their own guilt while sometimes imputing culpability to others. Under cross-examination by Shumacker, for example, a former company commander denied having ordered prisoners of war to be shot in Stoumont but asserted that he had "heard" on December 19, 1944, that one of his subordinates, also a defendant, had killed prisoners that day. In like manner, an ex-platoon leader denied all wrongdoing but testified that he had received unequivocal preattack orders from his company commander, one of the seventy-four defendants, to the effect that prisoners of war were to be shot. The witness claimed, however, not to have conveyed these orders to members of his platoon.[44] It had been in anticipation of precisely this problem of mutually antagonistic defenses that Narvid had moved in vain for severance at the start of the trial. Having tried in every conceivable way to nullify the impact of the pretrial sworn statements, Everett now looked on in dismay as some defendants lent additional credibility to the crucial documents. In a desperate attempt at damage control, the defense requested on the afternoon of June 27 that the court impose limitations on the prosecution's latitude in cross-examination. Rosenfeld's denial of the motion the following morning prompted Everett to immediately request a recess to permit consultation with the defendants on the advisability of resting the case, rather than to allow the accused to imperil one another by their testimony. In the course of a thirty-minute intermission, Everett now argued vigorously in favor of closing, convinced that the defendants were hanging themselves by their own testimony, but the Germans, desperate to refute their earlier depositions, were adamant. The next day, Everett wrote despairingly of the results. A defendant against whom the prosecution case had been weak had taken the stand and had succeeded, he feared, in hanging himself and seven others.[45] Even the leading defendant, Jochen Peiper, was dismayed, albeit for other reasons. He wrote to Everett in sometimes awkward but powerful English that

> Although my men's attitude during the Battle of the Bulge was better than during the Battle of Dachau, nevertheless I'm glad to share the fate of my comrades. From the point of view of the old commander, I have to feel ashamed of my outfit, especially of some officers. But attitude without support is rare!
> When hearing of investigation circumstances, the old front-line soldier can only be silent scornfully and smile ironically. From a psychologist's standpoint, the development is naturally quite easy to understand. I also try to see it with these eyes. Besides, I'm on the point [sic] to become a philosopher owing to the splendid isolation in American custody. My boys may charge me with all they want. The main thing is, it helps them. They are not evil and no criminals.
> They are the product of total war. . . . The only thing they knew was to handle weapons for the Dream of Reich. They were young people with a hot heart and the desire to win or to die. . . .[46]

It was a remarkable unburdening, which amounted to a rejection of the testimony of other defendants on their own behalf and suggested skepticism on Peiper's part with regard to at least some of the defendants' claims of duress, in addition to reinforcing his implicit concession while on the witness stand that *Kampfgruppe* Peiper had been guilty of spontaneous excesses.

But, in the days that followed, the defense was able to introduce additional evidence that suggested that the prosecution was guilty of exaggeration. Prosecutors had claimed, for example, that Peiper's battlegroup had murdered at least nine civilians in Büllingen. But Everett had dispatched Miles Rulien, a civilian attorney assigned to aid the defense staff, to the village to investigate. Büllingen was a community of around three hundred souls and several dozen houses, and it had not been difficult to keep track of the inhabitants, as the village mayor had customarily done. Rulien had returned with an affidavit from the official in which he stated that only two residents had died since the beginning of the Ardennes offensive, and one of them had expired of natural causes after the war. In still another affidavit submitted as defense evidence, Anton Jonsten declared that his wife had been killed on December 16 or 17 (Jonsten was not sure which) by shrapnel from American artillery fire as she ran down a street seeking shelter from the bombardment. The affidavits secured by Rulien were not conclusive refutations of the prosecution's charges, for it was conceivable that, in the confusion of combat, transient civilians might have fallen victim to Peiper's men and their deaths never recorded. But the affidavits should have introduced a strong element of doubt concerning the alleged murders.[47]

La Gleize was an equally small community where, the prosecution had alleged, "one hundred seventy-five to three hundred eleven" American prisoners had been killed. Lieutenant Colonel Hal Mc-Cown had testified that during his several days of captivity in La-Gleize he had seen no bodies of American POWs. McCown had admitted under cross-examination that he had not seen all parts of the village, but the defense was now able to offer affidavits from residents of La Gleize that corroborated McCown's testimony. Father Louis Blockian, the village priest, had remained in La Gleize from December 18, 1944, when German troops had entered, until December 24, when American forces retook it. During that time, the only dead American the cleric had seen was a charred body hanging from the hatch of a burned-out Sherman tank. Three other residents of the village who were interviewed by the defense had seen no evidence of German atrocities; on the contrary, SS medics had been observed caring for American wounded. If four citizens of La Gleize and a major of the United States Army had failed to detect evidence of so much as one murder, much less several hundred, could much credence be reposed in the prosecution's contention or, more significant, in the sworn statements that formed its foundation? With that question left in high relief, the defense staff and the defendants were at last able to agree that the time had come to rest their case.[48]

Ellis and his prosecutorial staff sought to patch whatever holes had been torn in the fabric of their contentions. Defense witnesses and defendants had testified with wearisome repetitiveness to various deceptive and coercive methods employed by pretrial investigators to extract the sworn statements on which the prosecution case was largely built. Now, the men who had extracted these statements were called to the witness stand and, not surprisingly, denied most of the accusations that had been made against them, but not all. The allegations of investigative misconduct had been so numerous that it would have been difficult to have responded to every one. But the investigators' silence on some charges may have been significant. Ellis questioned Lieutenant Perl concerning Peiper's allegation that, during an interrogation session at Zuffenhausen, Perl had informed him that his case was hopeless, because the sons of a U.S. senator and a business tycoon supposedly had been victims of the crossroads massacre. Perl denied making this comment, but was not asked whether he had told Peiper that he could never be given his freedom, that his life was now "ruined" and without meaning, and that he could spare his men suffering by "admitting everything." Harry Thon, another investigator, was examined concerning his interrogation of a German witness who, in the Dachau courtroom, had testified for the defense that he had been beaten, threatened with hanging, and told that his parents, living in Poland, would suffer unless he produced an acceptable statement. Thon was questioned by the prosecution concerning the alleged beatings, which he denied, but he was not examined on the other elements of the accusation.[49]

The prosecution had clearly been stung by the defense's success in raising doubts about the alleged murders in La Gleize, and it chose to conclude its rebuttal of the defense case by addressing this issue. It was an ill-advised effort. Affidavits from two German prisoners of war were so nebulous as to prove nothing, while statements secured from two former GIs, purporting to describe the recovery of about two hundred bodies of American prisoners of war at La Gleize, dated the event at December 22, 1944, when the village was still in German hands, and appear to be garbled accounts of the removal of corpses from the crossroads south of Malmedy.[50]

It was on this less than edifying note that the submission of evidence in the case of *U.S. vs. Valentin Bersin, et al.*, concluded on the morning of Tuesday, July 9. Following a one-and-one-half-hour recess, the court reassembled to hear the prosecution's concluding arguments, delivered by Captain Raphael Shumacker. In his summation of the relevant law and evidence, Shumacker called for rigorous justice to be meted out to the murderers of American prisoners and Belgian civilians and to those who had encouraged murderous acts "by speeches and orders" and had incurred thereby as heavy a burden of guilt as that borne by those who had actually sent bullets thudding into human flesh.

"Today in America," Shumacker informed the court, "the survivors of these massacres, the mothers, fathers, wives and children of these comrades of ours who so needlessly fell, not on the field of battle, but from the tender mercies of the SS, are awaiting your findings. . . . Let their punishment be adequate for their crimes."[51]

The turn of the defense came the next morning. Everett had been agonizing for the previous week over the organization of his final opportunity to sway the court. He worked individually with those defendants who wanted to make final statements and allocated speaking slots to defense attorneys, American and German, irritating some by limiting the time available to them and distressing others by excluding them altogether on the grounds that they had seemed to annoy the court. Everett labored on his own summation, spending the whole of Thursday, July 4, on his closing arguments while clad in his shorts, as the day was a hot one. He had thereby forgone the Independence Day celebrations at the officers' club but felt better as a result in regard to "those 74 accused," although he assessed the result of his efforts, with characteristic self-deprecation, as "pretty poor."[52]

The defense summations simply reflected the complexities of the case and the appalling difficulty of defending seventy-four defendants ranging in rank and responsibility from private to general. References to the doubtful character of many of the sworn statements were combined with reminders that the mad desperation of combat often obscures the neat distinctions between criminality and legality so easily made in the staid atmosphere of the courtroom. But, in a performance reminiscent of the fratricidal testimony of some of the defendants, lawyers defending the several categories of accused—commissioned officers, noncommissioned officers, and enlisted men—lent credence to the prosecution case by attempting to justify the murder of prisoners of war on the tenuous grounds of "military necessity" or "superior orders."[53]

It was left to Everett to attempt to neutralize the damaging contradictions in the defense case by appealing, as trial attorneys commonly do, both to the intellects and to the emotions of those sitting in judgment. In a slow, deliberate cadence and in accents that only hinted at his Georgia roots, he recalled the initial difficulty that he and his team had experienced in gaining the cooperation of the defendants, a problem rooted in the distrust that they had felt for all Americans as a result of their ostensibly harrowing experiences at the hands of brutal and unprincipled Army interrogators. Gradually overcoming their suspicions, Everett explained, he and his staff had come to understand that many of the accused had been so disoriented and frightened by the tactics of the investigators as to have been willing to sign anything placed before them. Everett awkwardly attempted to undo the damage done by the testimony of those defendants who had tried to shift blame to their comrades by attributing it to continued terror of the investigation-prosecution team.

> You may have wondered why these accused discontinued appearing in their own behalf. That was my decision, because the fear of the Prosecution still lingered in their minds after months of solitary confinement. . . . A complete picture of these tricks, ruses and beatings would have been shown, except for my decision.

Everett continued his summation:

> My observation of both military and civil justice as administered by our great nation is that there is no power so unrestrained that can lurk within our halls of justice to deprive any person, even an enemy soldier, of his life, based on admitted ruses, artifices and ceremonies. The prosecution offers you no proof of acceptance of American soldiers as prisoners of war. Instead, they attempt to prove cold-blooded murder by admissions of one accused against another, cunningly dictated as a further form of stratagem. It is felt that such a sentence [sic] would be unworthy of the traditions of the American people or of the immense sacrifices that they have made to further the spirit of democracy and common ideals to mankind.[54]

It was a statement unfortunate in its less than felicitous use of language and unfortunate, too, in its implicit discounting of the testimony of American survivors of the crossroads massacre that they had, indeed, unambiguously surrendered to German forces, had been assembled in a field with hands raised, and then mowed down by machine-gun fire. Each of the judges was then asked to consider:

> that primitive impulses of vengeance and retaliation among victimized peoples are often called forth in the heat of battle or as the culmination of a war-weary last struggle against an overwhelming enemy.

Thus the spiral of inhumanities mounts which have [*sic*] always been
the inevitable by-product of man's resort to force and arms, whether
he be enemy or ally.[55]

Here, Everett was on firmer ground, although he appeared now to
be admitting what he had earlier questioned, while attempting to minimize its legal and moral burden by means of historical relativization.
He went on to suggest to the court that a fair and dispassionate judgment in the Malmedy case would assist in nurturing a new "democratic
nationalism" among the German people and concluded his address
with words of Tom Paine that had been used a short time earlier by Justice Wiley Rutledge in his dissent from the majority opinion that the
U.S. Supreme Court lacked jurisdiction in the trial of the Japanese general Tomoyuki Yamashita, a case that bore some similarity to the Malmedy proceedings: "He that would make his own liberty secure must
guard even his enemy from oppression, for if he violates this duty, he
establishes a precedent which will reach himself." The statement had
not been a great piece of courtroom oratory, but it was intensely moving to those whose lives hung in the balance. Fritz Kraemer, former
chief of staff of the Sixth Panzer Army, wept openly, while Sepp Dietrich, the highest-ranking defendant, bowed to Everett in gratitude.[56]

    Before the officers occupying the bench retired to consider their ver-
dicts, the proceedings were interrupted by the incongruous intrusion of
one of the territorial consequences of German defeat. The prosecution
announced that, by verbal order of General Joseph T. McNarney,
USFET's commanding general, all charges against Marcel Boltz, one of
the enlisted defendants, were being withdrawn. Boltz had been born in
Alsace, as the area is called when under French sovereignty, or Elsass,
when it is German. Alsace became Elsass in 1940, and Boltz was re-
cruited for the Waffen-SS. By 1946, Elsass was again Alsace, and Marcel
Boltz was once more, as he had been born, a citizen of the French Republic. France had sought to reclaim its wayward son from American
custody and had succeeded by means of State Department intervention
with McNarney. Everett recalled the visit that a French attorney had
made to Dachau in an effort to effect Boltz's release and derived some
satisfaction from the fact that the objective had been achieved with his
assistance. That Boltz was soon to be released by French authorities
who had not been convinced by the evidence against him was to encourage Everett's powerful reaction to the trial's outcome.[57]

Several thousand pages of evidence and testimony had been accumulated since the opening day of the trial nearly two months earlier. Colonel Claude Mickelwaite, advanced to the position of theater judge advocate, had arrived at Dachau from Wiesbaden, and Everett suspected, although without evidence, that the purpose of his visit was to instruct the army judges to return verdicts of "guilty." Whether or not his suspicion conformed to truth, a decision was reached with remarkable dispatch. After two hours and twenty minutes, the bell sounded, announcing the reconvening of court. Defendants, defense and prosecution staffs, and judges filed back into the forward areas of the courtroom, while spectators, including wives of many of the accused, took their places in the rows of wooden seats reserved for them. Banks of floodlight were once again illuminated, and cameramen squinted through their viewfinders as the president of the court, General Dalbey, called upon the defendants and the two legal teams to rise. "The Court in closed session," Dalbey solemnly intoned, addressing the defendants, "at least two-thirds of the members present at the time the vote was taken concurring in each finding of guilty, finds you of the particulars and the charge guilty." The verdict was translated into German, and all resumed their seats.[58]

Thus, without exception, the seventy-three remaining defendants were found guilty of the "killing, shooting, ill-treatment, abuse and torture of members of the armed forces of the United States of America, and of unarmed Allied civilians," verdicts reached after periods of deliberation that averaged less than two minutes per defendant. Sentencing was yet to come, but each man was first to have the opportunity to make a final plea for mercy, last words, in effect, as far as the trial was concerned and for some, perhaps, within hailing distance of finality in absolute terms. Slightly more than half of the defendants, primarily the younger enlisted men, chose to address the court. A majority of these (approximately 62 percent) were essentially noncommittal as to personal guilt, stressing, rather, hardships endured during youth, family responsibilities, kin killed in Allied air raids, and other factors that, the defendants hoped, might incline the judges to leniency. Almost all, however, emphasized that as SS men they had been rigorously trained in the necessity of unquestioning obedience to even "impossible" orders. In some cases, this oft-repeated observation probably represented a tacit admission of guilt, particularly when coupled with emphatic assertions that to have refused to carry out orders in a combat situation would have resulted in the speaker's death. Thirty percent of those who chose to make a final appeal specifically denied the charges against them. One twenty-seven-year-old enlisted man, accused of having shot American POWs in La Gleize, declared that he had not fired a single shot during the entire offensive. The remainder, by far the smallest group, admitted having committed the crimes of which they had been accused but claimed extenuating circumstances. A nineteen-year-old youth told the court that he had shot two male civilians in Wanne on orders of a superior. Disobedience had been out of the question, for he had seen five comrades shot for insubordination. Another young man expressed regret for having shot a single American prisoner of war but also claimed superior orders. A former sergeant of the 9th *Panzergrenadier* Company conceded that he had killed an American prisoner near Cheneux, an act for which he pleaded the multiple extenuation of exhaustion, nervous instability (he had never fully recovered, he claimed, from having been buried in debris in Normandy during the summer of 1944), the heat of combat, superior orders, and incitement by his comrades. Yet another defendant sought to excuse his shooting of Belgian civilians in Wanne on the grounds that the Ardennes offensive had been his first combat experience and that he had been so terrified that he had obeyed orders without question but that he had not been conscious of committing a crime, for the civilians he had killed had been alleged to have been guerrillas who had killed German soldiers.[59]

The balance of the afternoon of July 11 and the morning of the following day were occupied with the reading of pleas. It was a scene to excite varied emotions. Forty statements, some simple and seemingly sincere, others transparent attempts at pathos and melodrama, a few with pretensions to rhetorical elegance, most the crude efforts of ill-educated minds, were read by men whose youthful physiognomies (their average age was less than twenty-two) belied the fact that many of them had experienced the horror and exhilaration of war over a longer period of time than had any American soldier in the Dachau courtroom. Their soldierly bearing was demonstrated in the snaps to attention with clicking heels and the military strides that characterized their movements between the prisoners' dock and the point before the elevated judges' bench from which they read their statements. An American officer might accord them respect yet desire vengeance against those who had murdered other American soldiers. It was to determine punishment for them and their silent comrades that the court adjourned at noon, accompanied by Everett's grim request that death penalties, where assessed, be executed by "musketry," the honorable soldier's capital punishment, rather than the common criminal's death by hanging. The petition had been Peiper's. A week before, he had written to Everett, "I beg you to tell to the court that these ones [sic] who have to die may die as soldiers. After having served six bloody years in all theaters and burning points, I think we have merited a firing squad!"[60]

6

Death by Hanging

IF THE VERDICTS for the Malmedy defendants had been reached with unseemly haste, the same could not be said of the assignment of punishment, which occupied the better part of a week. In the meantime, both defense and prosecution staffs sought to release the tensions accumulated in the course of the previous months. Everett organized a party for the evening of July 12 at the Munich home of one of the German defense attorneys. Dr. Pfister supplied the venue and Everett the all-important food and drink. Although an abstainer from hard liquor, he provided liquid cheer for his colleagues and joined mess sergeant Hilliard in making sandwiches from canned turkey, salmon, and lettuce secured from army stores. The food was a luxury almost unimaginable to the German guests, and Everett delighted in their demonstrative enjoyment of the choice comestibles. The feast drew other Germans uninvolved in the trial as the evening wore on, and Everett was introduced to a well-known cardiologist, with whom he discussed his daughter's long-standing heart problems.[1]

He was exhausted but managed to hold on until the wee hours, finally returning to his room at around 2:00 A.M. Clearly still anticipating an appointment as chief of war crimes operations at Dachau, he spent much of the next day studying the unit's organizational structure, although the festivities of the previous evening exacted a nap that afternoon. "I am really worn out after 3 months of constant strain on this case. But I guess I can take more," he confided to Mary. As he was returning to his room after dinner, planning to do a bit more work and then turn in, his phone rang. On the other end of the line was a member of the defense team, Lieutenant Colonel John Dwinell, with whom he had dined that evening. Dwinell was now at the officers' club, where, he informed Everett, there was "trouble." Everett hurried to the club, where he found two prosecution investigators in the company of the wives of three of the German defendants. The imbalance in gender of the group was the result of overindulgence by one of the investigators, who had been taken to his room "dead drunk." Everett's belief in the moral turpitude of those who had prepared the Malmedy case thus received additional reinforcement. It was with a combination of disgust and satisfaction that Everett phoned a resident JAG officer, Colonel William Denson, to report the incident. Denson appeared at the club and instructed the remaining American revelers to return to their quarters. The indiscreet conduct of the investigators produced no further consequences, although an unnamed member of the court had been present and, according to Everett, was "really burned up" over the "disgraceful" conduct he had witnessed. But, he reported to Mary, such behavior was "typical" of the prosecution.[2]

While awaiting the handing down of sentences, Everett returned to fantasies of being joined by his family. He looked forward to recreating in Germany, for the remainder of his tour of active duty, some semblance of his comfortable life in Atlanta, complete with friends suitable for membership in the Piedmont Driving Club. He was sure that Mary would like a doctor and his wife with whom he had had dinner and would be "crazy" about their house and yacht, the latter presumably used for cruising on one of the lakes south of Munich. No doubt, he was attempting to find distraction from the depressing realization that the trial was about to culminate in what would likely be death sentences for a significant fraction of the defendants, conceivably for all of them. Certainly, nothing in his correspondence for the period between the handing down of verdicts and sentencing suggested optimism.[3]

Optimism would have been misplaced. Court reconvened at 1:30 on the afternoon of Tuesday, July 16. The prosecution and defense teams were not fully represented. One member was ill; three others had been excused. Everett, grim-faced, assumed his position at the long table in front of the prisoners' dock. The president of the court, Brigadier General Josiah Dalbey, deepened the already oppressive atmosphere by opening the proceedings with a response to the prisoners' request that the firing squad be substituted for the gallows as the means of executing whatever death sentences might be imposed. The court, he announced, had been directed by General Joseph McNarney, commander of USFET, to impose the punishment required by regulations, namely hanging, but might make its own recommendation in the matter, which Dalbey grimly informed the prisoners it would do. Then, with a warning to the spectators' gallery to remain silent during sentencing, Dalbey began: "Valentin Bersin." Bersin rose from his place, strode to a point before General Dalbey, and stood at rigid attention. To his left stood Everett, also at attention, as he would stand throughout the sentencing. "Valentin Bersin, the court in closed session, at least two-thirds of the members present at the time the vote was taken concurring, sentences you to death by hanging at such time and place as higher authority may direct." For close to an hour, Dalbey droned alphabetically through the list of prisoners. Forty-three, including Peiper, were sentenced to death; Sepp Dietrich was given a life sentence; Priess received twenty years, Kraemer ten. Of those not sentenced to death, twenty-two received life imprisonment, the remainder, terms of ten, fifteen, or twenty years. The grim old German prison at Landsberg west of Munich, where Adolf Hitler had been held following his abortive "Beer Hall *Putsch*," was to be the place of incarceration and execution. At 2:20, the court adjourned sine die.

General Dalbey gave a party that evening for the U.S. Army participants in the trial that Everett attended reluctantly. His head "whirling, splitting and hammered" as a consequence of the trial's outcome, he ate nothing and made clear that he was in no mood to discuss the events of the previous two months. The Malmedy trial was over; *l'Affaire* Malmedy was about to begin.[4]

On the evening of the day following the sentencing, Everett composed a long letter to his wife in which most of the elements of his later campaign to nullify the trial were present. He admitted to minimal satisfaction that forty-three defendants, rather than the sixty to seventy that some had predicted, had been sentenced to death, noting that, after the volume of "rot" that had been allowed into evidence, he, too, had been fearful of more capital sentences. Everett tacitly conceded that some war crimes had been committed but declared his heart to be "crushed" by the principle that a "young kid" who knew nothing else could be sentenced to death for carrying out an order that would have meant death to refuse. He professed admiration for the courage of those same "kids," not one of whom had flinched as the sentences were pronounced, and judged Peiper and his wife (who had attended the trial) to be "cultured people." Frau Peiper, whom Everett judged to be "very brave," had expressed concern for her safety and that of her three children, and he had promised to do what he could to ensure their security.[5]

It had been "one of the most farcical trials imaginable," he raged, but who had been responsible for this miscarriage of justice? In his view, the officers who had determined the verdicts and sentences had been simply instruments in the hands of corrupt and sinister forces. He and General Dalbey had spoken twice since the court had adjourned, once in the officers' club and again in Everett's office. On both occasions, at least as he recalled it, the general had offered words both encouraging and sympathetic. Everett concluded that Dalbey agreed with him that the case should never have come to trial, in part, it appears, because Dalbey was aware that the killing of prisoners of war was an offense of which many U.S. officers and men who had fought in the European Theater were also guilty. That knowledge, he confided to Everett, had made judging the Malmedy case "the hardest thing he had ever done." Two other officers who had served with Dalbey on the court had seemed to express agreement but had noted that they had been "under orders," which Everett may have interpreted as support for his suspicion that the verdicts had been, in effect, dictated by higher authority. But Everett's rational, although not necessarily always accurate, assessment of the trial was once again clouded by his anti-Semitism. He seemed to suggest to Mary that Jewish machinations were, in some sense, at the root of or at least an important factor in what had gone wrong in the investigation and trial of the Malmedy case and much else besides. He expressed despair at the "over-production of Jews" in military government, war crimes investigations and trials, and UNRRA (United Nations Relief and Rehabilitation Administration). The last reference was particularly unfortunate in that UNRRA had responsibility for the care and repatriation of persons "displaced" by the war, including thousands of Jewish survivors of the Holocaust. Everett was far from unique in his inability to empathize with Jewish victims of Nazism. He never expressed support for Nazi anti-Semitic policies, as did some officers of the U.S. Army stationed in Germany, but undermined the ethical character of his stance in regard to the Malmedy case with diatribes on the calamitous consequences of another two years of "Jewish occupation" of the U.S. zone. The corruption rife in all facets of military government could provide stories, he believed, worth "millions" to the press, and he encouraged his wife to "blast loose" to their friend Bill Howland, Time-Life's bureau chief in Atlanta.[6]

Mary Everett showed little inclination to become actively involved in the Malmedy controversy, while her husband's attentions were momentarily divided between his smoldering resentment of military government and a new assignment. He did not receive the top Dachau job;

Colonel Howard F. Bresee was appointed to the position, and Everett's "sour grapes" response suggested disappointment tinged, perhaps, with relief. At least now, he wrote, he would not have responsibility for that "stink hole," although there was an absence of preferable opportunities as "everything over here stinks." Bresee, "a nice little 'yes' man," was better suited to the job than he.[7] In the wake of the Malmedy trial, ironically, he found himself briefly involved in a classic case of corruption within the army of occupation. A colonel with twenty-nine years of army service had been charged with having tried to smuggle $12,000 in black market gold into Switzerland, and Everett was appointed to assist in his defense. Compared to the proceedings just concluded, it was a simple assignment, but Everett was physically and psychologically exhausted and, in addition, lacked sympathy for his client, who claimed to remember very little about the events that had led to his indictment. "Well, it doesn't make sense as to honest dealings [sic]," Everett wrote. The court martial, which opened in Frankfurt on August 5, lasted barely two days and resulted in the defendant's conviction with the token punishment of a $2,500 fine. Although Everett was disdainful of the officer he had defended, his professional pride had again suffered; "as usual," he had lost, he wrote to Mary on August 6.[8]

But Everett had not forgotten the Malmedy case. While in Frankfurt, he had approached an aide to General McNarney and shared with him his perceptions of the recently concluded trial. Everett's comments reached the ears of McNarney's chief of staff, General Harold Bull, who notified theater judge advocate Colonel Claude Mickelwaite. Mickelwaite, of course, had been apprised of allegations of irregularities in the pretrial interrogations of German suspects in April but had probably hoped that the conclusion of the trial would plunge that and other awkward aspects of the Malmedy case into welcome obscurity. The facilitation of that result seems to have been the purpose of a phone call made by Mickelwaite to Everett at the end of July, in which the judge advocate expressed uneasiness over Everett's posttrial comments and urged the Georgian to forget the matter and move on.[9]

Part of Everett seemed willing. The skin around his eyes was black with fatigue, which made him look, he said, as though he had been in a fight. He thought he might need to check himself into a hospital and threatened to do so if he were assigned to another case at Dachau. He described himself as "completely drained" and wrote to his daughter and son-in-law on August 11 of the previous night's profound despair during which he had been unable to sleep and had walked under the stars until 3:00 A.M., growing increasingly depressed. His deepening depression was the result in no small measure of the perception that his links to his family were breaking down after six months of separation. He continued to be at pains to assure a suspicious wife of his fidelity in the face of abundant opportunities for infidelity, but that, as before, seemed a futile endeavor.[10]

Everett attempted to extricate himself from his psychological desolation by attending a parade through the streets of Dachau, complete with brass bands, wagons, flowers, and residents in traditional folk costumes, but he could think only of how much his family would have enjoyed it. A visit to the home of Dr. Curry, his newly found yachting friend, provided an opportunity to play with the four- and six-year-old children of the physician's German assistant and to present them with cookies, candy, and oranges, the first of that fruit they had ever seen. But he was reminded of his longing, never far from his mind, for his own children.[11]

By the middle of August, Everett was ready to apply for release from active duty and return to the United States. He was prepared to argue that the army had reneged on its commitment to transport his family promptly to Germany, and, in any event, the economic loss occasioned by separation from his civilian law practice was not justified by the limited use that the army now seemed inclined to make of his legal talents. He hoped that Mickelwaite would be happy to support the departure of a troublesome malcontent. To his chagrin, the theater judge advocate attempted to dissuade him from making formal application for a return to civilian status, but without success, as Everett was determined, he wrote to his wife, to "let these worthless guys run this show in their own sweet way." Mickelwaite gave up and advised Everett to pursue his case for discharge from active duty in Wiesbaden where, he learned, the process would require up to two months with no guarantee of success. But exciting news arrived a few days later. Mary and young Willis would be on their way to Europe by the end of September. Everett hurried to secure housing and pondered his future with the U.S. Army in Germany.[12]

As he awaited his wife and son's arrival, his determination to return to civilian life in the United States hardened. Had he been reassigned to military intelligence, the function in which he had gloried during the 1930s and the war years, he might have reconsidered. In

Wiesbaden, he had encountered WAC Major Ellen V. Hayes, his wartime intelligence chief in Daytona Beach, who informed him that she had seen a written request for Everett's posting to a G-2 position in Berlin, a prospect that, even in the depths of his disgust with the army, he might have found appealing. But, whether out of vindictiveness or, more likely, a reluctance to set an example that would encourage the flight of additional scarce personnel trained in the law, Mickelwaite had made clear his intention to block such a transfer. Faced with the alternatives of continuing service with the Judge Advocate General's Corps or relief from active duty, Everett chose the latter. "The whole sloppy matter is repulsive to me," he declared to Mary, "and I am through [underlined in original] with the Army for their treatment of, #1, you and Willis and, #2, myself. . . ." He recognized, however, that application for discharge before his wife and son had departed for Europe might result in the army's canceling their travel arrangements with at best the deferral of a reunion until the discharge was approved and he had secured transportation to the United States—possibly several months—or, a far worse possibility, the denial of his application and Mary and Willis's return to the bottom of the priority list for shipment to Germany. Everett chose to bide his time.[13]

Following the conclusion of the smuggling case, Everett does not appear to have been assigned additional trial duties. This may have been the result of the recognition by Mickelwaite and his deputy for war crimes, Lieutenant Colonel Clio Straight, of Everett's evident exhaustion and of his disaffection for the army's legal system. Certainly, both men were loath to involve this man of prickly conscience in another high-profile case. In a two-hour staff meeting on September 7, Everett and several other officers had given Straight an "earful," leading the latter to conclude bitterly that, from their perspective, nothing seemed to be functioning properly at Dachau. Only Bresee had offered Straight a more positive assessment, but Everett dismissed both Bresee and Straight scornfully as he had earlier assessed Bresee, as "yes men."[14]

The meeting of September 7 was followed five days later by a larger conference presided over by Straight in his capacity as commander of the 7708 War Crimes Group, which he later described as "an organization created by the theater for administrative purposes, to facilitate the handling of the assignment of personnel and equipment and so forth."[15] Everett seems not to have been present, for had he been, he would surely have expressed outrage at Straight's remarks, which went far beyond matters of administration. The meeting clearly was intended to move the war crimes trial program ahead with maximum efficiency and minimal attention to legal "technicalities." The defense in the Malmedy case, Straight opined, had been given too much access to prosecution evidence and witnesses, an error that should not be repeated in future cases. An objection raised to the practice of not allowing defendants to testify on their own behalf under oath as detrimental to the defense was brushed aside by Straight as "legal mysticism." That considerable discomfort with Straight's position was expressed by at least one civilian participant in the conference provided further evidence that Everett was not alone in his critical assessment of army war crimes justice.[16]

While awaiting his family's arrival, Everett set to work on a formal analysis of the Malmedy trial that would later constitute an appeal to the U.S. Supreme Court, but his schedule permitted time to shop for presents for his son: *lederhosen* and two German helmets, both in new condition. Romance had blossomed between Irving Hayett and Sally Rose, court reporters for the Malmedy trial, and the two invited Everett to serve as best man at their wedding in September. Everett was surprised, but pleasantly so. Both were Jewish, although, he was quick to note, "hard working" and "very nice." The civil ceremony was performed by the *Bürgermeister* of Dachau (a rabbi conducted a religious service some days later in the Officers' Club) and was followed by a reception catered by the indispensable Sergeant Hilliard. Everett arranged for a room for the couple in a hotel in Garmisch and provided his Opel and Hans Stengel, his German driver, as transport. Everett found it a delightful affair, one that he may have enjoyed more than did the groom, who became ill toward the end of the celebration.[17]

The steamer *George Washington* discharged Mary and young Willis along with the families of many other officers in Bremerhaven in mid-October. The longed-for reunion temporarily drove Dachau and Malmedy from Everett's mind, and USFET helped facilitate the process. A leave of absence in November permitted the three to vacation on the French Riviera, while, shortly after returning to their requisitioned house in Munich, Everett learned that his application for relief from active duty and return to the United States had been approved.[18]

Prior to their departure, he, Mary, and young Willis were free to wander the south German countryside in the Opel, although not without occasional friction with Hans, whose aggressive driving sometimes prompted Everett to remind the Wehrmacht veteran that he was no longer operating a tank on the Russian front! In December a snowy drive southeast of Munich to the Chiemsee in the company of another officer and his wife culminated in a revealing visit with an elderly countess whose daughter had married a United States citizen. In "beautiful English" the countess related her experiences with the U.S. army of occupation, which, as Everett approvingly recounted them after his return to Atlanta, harmonized with his own perspective on Germany under military government. The ancestral *Schloss* had been deeded by the countess to her daughter, now an American citizen living in Egypt, shortly after her (presumably prewar) marriage. But the postwar fate of the aristocratic homestead filled Everett with indignation:

> The Americans took away this <u>American property</u> [underlining in the original] and housed 1100 Refugees therein. They [the countess and her family] could only get out a few priceless articles, and the rest had to be left. Gold embroideries [*sic*], draperies, rugs, chairs and everything. Several months after the Refugees were moved into American property without permission, the Countess had to look into something at the castle and what a barren waste—nothing left.[19]

Offense had been heaped upon despoliation. According to Everett's hostess, she had been given permission by a U.S. Counter Intelligence Corps team to keep a pistol for self-defense but had been arrested by other CIC operatives for being in possession of the weapon. But the countess, Everett enthused, had a "wonderful psychology of life." While incarcerated for the "pistol incident," she cleaned up the jail and taught her fellow prisoners hymns and passages from the Bible. In spite of her misfortunes, Everett noted, she "simply radiated happiness."[20]

Several constants of Everett's mindset are evident in his telling of the story. First, he empathized strongly with Germans in their postwar misery and degradation, particularly if the Germans in question were of "good breeding." Second, the U.S. Army was a source of arbitrary oppression, not only of Germans but of Americans as well (he was as much offended by the fact that the requisitioned property belonged to a U.S. citizen as he was by the expulsion of a charming German aristocrat from it). Third, he had little sympathy for the victims of Nazi persecution. While his anti-Semitism was in part responsible for this lack of feeling, at least as much was owed to the fact that, while he interacted with Germans on a daily basis, survivors of German oppression he saw seldom, if ever. Willis Everett was a man of deep sensitivity and humanity, but he dealt poorly with abstractions.

On December 19 he was formally relieved of his assignment to the 7708 War Crimes Group by Straight and ordered to report with his family to Bremerhaven following the holidays for transportation to "the Zone of the Interior" by the first available ship. By mid-January, the family was on its way home, and landfall in New York was followed by the train trip from New York to Atlanta, a journey that Everett's assignment the previous year to Columbia University had made familiar. The army's bureaucracy continued to rumble toward its preordained end. Separation formalities were completed at Fort Benning, with June 15, 1947, the effective date of Everett's discharge from active duty.[21]

7

A Troublesome Conscience

ONE OF THE last official communications received by Everett while on active duty with the 7708 War Crimes Group was a Christmas greeting from Colonel Bresee to the U.S. Army staff at Dachau. As a stimulus to holiday joy, it was woefully ineffective. Perhaps nothing joyful could emerge from Dachau, the scene of the frightful suffering and death of tens of thousands during twelve years of Nazi tyranny and of a sometimes arbitrary and maladroit endeavor to impose justice on the perpetrators of those and many other German crimes. The inside of a card proclaiming "Christmas 1946 War Crimes" expressed the "hope that despite the grim reminders of the immediate past at Dachau, your Christmas will be a happy one and that your contribution will assure [sic] that 'peace on earth, good will toward man' [sic] will never again be an empty and meaningless phrase to millions of people." It was a sentiment as utopian as it was infelicitous.[1]

To what degree had the conviction of the Malmedy defendants contributed to the achievement of that worthy, if unlikely, end? The prosecution had presented the case as a conspiracy, which had expressed the essence of the Nazi evil. Adolf Hitler had supposedly required of his troops that they conduct themselves in a brutal and lawless manner in the offensive of December 1944. *Kampfgruppe* Peiper had been a particularly appropriate and efficient executor of these orders. It was an element of the *Leibstandarte SS Adolf Hitler*, a unit that had been established in 1933 under the command of Josef "Sepp" Dietrich as an instrument of violence with unique ties to the person of the *Führer*. Jochen Peiper was not only the commander of the organization's spearhead but a former adjutant to Heinrich Himmler, *Reichsführer-SS*. Although the prosecution had not explicitly made the point, the fact that Himmler's SS had operated the concentration camps that had so horrified and outraged liberating U.S. forces would have been lost on few. The Malmedy massacre and Buchenwald could be seen as facets of an overwhelming complex of singular evil.

The reality, in fact, was more complex. The world of the concentration camps and the Holocaust was a singular evil. The killing of prisoners of war was not. German and American troops had regarded each other during World War II as members of the same species, in contrast to their "subhuman" Soviet and Japanese adversaries, against whom war was waged *à outrance* and in frequent disregard of international law. By and large, German and American combatants had endeavored to respect the limitations on the destruction of human life imposed by the Hague and Geneva Conventions, although some erosion of this commitment over the period from November 1942, when Germans and Americans first faced each other in large-scale combat, until the end of the European war, is evident. Nevertheless, violation of the "laws and usages of war" were perpetrated by both sides in the chaos and fury of combat, and the Malmedy massacre and related atrocities were hardly crimes that, in their typology, were uniquely German. An event that paralleled Malmedy had occurred on July 14, 1943, near the Sicilian town of Biscari. In two closely related mass murders, troops of the U.S. Forty-fifth Infantry Division had shot and killed approximately seventy-five Axis prisoners of war, some German but most Italian. Although approximately two dozen GIs had been involved and some of them had volunteered their participation, only two men were court martialed for their roles in the killings. One of them, a sergeant, was found guilty of murder and sentenced to life imprisonment, although he was returned to active duty after about a year. His reinstatement, ironically, was ordered by none other than Lieutenant General Joseph McNarney, then deputy commander of the Mediterranean theater, little more than three weeks prior to the Malmedy massacre. The other defendant, a captain, was acquitted on the grounds that he had been following orders issued by General George Patton shortly before the landing of the U.S. Seventh Army in Sicily. Multiple witnesses had testified to the fact that Patton had strongly discouraged the taking of prisoners, particularly if they had continued to resist to within two hundred yards of the American advance.[2]

The Biscari massacre was unusual in having left behind a highly detailed record, but numerous recollections of GIs involved in combat in the European theater contain references to the killing of German prisoners. Most of these were spontaneous products of the rage of combat, but not all. Prior to D-Day, General Maxwell Taylor instructed the men of his 101st Airborne Division to take no prisoners, and similar orders may have been issued to other units involved in the initial assault, on the grounds that every man would be required to fight and could not be distracted by the taking and holding of prisoners.[3] Everett himself had received a letter from Theodore L. Bailey, a veteran of World War I, who broadened the historical perspective on Malmedy by noting that he had witnessed the shooting of German prisoners in the earlier conflict. He revealed more relevantly that he had been told by an American officer who had served in Italy during World War II that he had been ordered to send one prisoner per day to the rear for intelligence purposes; when more than one surrendered, the surplus had been promptly killed.[4]

General Dalbey had undoubtedly been aware of American counterparts to Malmedy, accounting for his uneasy posttrial conscience. And, in spite of the fact that the War Department had imposed tight secrecy on the case on the grounds that public knowledge of it "would give aid and comfort to the enemy and would arouse a segment of our own citizens who are so distant from combat that they do not understand the savagery that is war,"[5] there can be little doubt that awareness of the Biscari massacre was widespread among American judicial officers. The Seventh Army's judge advocate, Colonel Homer Jones, had been reassigned to duty in Washington, D.C., following the Biscari trials and had described the case to officers of the Judge Advocate General's Department in the course of a discussion of offenses likely to be encountered by judge advocates in the field.[6] Although he was unaware of the Biscari massacre, Everett knew enough to be conscious of the hypocrisy implicit in the Malmedy verdicts and sentences—a major, although secondary, element in his inability to follow Mickelwaite's suggestion that he put the case behind him. But it was the internal character of the investigation and trial, rather than the broader historical context of the "massacre," that had been the primary source of Everett's outrage during the proceedings. This, in combination with an ill-defined but intense feeling of personal guilt for the outcome of the trial, situated within his view of the army as both negligent and corrupt, continued to grip him following his return to the United States. He was not alone in holding a highly negative view of army justice in Europe. An article in the St. Louis *Globe-Democrat* of September 17, 1946, described the efforts of Captain Earl J. Carroll to correct gross deficiencies in the army's judicial and prison systems. Carroll had been outraged by the physical brutality and "gross indignities" inflicted upon U.S. enlisted men accused of offenses under the Articles of War in England and had resigned his position as assistant adjutant general in protest. Conditions in Germany, he believed, were even worse, and he planned to involve himself in the defense of a number of men who were facing prosecution in the U.S. zone of occupation. Carroll, the article noted, was only one of many who were critical of "American Army rule in Europe."[7] Everett became aware of Captain Carroll's allegations and could only have found support for his own conviction that the Malmedy investigation and trial had been ethical abominations. A penal system capable of brutalizing soldiers of the U.S. Army would have few reservations about denying substantive justice to Nazi war crimes suspects.

War crimes trial regulations did not allow for formal appeals of verdicts handed down by military government courts. While still in Germany, Everett began to consider an attempt to circumvent this obstacle by appealing to the United States Supreme Court and to use the threat in order to suggest to the army the wisdom of caution. By the time of his departure for the United States, he and John Dwinell, the former member of the defense team whose indignation was closest in intensity to his own, had prepared a 228-page critique of the investigation and trial, the essence of which was the claim that the seventy-three convictions had been secured primarily on the basis of "illegal and fraudulently procured confessions." Everett sent the document to Straight's office for inclusion in the internal review process that was mandatory before verdicts and sentences became final, but his allegations quickly became public knowledge. Edwin Hartrich, of the *New York Times*, reported from Frankfurt that the petition had been forwarded to the deputy theater judge advocate but that its contents would remain secret until the case was "disposed of" by General McNarney: "By its action, American headquarters here is trying to pull down a legal curtain on one of the most controversial incidents of the war." Everett's relativistic perspective was reflected in Hartrich's observation that the integrity of American military courts was at stake, because many Germans were saying that American troops and airmen also committed atrocities that should make them eligible for trial.[8] The article produced consternation within the army's war crimes trial program and a search for the source of the damaging information. Everett's departure had exposed Dwinell to the wrath of Straight and Ellis, although his apparently sincere professions of innocence probably suggested the likelihood that Everett himself had been responsible for the "leak." In fact, as Tom Reedy of the Associated Press's Munich Bureau later informed Everett, an unnamed enlisted man at Dachau had made available to the press the explosive information. The *Stars and Stripes* immediately jumped on the story and, on January 27, reported the "surprise" expressed by war crimes branch officials at "Lt. Col." (how that must have irked him!) Everett's intent to carry his accusations of prosecutorial and judicial malfeasance to Washington. "Legal experts" who had prepared the case against the German defendants had assured the armed forces newspaper that the trial had been fair and that the accused had been proven guilty "beyond a doubt," and unnamed officers of the war crimes branch, making no pretense of neutrality, were in agreement. Nevertheless, the *Stars and Stripes* was assured, Everett would be given every opportunity to challenge the verdicts.[9]

Although Everett arrived home shortly thereafter, he remained technically on active duty, and he may have been made uneasy by the recent press revelations. In any event, he immediately cabled assurances of his future discretion to Colonel Claude Mickelwaite, judge advocate for the European theater: "According to WD [War Department] policy no statement will be issued unless approved while on AD [active duty]. After that only the highest code legal ethics will govern. The record of trial speaks for Malmedy case."[10] But discretion was fast becoming irrelevant. McNarney's office, perhaps stung by Hartrich's implicit criticism, reversed itself and made public Everett's detailed critique of the trial. "Army Reveals Defense Brief in Trial of Nazis: 'Malmedy Massacre' Case is Called Parody on Justice; Confessions are Impugned," read the heading of a second story by Hartrich in the *New York Times*, this one on January 29. Hartrich noted that the petition contained two basic themes:

1. It was a parody on justice to German soldiers for shooting Americans, when it was well-known by those who participated in the war that the Americans and the other Allies were also guilty of these violations of international conventions. "There was no abnormal or inhuman conduct proved in this trial which is not mirrored many times in our American war record both in Europe and in the Pacific," the brief said.
2. The "Malmedy massacre" trial was carried through by a victorious power, which was determined to punish the German SS men who

shot GIs regardless of the juridical principles involved. The petition charges specifically—and the defense counsel documented their case with copious references from the stenographic record of the Malmedy trial—that the conviction resulted from a desire for vengeance; that confessions were obtained by beatings and high-pressure methods of pre-trial interrogation; that the military court rendered unfair, impartial [sic] and incorrect rulings, and that one defendant with no evidence against him was convicted. The defense counsel charged that "80 to 90 percent of the evidence adduced at the trial consisted of these illegal and fraudulently obtained confessions."

Here, minus the anti-Semitic trappings, was Everett's challenge to the decisions of the Dachau court. Hartrich was, if not sympathetic, then at least intrigued. USFET's effort to minimize the impact of Everett's and Dwinell's allegations by noting that the same claims had been made during the trial were challenged by the correspondent with the observations that the brief "had not been made a part of the public record of the trial when it was filed with the War Crimes Division of the Army in December" and that it represented, moreover, "the considered finding of two American defense attorneys who are members of U.S.F.E.T.'s Judge Advocate General's section."[11]

By the end of February 1947, Everett was back at his desk in rooms 401–402 of Atlanta's Connally Building, the offices of Everett and Everett, Attorneys and Counselors at Law. But his mind was still primarily on Malmedy. On his way home from New York, he had stopped in Washington for a few days' visit to the office of the army's judge advocate general, where he outlined his concerns to seemingly sympathetic listeners although, as he candidly noted, "they were only hearing my side of it." More substantive conversations with members of the War Crimes Branch brought confirmation of what the Malmedy trial had seemed to imply. Colonel Gunn of that agency, he recalled, declared that as soon as the "finger of suspicion" pointed at a war crimes suspect, that individual lost all rights and had to prove his innocence, as his guilt was assumed.[12] There is no independent corroboration of Gunn's conception of the rights (or lack thereof) of war crimes suspects, and Everett may have colored what he had heard to conform to his assessment of the manner in which the Malmedy defendants had been handled. Nevertheless, the presumption of innocence was not a principle formally recognized in U.S. Army war crimes trials, a fact ambiguously acknowledged later by the deputy theater judge advocate, Lieutenant Colonel Clio Straight, with the proviso that, in the absence of a "suitable prescribed standard," the presumption was, in practice, honored.[13]

But Everett's apprehensions concerning the character of war crimes justice had been reinforced. He feared that the army's review of the case would be summarily pro forma and that the forty-three death sentences would be carried out before he could bring the matter to the attention of the U.S. Supreme Court. On February 28, he dispatched a memorandum to USFET's judge advocate, Colonel Mickelwaite, characterizing the trial as one invalidated by "certain errors committed during the trial, and certain acts and procedures followed prior to the trial" and expressing the fear that "regulations now in force . . . require the execution of certain sentences within a short limited [sic] time, and therefore insufficient opportunity would be afforded this officer to find out the final results of the review . . . and prepare an appeal to the United States Supreme Court." He therefore requested of Mickelwaite that he be granted "sufficient time to prepare the necessary appeal, briefs and allied papers to the Supreme Court . . . after notice has been received of the final judgement [sic] in this case."[14]

Had Everett been aware of the course that the review process had taken since the close of the trial, he might have been less apprehensive. The record of the case was first to be scrutinized in Straight's office, the results to form the basis of a second review by the theater judge advocate. Primary responsibility for the initial review had been assigned in August 1946 to Maximilian Koessler, a civilian attorney who was an Austrian by birth who held law degrees from the University of Czernowitz and from the law school of Columbia University. He had been urged to complete his review expeditiously but by February 1947 had managed to finish analyses of only fifteen convictions. Koessler was, he admitted, "defense-minded" and thought it his obligation to compensate for the fact that the Malmedy judges, conforming to the regulations governing army courts, had provided no explanations of their verdicts. He therefore examined the trial record with extreme care. He recommended the confirmation of guilty verdicts in twelve cases but concluded that the evidence against three defendants, one of whom had been sentenced to death and two of who had received life imprisonment, had been insufficient. But he was also uneasy about several general characteristics of the trial. The charge sheet had been insufficiently specific and the number of defendants too large. That, Koessler concluded, had made it extremely difficult for the judges to distinguish one prisoner from another, with the result that the substantial evidence of guilt against some had tended to damage all. Koessler's suspicions were aroused by what seemed to be unnaturally similar wording shared by a number of the sworn statements, and he deemed the use of hoods, false witnesses, and mock trials during the pretrial investigation to have been improper.[15]

Koessler's incomplete review but not its fate would have gladdened Everett's heart. Koessler had been relieved of the assignment in January 1947. The ponderous pace at which his work was progressing would have required another two years for finality. But Straight might have been troubled by Koessler's conclusions, as well. When, two years later, he was asked why he had chosen to disregard Koessler's effort, he was hard pressed to offer a cogent explanation: "I did not believe that it accurately portrayed the record. It was not editorialized in such a manner that it facilitated my work or my superiors [sic], but it accurately portrayed what was in the record."[16] English was not Koessler's native language, and his syntax could be tortured and extremely prolix. Straight could reasonably hope for better from William D. Denson. Denson was a graduate of West Point and Harvard Law School and had served as chief prosecutor in the Dachau and Mauthausen concentration camp cases, proudly noting on his resume that he had secured convictions of all 101 defendants in the two trials and ninety-four death sentences.[17] As reviewing responsibility in the Malmedy case was passed to him by Straight, he was scheduled to assume the chief prosecutorial role in the Buchenwald concentration camp trial, in which he would achieve comparable success (all thirty-one defendants convicted, with twenty-two death sentences).[18] Denson needed to work quickly, in light of the scheduled commencement of the Buchenwald trial in April, but he succeeded in completing his review. It, too, failed to win Straight's approval. Again, the deputy judge advocate had difficulty in articulating his objections:

> Mr. Denson did very good work. However, if he were to look at that he would probably say it doesn't bear much resemblance to what it did, for the reason that he expressed himself, his review was extremely long and the review of the case, in order to portray it for

one's self, or for anybody else, was extremely difficult in view of the nature of the charges. . . .[19]

A third attempt by Straight to make sense of the Malmedy trial would not bear fruit until October.

Everett was unaware of the legal fumblings in Straight's office and was led to expect better. Near the end of March 1947, Lieutenant General Clarence Huebner, chief of staff to the new U.S. commander in Europe, General Lucius D. Clay, informed Everett that the record of the Malmedy trial was being reviewed by the deputy judge advocate for war crimes. That process was likely to be finished within a month, following which the European Command's judge advocate would make recommendations based on his own analysis to General Clay. Everett was advised to remain in close touch with the War Crimes Branch, Civil Affairs Division, in Washington for information on the progress of the review process and was assured that no sentences would be executed until at least sixty days after Clay had reached a final decision.[20]

Everett's determination to see justice done in the Malmedy case was beginning to be noticed by Germans as well. United States occupation authorities considered the war crimes trial program to be important not only as the means of punishing German criminality but also as a key part of the process of reeducating the German people in the ways of democracy and the rule of law. The reaction of the German population in the U.S. Zone to the trial of German leaders before the International Military Tribunal at Nuremberg, whose sentences had been handed down on October 1, 1946, had been overwhelmingly positive, a phenomenon that may have contained an element of scapegoating as well as sensitivity to the demands of justice. The trials of lesser figures, however, evoked a different response. Almost all Germans had close relatives who had fought in World War II, if they were not veterans themselves, and they empathized with ex-soldiers who were prosecuted and punished for offenses that, in many cases, seemed to be the unavoidable consequences of a brutal war, offenses of which Allied combatants had also been guilty.[21] Needless to say, empathy for the Malmedy defendants, many of them under sentence of death, was particularly intense among their former comrades of the Waffen-SS.

Dietrich Ziemmsen had been operations officer on the staff of the First SS Panzer Division, *Kampfgruppe* Peiper's parent unit, at the time of the Ardennes offensive and had been seriously wounded by American artillery fire on December 21, 1944. He had been a witness for the defense during the Malmedy trial, refuting the prosecution contention that the killing of prisoners of war had been ordered and testifying that he had established two collection points for prisoners of war and had seen roughly eight hundred captured GIs being funneled into them. Ziemssen's testimony had carried some weight, for not only could he claim direct knowledge of several factors crucial to the Malmedy case but he had made written application to testify for the defense, an act not without risk, for he himself was a potential defendant. Captain Shumacker, cross-examining for the prosecution, had suggested that Ziemssen's memory had been conditioned by the realization of his own culpability in the transmission of criminal orders, to which Ziemssen had responded, to the delight of the defense, that the prosecution had in fact threatened him with criminal charges if he should testify on behalf of the Malmedy defendants.[22]

Like Everett, Ziemssen was held captive by Malmedy, although, perhaps, for reasons that had more to do with comradeship than justice. As Denson was completing the review that Straight would find wanting, Ziemssen addressed his first letter to Everett. He was clearly aware of the published accounts of Everett's challenge to the Malmedy investigation and trial and expressed the "great joy and high satisfaction" that he shared with other defense witnesses at Everett's evident determination to see the outcome revised. But Ziemssen's purpose went beyond congratulation. He and his comrades, in their "unlimited confidence that we . . . have got in your person," were eager to support Everett's effort by providing additional documentation of the U.S. Army's investigatory transgressions, "above all . . . valuable information concerning Schwäbisch Hall. . . . Our aim is not to neglect anything fit to get justice for our comrades." But, Ziemssen indicated, more than justice for seventy-three former members of the Waffen SS was at stake. "We are convinced that your measures will be better suited to put aside the hatred among nations and to establish a real peace than many other things we have seen and endured. In favour of our comrades and moreover in favour of both nations we heartily wish that you will succeed. . . ."[23]

There was surely an element of cant in tying Malmedy to international reconciliation. Moreover, it was not at all clear that "justice" had quite the same meaning for the two men. For Ziemssen, justice was synonymous with freedom for the Malmedy prisoners. He would likely have been distressed had he seen Everett's letter of mid-June to Cecil Hubbert, acting chief of the War Crimes Branch, Civil Affairs Division. Everett was becoming increasingly uneasy. General Huebner had told him in March that Straight's review of the case was expected to be completed within a month, but he had heard nothing. He was contacting Hubbert, in part, to remind him of Huebner's promise of timely information on the status of the review but also to provide his definition of "justice" in the Malmedy case. Before leaving Germany, he noted, he had been asked by an exasperated Straight what he thought was the solution to the Malmedy imbroglio—"turn them loose, or what?"

> [M]y reply always has been to send the case back for retrial after a careful analysis has been made of the evidence or keep them in jail and never try it. Again I insist that this is the only feasible way out because it certainly would be a blotch on our judicial system to allow sentence to be affirmed under such doubtful practices. Personally I do not wish to further fight this matter but an obligation greater than you may realize exists within me . . . to defend justice and moral rights, especially when forced to defend these Germans.[24]

Although he had earlier assured Mickelwaite that he would make no public statements in regard to Malmedy without the approval of the theater judge advocate, circumstance had changed. Not only were his anxieties increasing in the absence of definitive information on the status of the case review, but, as of June 15, Everett was a civilian and no longer under military discipline. And Claude Mickelwaite, with whom Everett had had a mutually friendly relationship, had been replaced by Colonel James Harbaugh as judge advocate of EUCOM (European Command). Everett now felt free to threaten to "go public" with his accusations of investigatory and judicial misconduct in the Malmedy case unless corrective action was forthcoming. "It is further requested that you use your good offices to encourage such a course in order that it will not be necessary for me to make further attempts to correct wrongs. Newspapers and editors have been and still are hounding me for the inside story."[25]

The War Crimes Branch was sufficiently stimulated by Everett's appeal to cable to EUCOM an inquiry as to the status of the review. Given the disarray in Straight's office, it is not surprising that a reply was slow in coming, but on July 10 Colonel Edward H. Young of the judge advocate general's War Crimes Branch was able to inform Everett that the deputy judge advocate for war crimes would complete his review in three weeks; Harbaugh would require an additional three weeks to weigh Straight's recommendations and to formulate his own for the guidance of General Clay, whose final decision would be rendered a week later. It seemed reasonable for Everett to expect that by early September 1947, more than a year after the announcement of verdicts and sentences, the final official judgment on the Malmedy trial would be rendered.[26]

But Everett was not above using personal friendships and regional affinities in an effort to sway the outcome. He had a contact in Clay's headquarters in the person of Judge Charles S. Reid, an old Atlanta friend who was serving as Clay's property control officer and who, after his return to the United States, would make headlines by leaping from the window of his twelfth-floor office. In a "Dear Charlie" letter dated July 26, 1947, Everett outlined his version of the Malmedy case, with the disingenuous assurance that it was not his "purpose to influence the decision of our fellow Georgian" (Clay was a native of Marietta). Nevertheless, Everett clearly hoped that Reid would bring to Clay's attention the use by army investigators of "mock trials" and phony witnesses to extract damaging sworn statements from German suspects and would remind him that American troops had been guilty of violations of the laws of war similar to those of which the Germans had been convicted.

> The Germans know of some of these incidents. Warfare is no gentleman's game as much as we would like it to be. . . . If we condemn a private for carrying out a command in the heat of battle, what discipline can we expect? If we condemn others for what we, ourselves, have done even to a lesser degree, what mercy can we expect for our children and grandchildren?

As he had suggested to Hubbert in June, Everett argued that justice demanded a new trial for the Malmedy condemned, one from which, presumably, the tainted sworn statements would be excluded and in which evidence of comparable American crimes would be admitted. But he doubted the ability of the U.S. Army to do it. Better to keep "the 74 defendants [he had seemingly forgotten about Boltz] in prison in the interim. Then, sooner or later, the Army will be relieved of trial responsibility and let some other agency bring these enemy combat soldiers back to trial. . . ." Reid brought the matter to Clay's attention, but, at that point, the military governor showed little interest.[27]

Everett's passion for justice would frequently exceed his ability to clearly articulate it. Reid assured him that the letter had been delivered to General Clay, although Clay had not yet received the recommendations of Colonel Harbaugh and would not until March 1948, half a year later than the date by which Everett had been led to expect a decision. If the army was proceeding at a glacial pace, it was in part because of the threat of public censure represented by Everett himself. But it was also the product of tension between the growing realization among army jurists in Europe that there had been something unsettling about the Malmedy proceedings and the reluctance of the judge advocate general's office to admit it. Although official confirmation of this conflict was slow in coming, Everett had reason to be encouraged by what he learned informally from Tom Reedy, a correspondent for the Associated Press in Munich whom he had come to know while in Germany. "Everybody is afraid of Malmedy here," Reedy reported in August, "and the jailers at Landsberg say that Peiper will never hang." The former president of the Malmedy court, General Dalbey, had remarked that the trial was "the worst mess he had ever got [sic] mixed up with and he surely wishes it had never happened!" The consensus seemed to Reedy to be that Everett was right about Malmedy but that there was an understandable reluctance to say so.[28]

Everett's resentments and prejudices received reinforcement from other disaffected army officers who had served the war crimes trial mechanism. A colonel who had clearly found the experience less than satisfactory wrote bitterly to Everett of "that farce of an Army officer Colonel Straight," who "shanghaied" a number of colonels (himself among them) out of Dachau because they would not vote the way he had instructed them, to the detriment of their careers. He intended to press his case with the inspector general and wondered if he might use Everett's name, as he had been given to understand that Everett, too, had been a victim of Straight "and his Jewish cohorts." Later missives would rail against "the Commies and Jews" in control of Dachau. Whatever satisfaction Everett might have derived from this correspondence, he wisely abstained from replying to it.[29]

In the wake of Straight's disappointment with Koessler's and Denson's evaluative efforts, the deputy judge advocate collaborated with another civilian attorney, Richard Reynolds, in an extensive revision of Denson's draft, which was forwarded to Harbaugh on October 20. Straight's review reached conclusions that were, in some respects, different from those of the trial judges. Of the forty-three death sentences that had been handed down at Dachau, only twenty-five (including Peiper's) were recommended for confirmation. In the eighteen cases in which Straight did not believe the death penalty to be justified, commutation to life imprisonment was suggested in seven instances and commutation to prison terms of ten, fifteen, or twenty years in ten. Twenty-two life sentences had been imposed at Dachau. The deputy judge advocate recommended only five of these for confirmation, urging that the remainder be reduced to sentences of ten or fifteen years' imprisonment. Reductions were recommended in most of the lighter sentences handed down in July 1946. But, with the exception of one defendant sentenced to death whose guilt did not seem to have been adequately proven, Straight's ameliorative recommendations were based not on insufficiency of evidence but, rather, on the tender years of the defendants. In twenty-nine and possibly thirty of the thirty-six instances in which Straight recommended the commutation of death penalties or the reduction of life sentences, the convicts had been under twenty years of age at the time of their alleged crimes; in no case was a death sentence or a sentence of life imprisonment recommended for confirmation if the convict had been in his teens in December 1944.[30] Straight later explained that

> these atrocities were closely connected with military operations; there is a difficult situation in the Army when superiors tell inferiors they will do something, particularly in connection with combat operations. Also, over and above everything else, I was of the opinion that these men . . . , some of them as I recall it were down to 17 or 18 at the time of these acts, had been brought up in the shade, they had not seen the sunlight, they had been taught doctrines that are quite far-reaching for our imagination to grasp and it occurred to me that they can be salvaged. . . .[31]

Intellectually and substantively, Straight's report was unsatisfying. Save in the single instance where the verdict and death sentence had been found to have been insufficiently supported by the evidence, the deputy judge advocate recommended the approval of all findings of the

Malmedy court, including all other death and all life sentences, but then suggested numerous commutations on the basis of the youth of the perpetrators and, in some cases, of ostensible evidence of repentance. His report might well be interpreted as indicating his uneasiness over the course and outcome of the investigation and trial, combined with reluctance to concede the possibility of error.

Straight's desire to skirt the central issues associated with the Malmedy investigation and trial is perhaps understandable, given the fact that he had been a central figure in the War Crimes Branch since its inception. To have found substantive fault with the Malmedy proceedings would have been an exercise in self-criticism, an activity in which human beings normally engage only with reluctance. In spite of the fact that Straight had seemingly subscribed to a fragment of Everett's critique of the trial—that many of the defendants had been kids who could not have been reasonably expected to disobey criminal orders—Everett would have been contemptuous of the report for its failure to confront the core considerations of investigative wrong-doing, evidentiary insufficiency, and American perpetration of similar combat excesses. But he received no official information, as Straight's evaluation passed into the hands of EUCOM's judge advocate. Everett had attempted to pump associates still involved in war crimes work in Germany for news but he had learned little. John Dwinell, who had been appointed law member to the court hearing the Buchenwald case, which Denson was prosecuting, knew nothing, save that he was "supersaturated" with the depressing business of Dachau and eager to return to the United States.[32] So desperate was Everett for news that he was driven to turn to the hated Colonel Abraham Rosenfeld for information. In his reply of October 8, Rosenfeld thanked Everett for his "kind letter" but confessed that, in spite of the fact that he had served for several months as chief of the 7708 War Crimes Group's trials branch, he had remained aloof from the Malmedy review because of his participation in the court and had no information about it. In fact, Rosenfeld was not being entirely truthful, for he had told Tom Reedy several months earlier that agreement had been reached on the reduction of twenty-three sentences. But he had visited Landsberg prison and had talked with "quite a few of the Malmedy boys," including Peiper, who had asked for news of Everett. This had not been a purely social occasion, as Rosenfeld had been chief prosecutor in the recently concluded Skorzeny trial, which he described as "interesting" but "unpleasant" for reasons that he would disclose later.[33]

In fact, the Malmedy and the Skorzeny trials were closely linked. The chief defendant in the latter was another *SS-Obersturmbannführer* who had played a significant and dramatic role in the Ardennes offensive. Otto Skorzeny had earned a reputation for daring improvisation in his spectacular rescue of Benito Mussolini from captivity in the mountain fastness of the Campo Imperatore Hotel in September 1943. In December 1944, Skorzeny's 150th Panzer Brigade, like *Kampfgruppe* Peiper, was to seize bridges over the Meuse River, which would carry German mechanized forces on their way to Antwerp. Unlike Peiper's force, they were to operate disguised as American GIs, using deception to achieve their objectives and sowing as much confusion behind U.S. lines as opportunity would allow. Skorzeny's operation petered out in failure as had Peiper's, and Skorzeny, too, was accused by the U.S. Army of committing war crimes during the abortive German offensive. In August 1947, he and nine other defendants were brought to trial at Dachau for the illegal use of U.S. Army uniforms and insignia and for the murder of more than one hundred American prisoners of war. Peiper himself had contributed to the latter charge by having testified in his own trial that, although he had not given orders for the killing of American prisoners, Skorzeny might have received such orders and, by implication, have carried them out.[34]

But the outcome of the Skorzeny trial was very different from that of the Malmedy proceedings. When called as a prosecution witness, Peiper did not give similar testimony, nor did three of his codefendants. An affidavit that had been generated by the Malmedy investigation and introduced by Rosenfeld as evidence was vigorously challenged by the defense, and prosecution efforts to secure corroborating witnesses were unsuccessful. Rosenfeld elected to drop the murder charges, noting that he did not want to try the case on affidavits alone. But it was in the matter of allowable defense evidence that the Skorzeny trial differed most dramatically from the trial of the previous year. Colonel Robert Durst's defense team was permitted to introduce extensive testimony that U.S. and other Allied forces had worn German uniforms in combat operations during World War II. On September 9, 1947, the defendants were acquitted of all remaining charges.[35] As Rosenfeld noted to Everett, "things have changed in the year since you were here."

While awaiting official word on the status of the Malmedy review, Everett had been kept aware of the human dimension of the Malmedy case, always of great importance to him. His uncritical sympathy for Germans in general in their postwar travail remained intense, as did the personal imperative to do something to alleviate it. While at Dachau, he had befriended Theodor Koerner, a former German officer who appears to have been held as a war crimes trial witness or suspect, and promised him assistance in building for himself and his family a new life after his release. Reminded of this by Koerner to the accompaniment of lavish praise for his chivalry and devotion to justice, Everett responded:

Your very kind and enjoyable letter of April 5th has finally reached me. It was indeed a pleasure to know that you were finally released after so long a time. Every effort was made by me to secure your release so as to have you spend Christmas with your wife and family as your wife had written me about this. It is my wish now that you are taking advantage of every minute with them. Again, I wish you and your people to know how sorry I am for the manner of handling certain affairs within your country but as time goes on my sincere prayer is that only right will prevail.

As to your request for assistance in coming to America, this is to advise you that it will be a great pleasure to sponsor or guarantee you and your family a living. At present I have over one thousand acres of land near Atlanta on which are houses and barns. There is a lot of very fine farming land and you would so enjoy the great freedom of our American life and especially the advantages for the children. You and your family are the type of people that make America truly democratic. . . . I have no idea as to the cost of travel and other expenses, but I have sufficient to defray any necessary expenses. . . .[36]

There is no evidence to indicate that Koerner accepted Everett's remarkable offer; Koerner had, in fact, expressed a preference for Brazil or Argentina. But the brief relationship between the two men vividly illustrates the perhaps naive but undoubtedly sincere humanitarianism that so powerfully motivated Everett. His father's encouragement to emulate "those who are always helping someone else and are thinking but little of themselves" had struck deep roots.

In Everett's mind, Koerner was a victim of the postwar injustices inflicted by the U.S. Army on the German people. As a former officer in that army, Everett felt it incumbent upon him to make a contribution to the rectification of those injustices. His sense of responsibility for the fate of the Malmedy defendants and their families was far more profound. Peiper had made an indelible impression upon him. Whatever might have been his culpability on the battlefield and as adjutant to Heinrich Himmler, Peiper impressed most Americans who met with him with his soldierly bearing, sardonic wit, and sensitivity, which he was capable of expressing in more than passable and often richly expressive English. A long letter that Peiper addressed to Everett in the days between the handing down of the verdicts and the sentencing is important, not for the insights it provides into his complex personality but as a means of understanding his impact on Everett.

Dear Colonel Everett,

When overlooking [sic] my life today, I may say that it has been a rich one! Should I begin it once more, I would march . . . the same straight way, the milestones of which were: idealism, faithfulness and sense of duty! . . . I fought and bled in all European theaters and became a preferred favorite of the god of hosts. In spite of all, it was a proud and heroic time! Where we were standing was Germany and as far as my tank gun reached was my kingdom! We had no personal aspirations. Our vision always has been the "Dream of Reich." In the end of war, when the Führer was needing his Leibstandarte the most, . . . fate had separated us from him and we were to fight a desperate way through Hungary and Austria. . . .

When seeing today the defendants in the dock, don't believe them to be the old Combat Group Peiper. All my old friends and comrades have gone before! These people who plead for mitigating circumstances are only the negative selection. The real outfit is waiting for me in Walhalla! Life of an old Prussian officer is not [sic] more worth living today! Better dead as [sic] slave.

Besides my charming children, I leave my wife, the best and bravest comrade I ever met. Unfortunately, I'm not able to do anything for her protection. In [sic] the contrary, I know that . . . my presence would do harm to her. The "thankful" population believes me to be a criminal and my family has to suffer from this fame. That's the worst, Colonel!

Everett as a young attorney, probably in the late 1920s. Courtesy of Willis M. Everett III

This photo of Mary Everett portrays the style and opulence of the 1920s and hints at Mary's suspicious nature. Courtesy of Willis M. Everett III

Everett as intelligence officer in the Fourth Service Command late in World War II. Combating "subversives" harmonized with his conservative principles. Courtesy of Willis M. Everett III

Bodies of U.S. soldiers at the crossroads south of Malmedy, tagged for identification. National Archives photo #111-SC-226895

Bodies of U.S. soldiers being uncovered. The body in the foreground appears to have its arms raised. National Archives photo #111-SC-226833

Peiper in a pretrial photograph. He preferred "Jochen" to "Joachim." U.S. Army photograph

Above: U.S. v. Valentin Bersin, et al., the most controversial of the post–World War II war crimes trials conducted by the U.S. Army, was played out inside this building at the former Nazi concentration camp at Dachau. National Archives photo #111-SC-249310

Left: Each defendant in the mass trial wore a numbered placard. Here, Sepp Dietrich, the former commanding general of the Sixth Panzer Army, stood as he was assigned number 11. U.S. Army photograph

Above: Among the U.S. Army officers who made up the Military Court during the Malmedy trial are Brigadier General Josiah T. Dalbey and Colonel A. H. Rosenfeld (fourth and fifth from the left). Although similar in some ways to a court martial, with a group of officers serving as judge and jury, the Malmedy trial followed dramatically different rules of evidence. U.S. Army photograph

Left: Everett (left) and Lieutenant Colonel Burton Ellis, chief prosecutor (right), shared a lighter moment in the courtroom. National Archives photo #111-SC-247940

Jochen Peiper, arms obscuring his placard and seated between defendants 45 and 7, looked on with contempt as the trial progressed. German defense attorneys are seen in civilian attire. National Archives photo #111-SC-249309

A reporter for the Akron *Beacon Journal* newspaper interviewed Colonel Everett (center) and Colonel Abraham Rosenfeld (right), law member of the court. U.S. Army photograph

Willis M. Everett Jr. addressed the court as defendants and white-helmeted army guards looked on. A stenographer recorded the proceedings, which were also filmed by U.S. Army cameramen. U.S. Army photograph

Everett stood beside each defendant as sentence was pronounced. Here, a young German learned that he had been sentenced to death. National Archives photo #111-SC-249329

The gallows at Landsberg loomed as a menacing presence and drove Everett's tireless efforts to see the death sentences overturned. Here, a German convicted in one of the flyers' cases is about to be hanged. National Archives photo #111-SC-221655

Senator Joseph McCarthy charged the Baldwin subcommittee with a "white-wash" in its investigation of the Malmedy trial. United Press International

Lieutenant General John R. Hodge (right), commander of the Third Army, presents a certificate of achievement to Everett for service to the army reserves (November 1950). The award came near the close of Everett's twenty-seven-year reserve career and was unrelated to Malmedy. Courtesy of Willis M. Everett III

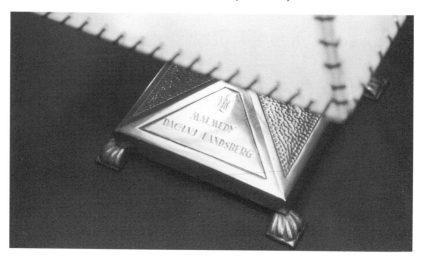

The lamp fashioned in Landsberg prison by Everett's "Malmedy boys." The base, made of brass, featured the LAH (Leibstandarte Adolf Hitler) monogram and the words Malmedy, Dachau, Landsberg. George Pearl

Willis Everett's children, Willis (left) and Mary Campbell, and Mary Campbell's husband, Kiliaen Townsend, relaxed on St. Simons Island in the mid-1950s. Courtesy of Willis M. Everett III

Willis Everett enjoyed the garden at his Lake Rabun summer home. Here, he stands in the midst of his dahlias. Courtesy of Willis M. Everett III

. . . I'm fearing that my wife has to undergo further reprisals when court is over. My great request is that she may be allowed to remain in connection with you. . . . My greatest sorrow is the fact that I don't know how she is going to get a living now. We have become the pariahs of the nation and may say with Shakespeare: "the evil that men do lives after them, the good is oft interred with their bones."

Before our steps separate, I want to thank you for all help you gave us as human being, as soldier and chief counsel of defense during the past eight weeks.

In a time of deepest human disappointments, you and McCown have returned to me much faith I already had lost. . . . I'm very glad to know that you are going to continue the work in my Germany. Time heals wounds! Only men with your character and chivalrous attitude are able to rebuild peace and to overbridge [sic] the strained relations between our countries. Perhaps our end will contribute a little to this goal. . . .

Joyfully to live, smilingly to fight, laughingly to die! That's my old watchword. It is with me also today. I'm going to die as one of the last soldiers of this terrible war, but not as a criminal! I have a good conscience. . . . May God give you a long and successful life and protect your family.

In sincere friendship I remain your devoted

Jochen Peiper

Colonel[37]

Peiper wrote the letter three days after having been found guilty by the Dachau court. He had no doubt that he would be sentenced to death and no reason to believe that the sentence would not be promptly executed. He was taking his leave of Everett and was probably as forthright as he was capable of being. Loyalty to Hitler to the end was combined with obvious contempt for many of his codefendants and a liberal dose of self-pity. Much in evidence was the rhetoric of soldierly self-sacrifice and devotion to duty, in part a cultural convention but also an accurate reflection of Peiper's self-image. But present, too, was the pathos of betrayal by countrymen and of a husband and father's separation from his family. With the exception of devotion to the *Führer*, the profound evil of whom he never fully understood, there was much in Peiper's self-portrait with which Everett could identify. And Peiper's assessment of Everett as a chivalrous officer able to put aside the rancor of war in a quest for justice was Everett as he wanted to see himself. Without Peiper, Everett would have worked hard for the revision of the Malmedy trial. With Peiper, it became a crusade.

Everett's memories of Peiper were kept vivid by poignant letters from Peiper's wife, Sigurd, who had taken up residence at Ronach am Tegernsee, south of Munich. She had initiated the correspondence, which mirrored her husband's despair, on the same day that Peiper wrote his putative farewell missive ("You did all the best you could do—but it was everything for nothing") but expressed a desperate hope: "I do not and cannot believe that this was the last word in this trial. I will hope as long as possible, and so long as I can hope, I will have the force [sic] to wait and work and live for my 3 little children. . . ."[38] She was correct in believing that the "last word" had not been spoken, and by June of the following year, with her husband still alive, there were additional grounds for hope. Frau Peiper was aware of Everett's visit to the War Crimes Branch in Washington after his return to the United States—the information had apparently come through an intermediary—and she expressed her pleasure but also her apprehension at news of the hangings at Landsberg of condemned from other trials: "we all are waiting for a sign from you which will give us any new hope and will take from us the uncertainty in which we are living. . . . My three kids are healthy and always cheerful and full of vital energy and waiting for the return of their father every day. What shall I tell them?"[39]

For someone of Everett's temperament, this was painful stuff. He hoped for definite information on the status of the trial review to share with Sigurd Peiper and, through her, with the kin of other condemned. If Rosenfeld had known anything, he had not shared it with Everett. Later in the fall, Everett appears to have been notified, probably by telephone, that final recommendations would be in General Clay's hands by November. In any event, he so informed Sigurd Peiper in a letter of November 6, 1947, which was received with "joy" as the first communication from him since he had departed Germany early in the year. There existed, she believed, reason for optimism. "Nobody in Germany can believe that the sentences will be done [sic] after such a long time and after all . . . we had heard about Schwäbisch Hall and the case."[40]

There would be no decision in November. Everett received driblets of leaked information about the progress of the review process, but this information was largely inaccurate. By January 1948, he was aware that the case was in the hands of Harbaugh's office but knew no details. His restraint in opening himself to the press was beginning to wear thin as the hold that the Malmedy case had upon him showed no signs of loosening. Everett did not express himself well by means of the written word. His letters are filled with misspellings and examples of tortured syntax, but he made up in persistence for what he lacked in eloquence. Perhaps his powers of expression came closest to matching his commitment in portions of a letter addressed to General Clay and dated January 10, 1948:

> Ever since returning from Europe I have made no statements and kept faith with Col. Mickelwaite and the Army, irrespective of repeated requests from the Herald Tribune, Associated Press and other large Eastern newpapers [sic] for the inside facts on the Malmedy trial. . . . In return, all I ask is that the Malmedy Case be sent back for retrial because of irregularities. What is done then is none of my official business but it is my business, what evidence [sic] was introduced and what methods employed in the original trial. Wars infect the spiritual and moral health of any country, no matter who wins them, and we were not immune. It is better to win than loose [sic] a war, but not much better. . . .
>
> Fear not only distorts normal judgment but it freezes the heart. The greatness of America is founded on the abundance of courage, imagination and fairness of its men and leaders. In everything that is vital and honorable in this nation of ours there is the history of courage somewhere by men who acted on their convictions.
>
> I strongly feel that your office will demonstrate that courage and fearlessly return the case against these soldiers for another trial or other disposition. . . .
>
> This letter could be termed a final personal appeal to correct those irregularities of trial as I am still determined to appeal this matter to our Supreme Court and any other battlefields I can honorably approach.
>
> As you know the last official communication received by me was a letter from General C.R. Haeber [sic], Chief of Staff, dated March 27, 1947.
>
> Current information on this Malmedy Case is desired.[41]

Similar impulses were in evidence as he wrote to Tom Reedy and his United Press counterpart in Munich, "Red" Wallens, on January 12: "I don't know why I can't forget about Malmedy and its affront to my dignity and sense of fairness. About 100 of my friends want me to forget about all that German stuff and live in the present. But I can't." He wrote wistfully about difficulties reviving his law practice, "failure to find a single old client, and my pet estate that I have kept in the courts for 13 years settled by my son-in-law." But the true purpose of the letter was evident: "Why can't you newsboys . . . give the topside some hell and make them remand the case for retrial."[42]

The "topside" was floundering. Colonel James Harbaugh, the European Command's judge advocate, had had no previous direct involvement in war crimes work prior to receiving his appointment. A West Pointer with many years of line service before transfer to the judge advocate's department, he had served with the Army Air Force as a staff judge advocate during World War II but had been in the United States when the Malmedy case had been investigated and tried. He had taken note of Straight's review and gave it, along with the trial record, to Colonel Howard F. Bresee, who had been regarded with some distaste by Everett at Dachau and was now chief of Harbaugh's review branch. Bresee, in turn, assigned the case to a review board chaired by a Colonel Scarborough for an advisory opinion.[43]

Bresee's report was not completed until February 8, 1948. It was very different from Straight's review of the previous fall and highly critical of it. Not only had the deputy judge advocate's report misstated crucial testimony in its analysis, but it had failed to address itself to the central question of the techniques used in securing sworn statements from the Malmedy defendants. Bresee's review board found "much evidence" of improper pretrial investigation, singling out "mock trials" in this regard and asserting that, in some cases, "confessions" had been the creations of investigators rather than factual statements. Pointed criticism was leveled at numerous procedural rulings made by the bench during the trial, which seemed to limit the defense in its examination of witnesses while allowing the prosecution greater latitude in its endeavors.

In fully twenty-nine of the seventy-three individual Malmedy cases, the review board found the evidence insufficient to sustain conviction and recommended disapproval of the findings and sentences.

Most notable in this category was the case of Sepp Dietrich, Hitler's sometime crony and commander of the Sixth Panzer Army during the Ardennes offensive. Dietrich's role in the scenario of slaughter outlined by the prosecution had been as transmitter of Hitler's murderous orders, and for this he had been sentenced to life imprisonment. But the evidence against the fifty-four-year-old former SS general had not convinced the board. No proof that Dietrich had ordered prisoners or civilians to be shot had been presented, nor had Dietrich confessed to having issued orders of that nature. He had conceded in his sworn statement that his orders had reflected Hitler's command that a "wave of fright and terror" should precede the attacking German forces, but, as the report argued, that was not a violation of the laws of war; the board pointed out that to create fright and terror in the minds of the enemy and thus break his will to resist must be the aim of any attacking army.

The board urged reductions of sentences in most other cases; in twelve instances, however, it found the evidence sufficient to sustain both verdicts of "guilty" and sentences of death. One of these was the case of Jochen Peiper. The board reached its conclusions on grounds somewhat different from those advanced by the prosecutors at Dachau. Peiper, the report declared, was criminally liable in that he had omitted giving his subordinates specific orders concerning the disposition of prisoners of war. It had, therefore, been left to the discretion of soldiers of lesser rank to decide whether to burden themselves with prisoners or to divest themselves of the encumbrances in the most direct and brutal way. Some had clearly chosen the latter course.

The logic and consistency of the board's report were not always compelling. Peiper was also held guilty of transmitting the illegal army order that had played so central a role in the prosecution's courtroom presentation. But the same board had recommended disapproval of the conviction of Dietrich and his chief of staff, Fritz Kraemer, on the charge of having issued illegal orders. From whom, then, had the criminal order supposedly circulated by Peiper come? Even in the absence of such an order, his willingness to permit prisoners of war to be killed seemed to be confirmed by his tacit consent to the killing of a half-starved GI captured at Petit Thier and by his possible acquiescence in the shooting of two other prisoners.

All of the eleven other instances in which the board recommended the confirmation of death sentences shared several characteristics: the defendants had held command responsibilities as officers or high-level noncommissioned officers, and all had been more than twenty years of age at the time of their alleged offenses. In every case, moreover, multiple pieces of testimony attested to the ordering of killings by the accused, their personal participation, or, at least, their personal acquiescence in such atrocities.[44]

The Dachau judgment had been left a shambles. Almost three-quarters of the death sentences had been found inappropriate, more than 60 percent of the life sentences had been recommended for reduction and, most important, in nearly 40 percent of the individual cases the evidence had been found inadequate to sustain conviction. Moreover, the board had openly accused the army investigators of conduct at best inept, at worst unprincipled, and held the judges guilty of consistent bias to the disadvantage of the defense. Much of Everett's negative assessment of the Malmedy investigation and trial seemed to have been confirmed by Bresee's board, and, had he known of it, he would have been pleased, although devastated by the support for twelve death sentences, especially Peiper's. The close agreement between Everett's views and the board's report was not entirely coincidental. And, arguably, it may not have been simply the product of rational minds reaching similar conclusions on the basis of the same evidence. Everett had not been alone among the defense staff in having taken exception to the investigative methods employed by the army in generating the evidence on which the convictions had been based and to the manner in which the Malmedy court had been operated. All questioned the propriety of the trial, although Everett was unique in the intensity of his feelings. One former member of the defense team had played a role in Bresee's review.

Lieutenant Colonel John Dwinell, Everett's chief strategist before and during the trial, had remained active in war crimes trial work in Germany after Everett's return to the States, serving as law member of the courts trying the Buchenwald and the Skorzeny cases. It was an index of the confusion that still reigned in the army's war crimes operation that Dwinell was named to Colonel Bresee's board. Bresee realized his error, and a replacement was found for Dwinell; surprisingly, however, Harbaugh insisted that Dwinell play a continuing, albeit less formal, role in the review process as adviser to Bresee's board during its three-month deliberation.[45]

Harbaugh's judgment in this regard may well be questioned, for Dwinell's involvement opened the board's recommendations to suspicion of bias in favor of the defendants; indeed, Dwinell later made clear that he believed, as did Everett, that a defense attorney's responsibility to his clients does not end with their conviction, and he proudly asserted that he had vigorously represented the defense position during his consultations with the board. Harbaugh would explain that the assistance of someone who possessed a working familiarity with the case was advisable to facilitate the work of the board. The trial documentation was intricate and of considerable bulk. More than a year had elapsed since the conclusion of the trial, while ominous rumblings from Atlanta suggested that a prompt resolution of the Malmedy affair was highly desirable.[46]

Harbaugh pondered the conclusion of Bresee's review board for several weeks and did some reading of his own in the trial transcript in preparing a final set of recommendations for General Clay. This final report was completed on March 8, 1948, and represented a cautious mean between the Straight and the Bresee reports. At the same time, Harbaugh sought to bring to Clay's attention the grave nature of the Bresee report's criticisms while implicitly disclaiming responsibility for them. He noted that the earlier report had recommended disapproval of twenty-nine convictions, most for lack of credible evidence. Dwinell's influence had been clearly reflected in the assertion that many of the sworn statements were worthless as a result of having been secured by promises of lighter punishment and that most had, in fact, been dictated by army interrogators; even had this not been the case, the Bresee report had noted a fundamental principle of Anglo-American jurisprudence, that a confession is admissible only against the party making it, a point that had been advanced by the defense during the trial but confuted on the "anything goes" evidentiary rules of war crimes trials. Harbaugh did not overtly associate himself with the review's conclusions and, in fact, expressed criticism of them. Nevertheless, there was substantial agreement between his recommendations to Clay and those made to him by Bresee. To be sure, Harbaugh found only thirteen cases worthy of disapproval; he urged confirmation of an equal number of death sentences, one more than had Bresee's board. Approval was recommended for Sepp Dietrich's life sentence, while a sentence of ten years was suggested for his chief of staff, Fritz Kraemer. In most other respects, the differences between the two sets of recommendations were slight.

With the exception of a death sentence reduced to life imprisonment, Clay accepted Harbaugh's recommendations and formally confirmed the remaining sentences on March 20, 1948. Thirteen of the Malmedy prisoners were freed from Landsberg; twelve, including Peiper, faced the gallows.[47]

8

An Old-Fashioned Sense of Justice

WHILE AWAITING OFFICIAL information from the army on the outcome of the review and on Clay's final decision, Everett prepared for a
counteroffensive, should the outcome not be to his satisfaction, as he
expected it would be. Heretofore, he had been operating largely as an
individual. Now, he began to muster forces for a concerted campaign.
The junior member of the defense team, Wilbert Wahler, had returned
to the private practice of law in Chicago. Everett hoped that Wahler
might have contacts on the *Chicago Tribune* and suggested "trotting up
there" with information on the less savory aspects of the Dachau trials.
And it might be well, Everett suggested, for Colonel Bresee, with whom
Wahler had gotten along rather better than he had, to receive a letter
from Wahler threatening to join Everett in exposing the "rottenness" of
the prosecution's conduct in the Malmedy case. Wahler did, in fact, contact the *Tribune* and discussed the case for several hours with a reporter
in his North Clark Street law offices. Wahler was more circumspect in
his evaluation of the Malmedy case than was Everett, a fact that was in
part the result of his desire for a reserve appointment in the judge advocate general's department. But he agreed with Everett that the Malmedy court had shown "utter lack of good faith" and that Mickelwaite's
visit to Dachau as the trial was drawing to a close probably indicated
that the outcome had been predetermined.[1]

The reason that Everett had asked Wahler to contact the *Chicago
Tribune* lay with a story that had been published in that newpaper on
February 23. Under the headline "Nazi Trial Judge Rips 'Injustice,'"
the *Tribune* printed an account of an interview with Iowa Supreme
Court Justice Charles F. Wennerstrum. The judge was on his way
home from Germany where he had served as presiding judge in *U.S.
v. List, et al.*, one of the secondary Nuremberg trials, which had tried
Field Marshal Wilhelm List and nine other German officers for war
crimes, including the killing of hostages. Wennerstrum had strongly

criticized the U.S. war crimes trial program as vindictive and believed it had failed to live up to the high ideals originally put forward
for it. Rather than contributing to their democratization, he thought,
the trials were simply convincing the German people that "their leaders lost the war to tough conquerors." Judge Wennerstrum also de-
plored the fact that Germans convicted of war crimes were denied a
formal system of appeals, which constituted to his mind a denial of
justice. Brigadier General Telford Taylor, chief counsel for war crimes
at Nuremberg, publicly castigated Wennerstrum for having made
statements "subversive of the interests and policies of the United
States"; this rebuke made Wennerstrum, too, in Everett's eyes, a victim of the army's preference for politics over equity.[2]

Everett recognized in Wennerstrum a kindred and potentially use-
ful spirit. He wrote to the Iowa jurist on March 8 of his enthusiasm for
Wennerstrum's stand and of his own fight, the struggle of a "Georgia
Cracker lawyer"

> against . . . rotteness [sic], intrigue and perpetuation of Nazi tactics.
> . . . You would scarcely believe that such things could be carried on
> in the name of America. . . . Frankly I have made it so hot for the
> Army, from within, that they are afraid to carry out the execution
> of the 43 death penalties. . . . Consistently I have told the Com-
> manding General EUCOM that I was going to the U.S. Supreme
> Court and the papers if they do not send the case back for retrial.
> Frankly I know of no way to get to the Supreme Court but have
> done a lot of "bluffing" along this line to force them to send the
> case back for retrial.

Everett had done some research on Judge Wennerstrum's religious
and political affiliations.

> Like yourself, I am an officer of the Southern Presbyterian Church and
> my father was moderator. . . . But we have no reputable Republican
> Party here, so there is no choice. We do not feel too kindly toward the
> Democratic Party now. As a result I have never been active in any po-
> litical work.

> May I conclude by saying that I admire you and respect your ability.
> We both think alike about war crimes trials except that I am a Rebel on
> the subject and you were gentle in your manner.[3]

Wennerstrum and Everett had a mutual friend in the Omaha attorney H. Beatty White, who had been a fraternity brother of the Iowa
Supreme Court judge and Everett's "opposite number" during the
war as director of military intelligence for the Seventh Service Command. White assured each man of the other's sterling qualities, writing to Everett that "Wennerstrum is a fine lawyer, judge and human
being and with a judicial temperament not usually given to scathing
denunciations of this type. I go for his sentiments and feel certain that
they were largely, if not wholly justified."[4] Of Everett, White wrote to
Wennerstrum:

> Willis Everett is a fine gentleman with a highly developed social con-
> science, a sense of fair play and an inbred hatred of despotism in any
> form. He is wholly sincere in what he is trying to accomplish, and is no
> "civil liberty" crackpot who hopes to feather his own nest or advance
> the cause of any ideology by his activity. He is a solid, down-to-earth
> citizen who believes in human rights in a constitutional sense. . . .
>
> I write you thus so you will know a little bit about your correspon-
> dent, and to assure you will find him honest and trustworthy in
> every respect.[5]

Wennerstrum would serve as a source of sympathetic but moderate
counsel for Everett in the months to come and would provide intro-
ductions to potentially supportive midwestern politicians. Meanwhile,
Wennerstrum had piqued the conservative *Tribune's* interest in possible
war crimes justice misfeasance under a Democratic administration, and
the newspaper made arrangements to send a correspondent to Atlanta
where, Everett assured Wahler, he would receive, in addition to "facts
from the record," "a lot of guidance as to what to look for and also some
'off the record' information they can investigate. . . ."; this on the understanding, however, that nothing would be published until after the
army completed its review and announced Clay's decision.[6]

To Sally and Irving Hayett, the Jewish court reporters for whose
wedding in Dachau Everett had served as best man and who had returned to civilian employment with Accurate Court Reporters in Detroit, there was a rather different approach:

> Greetings, welcome and love—just heard the other day that both of
> my children were back in the U.S. and how happy that made me feel

to know that you all had left that "mess" over at Dachau. How any of us stood it is a miracle. . . . Twenty months have elapsed and still no completed review of the Malmedy case and no final decision. I have fought the big Army boys in Germany and the U.S. since seeing you two kids last. Have not turned loose in any papers and will not until the Army decides what they will do. My price of keeping my mouth shut is that the case be sent back for retrial.

Sally, now that you are away from that mess can't you give me some details of what went on in Schabesche [*sic*] Hall? If testimony were demanded of you before some competent body what dope would you have to spill? I do not desire you to be disloyal but when they promised to give those damn Germans a fair trial it became my duty to see that they got one and I have not changed my opinion one bit since the trial that they were not accorded a fair trial as we look at one! Could you help me out on this matter? Anything you write would be treated as confidential because I would never get you or Irving in any trouble even if I had to go to jail myself.

How about a "kid" sometime soon? How about a trip to Atlanta sometime sooner? How about a letter about all the happenings since I saw you and news of yourselves *nunc pro tunc*.[7]

Otto Leiling had been the German defense attorney with whom Everett had worked most closely during the trial, in part because of Leiling's British wife and perfect English. By March 1948, he no longer knew Leiling's whereabouts but wrote to another former German member of the defense team, Eugen Leer of Munich, with a call to cautious action:

It has been a long time since I have seen you or your wife. Have had several letters from Mrs. Peiper and have written several to her. I have assured her of my continued fight which no doubt you have seen the results [*sic*] in one delay after another. . . . I am sure you have felt that invisible pressure that has continuously been exerted by me on behalf of trying to send the case back for a retrial. . . . You can help by pushing along the same lines through your German channels but you are so handicapped by being subject to military regulations. . . .

Would you be kind enough to discuss my activities on behalf of the defendants with Dr. Leiling and the other German Defense Counsel?[8]

The assistance of John Dwinell, Everett's chief strategist during the trial and a man with vastly greater trial experience than he, would be of crucial importance to continued challenges to the Malmedy verdicts if confirmed by General Clay. Everett was as yet unaware of the role that Dwinell had played in Bresee's review; had he been, he might have been less imperious in his letter of March 16: "Understand Col. Bresee is in Frankfurt and on the review of this case. Now write me back and let me know if that is correct. . . . Also send me what 'poop' you have on appeal to Supreme Court. Do this now John and don't put it off—write a personal note as you did last time but get it off to me."[9]

Dwinell had already been the subject of communication between Everett and Colonel E. H. Young of the War Crimes Branch, Civil Affairs Division, in Washington. Anticipating an unsatisfactory decision from Clay's office, Everett requested that Dwinell (and Leiling, too) be brought to the United States and made available for assistance in preparing the oft-threatened appeal to the Supreme Court. "In view of the fact that my entire legal services are free," Everett noted sarcastically, "this does not seem to be an unreasonable request."[10] The request was not entirely Everett's initiative and had, in fact, been suggested to Everett by Dwinell, who may have had ulterior motives. In a letter to Everett of February 13, Dwinell had revealed that "I am in an extremely difficult position. However, I have spoken to Col. Harbaugh, the Judge Advocate, about the situation and I told him that it was possible that you would request my services in connection with an application to the Supreme Court. I suggest that you obtain orders for me immediately. . . ." Dwinell's urgent desire to leave Germany may have been the result of discomfort over the somewhat dubious role he had played in the trial review, although his deteriorating relationship with Mrs. Dwinell, who resisted joining him in Germany, was also a motivating factor.[11]

Everett was informed that his request for Dwinell's and Leiling's services had been denied in a letter from the War Crimes Branch dated April 12.[12] By that time, he had already known for approximately three weeks of Clay's "final decision" in regard to the Malmedy case and had received from Sigurd Peiper a plaintive telegram: "Judgment confirmed—please your help."[13] Everett had been promised a period of at least sixty days in which to appeal to the Supreme Court, and the army's reluctance to move forward with the execution of the death sentences was suggested by the assurance that "any reasonable request for an extension of the sixty days stay of execution granted to the condemned will receive sympathetic consideration."[14] Everett hoped that, all else failing, the Department of the Army could eventually be forced to intervene, and he was willing to provide the necessary encouragement. In the meantime, as the opportunities for revision within the structure of military justice had apparently been exhausted, Everett turned to the Supreme Court for a writ of habeas corpus, the key defense against illegal and arbitrary imprisonment under Anglo-American law. This writ, if granted, could lead to the retrial of the Malmedy case, which Everett had long demanded as the appropriate solution to the Malmedy conundrum. The results of previous petitions of this nature were not encouraging. In the case of Japanese General Tomoyuki Yamashita, a majority of the justices had ruled that the Court lacked the authority to review the proceedings of military courts, although Justices Rutledge and Murphy had dissented. Nineteen days later, on February 23, 1946, Yamashita had been hanged.[15]

The petition had been roughed out by Everett and Dwinell while the two were still together in Germany. Now, it was a matter of refining the document and learning the means whereby the petition might be brought to the attention of the nine justices. Fortuitously, a heart attack suffered by his father brought Dwinell to New York City by late April, and none too soon, for Everett's inexperience was reflected in an effort to discuss the preparation of the petition with Supreme Court Justice Frank Murphy, an obviously improper approach that Murphy politely but firmly rebuffed. Dwinell arrived home not only with a superior understanding of court procedure but also with copies of all of the earlier reviews of the case.[16]

And there was judicial punctilio to be served. Former Georgia governor John Slaton and the prominent Atlanta and Washington attorney William A. Sutherland supported Everett's application for admission to practice before the Supreme Court. Forty copies of the 228-page petition were prepared, bound in brown covers in tablet form, and submitted to the clerk of the Court, a substantial undertaking in those days before word processors and modern photocopying machines, in which Everett's daughter, Mary Campbell, performed noble service. Everett noted in an accompanying letter that executions of the twelve defendants under sentence of death were scheduled for May 20, the end of the sixty-day stay that he had been promised, and requested that his motion be heard prior to that date; if necessary, he was willing to come to Washington "because the whole matter is close to my heart."[17] A reply from E. P. Cullinan, assistant clerk, assured Everett that the copies of the petition had been received and that the case had been docketed on May 13 as "No. 512 Miscellaneous October Term 1947" and was "immediately brought to the attention of the Court." The petition was formally presented to the Court on May 14, 1948. A note penciled in Everett's hand on the bottom of the letter from Cullinan reads: "telephoned 5/12/48 at 2:45 p.m. Court met for 20 minutes and adjourned. No news. Attention of court called to date of execution and urgency of matter."[18]

The two-inch thick argument was, in reality, an addendum to the single-page document that accompanied and had preceded it. The "Motion for Leave to File Petition" was presented by Everett on behalf of Valentin Bersin and the Malmedy prisoners still incarcerated at Landsberg as petitioner versus President Harry S Truman as Commander in Chief of the Armed Forces of the United States, James V. Forrestal, Secretary of Defense, Kenneth C. Royall, Secretary of the Army, General Omar N. Bradley, Chief of Staff of the U.S. Army, and Thomas C. Clark, Attorney General. The motion was addressed to Chief Justice Fred M. Vinson and the associate justices and, in the ceremonious language of judicial discourse, read: "Now comes the petitioner on behalf of the plaintiffs in the above styled case and respectfully requests permission and leave of this Honorable Court to file this original petition for a Writ of Habeas Corpus and that the same be placed on the Docket for hearing."[19]

In plain language, the Court had to accept jurisdiction before the case could be judged on its merits. The outcome could not have been closer. With Robert Jackson disqualifying himself because of his earlier service as U.S. chief prosecutor in the initial Nuremberg trial, the Court split four to four:

> The motion for leave to file a petition for an original writ of habeas corpus for relief from sentences upon the verdicts of a General Military Government Court at Dachau, Germany, is denied. The Chief Justice, Mr. Justice Reed, Mr. Justice Frankfurter, and Mr. Justice Burton are of the opinion that there is want of jurisdiction. . . . Mr. Justice Black, Mr. Justice Douglas, Mr. Justice Murphy, and Mr. Justice Rutledge are of the opinion that the motion for leave to file the petition should be granted and that the case should be set for argument forthwith.[20]

Jackson's abstention long rankled Everett, who believed that the Nuremberg trial before an international tribunal was sufficiently different from the purely U.S. Army Dachau courts so that participation in the former was not a disqualification for review of a case tried in the latter. For a time, it appeared that the error was Everett's in bringing his petition to the Supreme Court rather than to the district court of the District of Columbia, which was held in an appeal of a later case to have jurisdiction in a situation in which a person is deprived of his liberty by a United States official outside the territorial jurisdiction of a federal court. In that case, it was held by an appellate court "that person's petition for a writ of habeas corpus will lie in the District Court that has territorial jurisdiction over the officials who have directive power over the immediate jailer." But a subsequent ruling by the Supreme Court had the effect of denying habeas corpus review to any of the Dachau cases.[21]

Everett was immediately informed of the outcome by telephone and was not surprised; on balance, he was more encouraged than disheartened by the fact that he had come so close to bringing the Malmedy case before the highest court in the country. He already had secured the attention of the press, some of it distinctly sympathetic. "Secretary Royall would better serve the ends of truth and justice if he instituted court martial proceedings against the military prosecutors accused," fumed the *Chicago Tribune* on May 21. Now, he had a highly detailed, if somewhat exaggerated, account of what had transpired at Schwäbisch Hall and in the courtroom at Dachau that could be circulated where it would do the most good. The actual petition for a writ of habeas corpus, as distinct from the writ for leave to file such a petition, was a tendentious compendium of fact and allegation, rather than an effort at objective analysis of the Malmedy case. It was, simply, a defense argument intended primarily to save from the gallows men whose guilt Everett believed to be unproved. An objective discussion of the facts of the Malmedy investigation and trial was not to be expected in a document of this sort, nor was it to be found. The petition contained reasoned challenges to the jurisdiction of the Dachau court and well-constructed arguments asserting that the conditions under which the defendants had been held were in violation of the Geneva Convention of 1929, the "Magna Carta" of prisoners of war. These arguments were combined with repetitions of the familiar claims that Everett and his staff had been denied adequate time and resources to prepare a proper defense and that such defense as had been prepared had often been vitiated by biased rulings from the bench. The circumstances surrounding many of the alleged crimes were murky, and it seemed evident that some of the alleged crimes had not occurred at all.[22] And it was hypocritical, Everett argued, for the U.S. Army to prosecute former enemy soldiers for excesses committed in the heat of the offensive "knowing full well how 'walnut stained' our hands looked after a heated battle to crack some enemy position."[23] But alongside these sober representations stood hair-raising descriptions of beatings, starvation, and other torments allegedly used routinely to compel prisoners to confess to crimes that they had not committed. Mock trials, the petition seemed to suggest, had been the rule rather than the exception admitted by the prosecution and had been terrifying affairs in which eighteen- and twenty-year-old plaintiffs had been brow-beaten, confused by false witnesses, beguiled by prosecutors pretending to be their defense attorneys, and, if recalcitrant, led to believe that they would be hanged within a day or two. In other situations, Everett's petition alleged, prisoners had been promised immunity or light sentences if they signed confessions that implicated others. Much was made of the suicide of Arvid Freimuth, who ostensibly had been heard to cry, "I cannot utter another lie" shortly before having been found hanged in his cell.[24] Everett was not above intentional misleading, although it was not in him to do it adroitly. He alleged that the army had refused to provide him with a copy of the trial record, requiring him to work from memory in preparing his petition. The first assertion was true; the second was not. Everett had confided to Wilbert Wahler in March that, unbeknownst to the army and in defiance of instructions, he had taken a copy of the record home with him from Germany. In any event, readers of the petition might legitimately have wondered about the source of the lengthy excerpts from the trial transcript with which Everett had salted the petition.[25]

The Supreme Court had not received the only copies of the petition. Herbert Strong, the Jewish-German member of the defense team whose fluency in German had been invaluable to Everett and who was now an attorney with the Wall Street law firm of Scribner and Miller, proclaimed the allegations contained therein "absolutely true and correct."[26] Copies also went to several legislators, the most significant of whom was Everett's congressman, James Davis, with whom he was on first-name basis. Davis, a former member of the Ku Klux Klan, state legislator, and Superior Court judge, had earlier sponsored an effort in the Georgia General Assembly to establish a registration system that would have required individual Georgians to so inform the state if they had an "ascertainable" quantity of Negro blood.[27] There is no evidence that Davis was attracted to Everett's cause out of sympathy with Nazi racism or with the SS defendants in the Malmedy case. But the criticisms leveled against the U.S. war crimes trials program by other congressmen may have been. Everett had noted with approval and commended to General Clay an address made by Congressman John Rankin of Mississippi on the floor of the House in November 1947. Rankin was an unabashed racist and fervent anti-Semite and anti-Communist who linked his prejudices with the Southern experience of the Civil War:

> Mr. Speaker, as a representative of the American people I desire to say that what is taking place in Nuremberg, Germany, is a disgrace to the United States. Every other country has washed its hands and withdrawn from this saturnalia of persecution. But a racial minority, 2 1/2 years after the war closed, are in Nuremberg not only hanging German soldiers but trying to hang German businessmen, in the name of the United States. The Associated Press this morning said that 14 German military leaders . . . were indicted today by the United States on charges of crimes against peace and humanity. Is this done to stir eternal enmity between us and the German people? Will it commend the ingredients of our poisoned chalice to our own lips someday?

> Suppose you people who won the War Between the States had, 2 1/2 or 3 years after the war closed, hung Jefferson Davis, Nathan Bedford Forrest, . . . and all the other great leaders of the Confederacy, how do you think we would have felt over it, even at this late date?

> Suppose that Lee had won the Battle of Gettysburg and brought that unfortunate conflict to a close in our favor and we had proceeded to hunt down Abraham Lincoln and Andrew Johnson, U.S. Grant, General Meade, and all the other great leaders on the northern side and then gone into the business world and destroyed the people who fought on your side or supported your cause, how would you have felt over it?

> Remember that both sides in that war charged each other with every crime that could be committed. On April 23, 1862, Schuyler Colfax, later Speaker of the House and Vice-President of the United

States, charged on this floor that Confederate soldiers dug up the lifeless remains of Federal soldiers and converted their skulls into drinking cups.

Of course, nothing of that kind ever happened, but it shows the extent to which men will go in making charges against their adversaries in time of war. Mr. Speaker, I say it is time to stop those disgraceful proceedings at Nuremberg, Germany, and try to lead the world back to the path of peace.[28]

In his tendency to relativize and even to deny German criminality during World War II and to portray postwar Germany as the victim of a Jewish conspiracy, Rankin went well beyond Everett's position, and Everett did not seek out the support of the Mississippi congressman. Davis remained his primary ally in Congress and facilitated his contact with other legislators and government officials. Everett had placed a copy of the Supreme Court petition in Davis' hands prior to the Court's decision. Davis was disturbed by the allegations of U.S. Army misconduct that it contained. Although not entirely convinced of the truth of the claims, he promised his support and urged Everett to press on with his fight, even in the face of the recent disappointment.

I hope that you will not feel that you should drop the matter here. I feel that a great deal indeed depends upon a thorough, accurate, and impartial investigation being made. Such an investigation cannot be made unless someone like yourself who is familiar with all the facts and details will make it his (or your) business to follow through and see that the investigation is a real investigation, in fact.

I want you to know that I am at your service for anything I can do here to help you see that justice is done in this matter.

Again I want to commend you for your unceasing efforts to right something which, if you have been correctly informed, is a most grievous and shocking wrong.[29]

Davis need not have feared that Everett's spirits were flagging; Everett assured the congressman that "as long as there is any fight left in me I will continue until they grant a new trial or other disposition. Please be assured that I will stand up to anyone on this case."[30] But

Davis's assistance was critical. Following the receipt of Everett's Supreme Court petition, Davis conferred with Georgia Senator Walter F. George, and the two legislators agreed to carry the matter to the cabinet level of the executive branch. Davis met with Secretary of Defense James V. Forrestal, while George visited Kenneth C. Royall, Secretary of the Army.[31] Royall later claimed that his conversation with Senator George was his introduction to the Malmedy controversy. Given the publicity that the case had already received, this assertion may warrant skepticism. But Royall was sufficiently disturbed by the allegations to order an immediate stay of all executions pending further review of the case.[32] A more sympathetic attitude on the part of the army was indicated by its reconsideration of Everett's earlier request for Dwinell's assistance and an offer of Dwinell's services to Everett on a part-time basis. Dwinell would have been of great value if Everett had filed for a rehearing of his Supreme Court petition, a step that he considered but did not undertake. But the fact that Dwinell had been assigned to the Judge Advocate General's Department in Washington made him an extremely useful contact and a source of inside information, as well as an advocate for Everett's position, which he shared. Within a month of the Supreme Court's decision, Dwinell had participated in a lengthy conference on the Malmedy case with General Thomas H. Green, the judge advocate general, and Colonel Edward H. Young, chief of the War Crimes Branch. "The General wanted to be acquainted with the facts of the case," Dwinell wrote Everett, and the three had gone through Everett's petition for habeas corpus "page by page," with Green "stopping from time to time to ask me whether I was definitely of the opinion that these things were true. He got a positive 'yes' with a remark now and then that I felt that you had told only part of the story."[33]

Royall's order of a stay of execution for the Malmedy condemned had been accompanied by a directive to General Clay to investigate the allegations contained in Everett's Supreme Court petition. It was a strange request, in light of the fact that Clay had completed a review of the case a short time before, in full knowledge of Everett's convictions. But, under pressure from Washington, he directed that yet another review be undertaken by his Administration of Justice Review Board, a panel that he had established a year earlier to periodically examine the operation of U.S. courts martial and other military courts, primarily in regard to their handling of U.S. citizens, although nothing in the originating order prohibited the board from also investigating the impact of U.S. Army justice on Germans.[34]

Everett had long ago concluded that the army was capable of no more than "whitewashing" its judicial misdeeds, and the assignment of the case to the Administration of Justice Review Board provided no occasion for a revision of his opinion. Dwinell picked up from "confidential sources" information on the composition of the board and reported to Everett that "something has happened that I believe is the worst and damndest outrage that has ever been perpetuated in this whole affair."[35] Dwinell's indignation had been occasioned by the fact that one of the board members was none other than Colonel James Harbaugh, EUCOM's judge advocate, in the company of Colonel John M. Raymond, the director of Clay's legal division, and Professor Carl Friedrich of Harvard, then serving as adviser on governmental affairs to OMGUS. In fact, the membership of the board had been established at the time of its creation, long before it had been assigned the Malmedy matter, although Clay might have been faulted for not having established an ad hoc committee composed of persons who had had no prior contact with the case. And Dwinell would have done well to remember that it had been Harbaugh who had permitted him to exercise great influence on the Bresee review. In any event, it may have been Dwinell's protests to the judge advocate general that contributed to Royall's muddying of already turgid waters with yet another investigative agency in the summer, of which more later.

"Jim" Davis and Walter George were conservative Democrats whose ideological perspectives were not seriously at variance with Everett's. But they assisted him because they believed that his case had legal and ethical merit and because he was one of their constituents, and a moderately prominent and influential one, to boot. Another early congressional champion was a Great Plains Republican, Francis Case of South Dakota. Case was one member of an odd South Dakota triumvirate that emerged early in 1948 in support of Everett and his campaign against the Malmedy verdicts. Case had chaired a subcommittee of the House Select Committee on Foreign Aid, whose members had spent several weeks late in the summer of 1947 in Germany and Austria studying the complexities of economic recovery and who had impressed General Clay by their serious demeanor and hard work, although they had concluded that the U.S. denazification program was impeding German recovery.[36] On September 15, the congressmen had met with members of the Bavarian state government and with church officials, including Auxiliary Bishop Johannes Neuhäusler of Munich. Early in the spring of 1948, Neuhäusler addressed a letter to Case and four other congressmen in which he recalled that German reactions to war crimes trials had been a topic discussed at the earlier meeting. Neuhäusler reminded Case and his colleagues that he had expressed the belief that most Germans supported the Nuremberg trials but had noted that he had serious reservations about the trials at Dachau. Now, he reported, he had detailed information about one of those trials—none other than Malmedy. There followed the by now standard litany of allegations about investigative abuses used to extract statements from the suspects under duress, and praise for Everett's tireless efforts:

> The American defense counsel Colonel Willes [sic] Everett, Jr., as is everywhere recognized, has endeavored in every way to expose the shameful interrogation methods and the dubious character of the "statements," unfortunately without significant success. . . . Since the death sentences, thank God, have not yet been carried out, we all have the serious moral obligation to prevent a single man being executed, as long as there does not exist 100% certainty of his guilt. A new investigation, without threats and torture-like methods, appears absolutely necessary. It would be appalling if the truth emerged too late.

> Because of my struggle against Nazism, I spent 4 1/3 years in prison and in a concentration camp, and therefore have no reason to wish the crimes of the Nazis to go unpunished. I also need not elaborate upon the fact that I regard the shooting of defenseless prisoners and wounded as an abominable crime of the worst sort. But I am human being, Christian and priest enough not to want to have inflicted the most severe punishment possible upon someone whose offense is not fully proven. . . .[37]

Case sent a copy of Neuhäusler's letter to Everett at the request of "a mutual friend." Charles H. Whiting, an attorney in Rapid City, South Dakota, and later a prolific author on World War II, had come to know Everett while both men were assigned to duty in Europe. Whiting, too, had been at Dachau during his eighteen-month tour of duty, and he had come away with an opinion of operations there that was no more positive than Everett's. Early in May, he wrote to congratulate Everett on his decision to petition the Supreme Court and added: "It has been one of my fondest hopes that as a result of your petition to the Supreme Court, the whole stinking mess, which in my opinion was War Crimes as conducted at Dachau, will be brought to public attention and that our military justice as applied to the defeated enemy may receive the public condemnation which I believe it deserves."[38] Everett replied with gratitude in his characteristically ingratiating manner in a letter accompanying a copy of the petition:

> Your most welcome letter of May 1 was received. So often I have thought and talked about you. Your gentle manner and excellent knowledge of the law and justice placed you on the top of that "trash pile" at Dachau.
>
> Needless to say I have been fighting the Army for two years on this Malmedy Case. . . . I begged them to spare me the humility [sic] of stamping the Army and War Crimes as worse criminals than those they were condemning. It was all futile. . . . The Army thought that I would be jumping up and down that only 12 were to be hung. Frankly they can hang all 74 [sic] as far as I am concerned but not on that farce of a trial and the evidence they presented. Two additional copies of my petition are enclosed for your Congressman Case and Dr. Neuhäusler. I have not started any political fight yet but maybe the honorable Mr. Case can help me when I do start. This sure has been a single-handed fight against the whole Army.[39]

Whiting forwarded the copies of the Supreme Court petition to Case and commented:

> I strongly recommend that you read this petition as I think you will find it very interesting. Much of it will probably be unbelievable to you. It would be to me except for the fact that I know it to be substantially true as I heard various members of the prosecution staff and others connected with War Crimes at Dachau bragging at having used the very methods outlined in this petition.[40]

What Whiting knew "to be substantially true" seems to have been the "mock trials," whose existence the prosecution had admitted. But he challenged none of the allegations made in the petition and wished for its success, along with the result that "you not only save the lives of these German boys, but that also the whole mess is brought to public attention, and that Colonel Straight, Brassee [sic] Ellis and others receive the public condemnation that they are entitled to."[41] Receiving the news of the petition's rejection by the Court, he wrote to Everett:

> I scarcely know whether to congratulate or console you, as I have just read of the decision of the Supreme Court on your petition. However, I think that truly you are to be congratulated. It was quite an accomplishment to get four of the Judges to grant your petition and by doing so you have apparently forced the War Department [sic] to take action.
>
> While I fear that we cannot hope for an impartial investigation by the War Department [sic], perhaps if enough political pressure is put back of them, they may do something. I am taking the liberty of writing my friend Case, urging him to bring the matter up on the floor of the House. . . . What we really should have is a Congressional investigation of the whole War Crimes setup. Then the public would really have a chance to find out what has been going on in Germany. . . .
>
> If you have any suggestions as to how I can be of any assistance to you in your fight on this matter, let me know, as I would be only too happy to carry out any suggestion which you might have.[42]

His having sent the petition to Case quickly produced modest results. The South Dakota congressman read it, and the reading had the desired effect. Case, in a letter to Brigadier General G. L. Eberle of the War Crimes Branch's Civil Affairs Division, pronounced himself "a bit flabbergasted at the methods used for obtaining of [sic] evidence and the type of evidence considered in the mass trial."[43] Whiting reported with satisfaction to Everett on the impact of his petition on Case:

> We have apparently succeeded in arousing at least one Congressman to action. Case is a fearless fellow and if he makes up his mind to do something about this matter, I think we can be sure that he will make himself heard. As chairman of the Sub-Committee on Military Appropriations, he occupies a position such that he cannot hardly [sic] be ignored by the War Department.[44]

Everett's staunch Presbyterian loyalties did not keep him from entering into a cordial correspondence with the Roman Catholic Bishop of Fargo, South Dakota, who also became an active participant in the Malmedy controversy. Bishop Aloisius J. Muench was serving as liaison consultant in Roman Catholic affairs to the U.S. military government in Germany. He had become familar with Malmedy through Bishop Neuhäusler and had been visited by Magda Diefenthal, the wife of former *SS-Sturmbannführer* Joseph Diefenthal, a boyish-faced battalion commander in Peiper's battle group who had been implicated in the crossroads mass killing. He had stood in the courtroom at Dachau on his one remaining leg to hear his sentence of death, and that sentence had been upheld by General Clay. Frau Diefenthal had presented to Bishop Muench affidavits in which German prisoners who had made statements against her husband "under brutal duress" retracted their earlier testimony. Deeply moved, Muench had contacted General Clay and forwarded the documents to him. That Muench combined deep respect for Everett with the latter's anti-Semitism was obvious.

> May I say that no one in the whole case has done so much as you in clearing our fair name for right and justice, besmirched by men who, hardly American, played such a foul role in obtaining evidence. I hung my head with shame when I read what happened in the original trial, but raised it again with pride when I saw what you did to rehabilitate our good name.
>
> If there is anything further that I may do to assist you in your efforts, I respectfully offer my services.
>
> With sentiments of admiration and regard I am
>
> Yours very sincerely,
A.J. Muench
Bishop of Fargo
Liaison Consultant MG[45]

Case and Muench impressed upon the U.S. Army the necessity for extreme caution in dealing with the Malmedy affair, and all three South Dakotans reassured Everett of the rectitude of his cause. In Everett's later correspondence with Muench, "ungodliness" joined "corruption" as the targets of his wrath. But his convictions received reinforcement from others in Germany besides Muench. On May 14, 1948, Everett dispatched two copies of his well-traveled Supreme Court petition to Tom Reedy, of the Associated Press's Munich office, with instructions to convey the copies to the German defense attorney, Eugen Leer, with one to be given to Peiper. Everett hoped that they and others associated with the defendants would examine the petition and add details that he might have overlooked.[46] Leer was already active in securing affidavits from German prisoners in Landsberg and from others who claimed to have knowledge of the events that were the focus of the Malmedy trial. These were the foundation of Leer's own appeals to EUCOM, which were shared with Everett. In sometimes awkward but incisive English, Leer argued, as had Everett, that the evidence on which the convictions had been based was so unreliable and had been secured under such questionable conditions as to necessitate a new trial. Like Everett, he did not deny that a substantial number of American soldiers had been killed at the crossroads south of Malmedy, but he maintained that the deaths had occurred under obscure circumstances that did not clearly constitute a violation of the laws of war and by persons who had not been convincingly identified by the prosecution evidence.[47] Some of these affidavits alleged duress by specific members of the pretrial investigation team at Dachau. Hans-Georg Huebler, an eighteen-year-old enlisted man at the time of the Ardennes offensive, swore before the *Bürgermeister* of Michelstadt that he had been beaten and kicked in the genitals by Joseph Kirschbaum over a period of several days while in the prison at Schwäbisch Hall. This abuse, in combination with promises of preferential treatment and early release, had motivated Huebler to sign a statement dictated to him by Morris Ellowitz in which he implicated his company commmander and a comrade in acts of murder. He claimed to have written a retraction of the earlier statement later while in Dachau, only to see it torn up by Lieutenant Colonel Ellis, while Kirschbaum and Ellowitz had impressed upon him the futility of claiming duress while on the witness stand. Kirschbaum, "with a smile that could not have been misunderstood, . . . asked me whom the court would believe, him or me? From the experience in Schwäbisch Hall and this new indication of might of the prosecution, I was so depressed that I did not find the courage to retract the untrue charges."[48] Dr. Eduard Knorr, a dentist at Schwäbisch Hall, had been employed by the U.S. Army to tend to the dental needs of the inmates of the prison and had done so twice a week, usually on Tuesdays and Thursdays. In that capacity, he had sometimes treated young veterans of the Waffen SS who were being interrogated as witnesses in the Malmedy case. In an affidavit of May 29, 1948, which he swore before the district notary of Schwäbisch Hall, he alleged that "about 15 or 20" of these men had shown injuries to the mouth and jaw consistent with beatings. Knorr had asked one of these men how things were going for him, to which the man had supposedly answered, "How should things be going when one gets beaten almost every day, at least during each interrogation; look at my head!" Knorr asserted that the young man's head was covered with bruises. He continued:

> I can remember exactly two cases, once one tooth and another time 4 teeth of the lower jaw were recently knocked out. Moreover, once a lower jaw fracture was pointed out to me which I could only splint provisionally, because [the patient] was immediately admitted to an American hospital. All of the men made a most intimidated impression and replied to any questions either not at all or only very inexactly out of fear that their statements could become the grounds for further abuses.
>
> I know that private persons living in the vicinity of the prison heard the victims' cries of pain clearly. Therefore, there was great agitation and indignation among the population.[49]

Convict Willi von Chamier swore in an affidavit witnessed by Captain Lloyd A. Wilson, prison director at Landsberg, that the pretrial statement that he had made at Schwäbisch Hall, in which he admittted to having shot prisoners under orders from his company commander at the crossroads and had implicated six others in the murders, was false. He claimed that he had made the statement in response to a threat from Lieutenant Perl that if he did not confess, he would be hanged; if he did confess, nothing would happen to him. He had agreed to confess in the intimidating atmosphere of a nighttime "mock trial," in which he was led into a room illuminated by two candles and told that he stood before a court and was about to be condemned.[50] Most of the affidavits assembled by Leer did not speak to the allegations of duress and physical abuse but simply purported to demonstrate the inaccuracy of the sworn statements and testimony presented by the prosecution. Bernhard Bartels, for example, swore before a notary in Lübeck that he had been a platoon leader in *Kampfgruppe* Peiper during the Ardennes offensive but had received no orders regarding the killing of prisoners. On the contrary, his company commander had ordered prisoners to be brought to him or to the unit headquarters. "My company commander was a soldier and no brigand."[51] Defendant Rolf Reiser attested before Karl Morgenschweiz, the Catholic priest assigned to Landsberg prison, that prosecution testimony to the effect that former *SS-Obersturmführer* Friedrich Christ, one of the defendants still under sentence of death, had been present at the crossroads killings could not be true, because he had seen Christ in Honsfeld at that time.[52] Friedmar Jirasek, who had been assigned to the platoon commanded by former *SS-Unterschar-führer* Friedel Bode, sentenced to death for, among other offenses, participating in the crossroads killings, swore before a Munich notary, Dr. Josef Edel, that when his unit had passed the fatal intersection the Americans were already lying dead and no one had opened fire.[53] These and other affidavits were of uncertain persuasiveness, but no more so than the original sworn statements on which the convictions had been based.

Everett boasted to Wahler that he had "started enough fire this time to burn someone."[54] The American Bar Association was taking notice of allegations by Everett and others concerning problematical aspects of the U.S. war crimes trial program and was receiving some encouragement from within EUCOM's judge advocate's office to do so. In a letter of July 22, 1948, U.S. Air Force Lieutenant Colonel Donald McClure, himself a member of the ABA's committee on international law, urged the organization to draft "proper and appropriate procedures for the handling of war crimes cases" for implementation in the wake of possible future conflicts. Criticism of at least some aspects of the post–World War II effort was implicit:

As I have participated in the efforts of our Government in these matters, I feel justified in sincerely urging that the American Bar Association, which is always interested in maintaining high professional standards, have a study of this important matter made, and take a stand that will brighten the dark places we find in this field where the torch should be carried with honor.

I sincerely believe that some such steps as those outlined above must be taken in this field at this time to clarify and strengthen our position in the eyes of those who will some day judge us and our actions in these proceedings. . . .

Such an effort, McClure added, should involve officers familiar with war crimes cases, but their value would "be predicated upon absolute freedom from any attempt to justify past actions." The endeavor would also suffer, however, if it were undertaken entirely by lawyers "who are not thoroughly familiar with the trial of criminal cases as they are conducted under Anglo-American jurisprudence." This remarkable letter, written on the letterhead of EUCOM's Office of the Judge Advocate with a copy sent to Everett by Judge Wennerstrum, who had received it from Frederic M. Miller, chairman of the ABA's section on international and comparative law, indicated a growing sense of discomfort in Harbaugh's office and, perhaps, an understandable desire to "pass the buck."[55]

The uneasiness in EUCOM's judge advocate's office was matched by that in the office of the Secretary of the Army. Kenneth Royall, as noted earlier, had decided to supplement General Clay's re-examination of the Malmedy trial with a reviewing agency of his own, suggesting that he lacked confidence in the army's capacity to deal effectively, in both a substantive and a political sense, with the growing controversy. The three-man commission that he named on July 23, 1948, was ordered to investigate and review not only the twelve death sentences still in force against Malmedy defendants but also 127 death sentences that had been imposed in other trials conducted at Dachau and subsequently sustained by review. The chairman of the committee was Judge Gordon Simpson of the Texas Supreme Court. Joining Simpson were Judge Leroy van Roden, of the Orphan's Court of Delaware County, Pennsylvania, and Lieutenant Colonel Charles W. Lawrence, of the Judge Advocate General's Corps. All three men had been involved in the administration of military justice and were familiar with the general procedures and issues in question. In fact, the membership of the commission conformed rather well to the description of the investigative organ proposed the day before by McClure in his letter to the ABA. Coincidentally, and there is no evidence to suggest that it was anything other than coincidence, Leroy van Roden was well known to Everett from his tour of duty in Germany, and the two had roomed together for a time in the Carlton Hotel in Frankfurt. Van Roden was, in fact, an excellent choice for the assignment, as he combined training in the law and judicial experience with some personal knowledge of the battle-field, having gone ashore at Utah Beach on D-Day, for which he had been decorated with the *Croix de Guerre* with palms and a Bronze Star.[56] On August 4, the day that Everett learned that van Roden had been dispatched to Germany as part of Royall's Simpson Commission, he drafted a letter to van Roden's wife that contained information that he hoped would be forwarded for the enlightenment of the judge. The commission, he wrote, should be particularly cautious in dealing with Lieutenant Colonel Straight, who had, Everett believed, been covering up for the investigation team, and with Colonel Rosenfeld, who had a major role in "guiding the case and determining the verdict." Van Roden, on the other hand, was advised to consult Bishops Neuhäusler and Muench, as well as the German defense attorney, Eugen Leer, and Mrs. van Roden was assured that Everett himself was eager to cooperate and would furnish information "upon which your good husband and Judge Simpson can base an impartial report. . . ." Copies of sympathetic correspondence from Judge Wennerstrum and Congressman Case, as well as from Whiting, Strong, and Curt Stern, the last two described as Jewish refugees on the defense team "who were more indignant than others," accompanied the letter. Everett was promised by return mail that the information would be forwarded to van Roden as soon as his address in Germany was known.[57]

Everett's letter to van Roden and the supporting materials initiated an odd correspondence between the two during the approximately six weeks that the Simpson Commission remained in Germany, a fact that, if it had been generally known, would have made van Roden's later public remarks on the Malmedy case even more controversial than they proved to be. On official EUCOM stationery, van Roden affectionately acknowledged the mailing from "Dear Old Timer" and noted that he could make no comments about the Malmedy case because the commission had not yet gotten to the record and, almost as an afterthought, because "it wouldn't be appropriate."[58] In a subsequent letter, van Roden shared with Everett the information that General Clay had apparently decided to commute one of the remaining death sentences and invited Everett to send him his thoughts on which of the other eleven condemned also deserved clemency. The implication that Everett had become, in effect, a "shadow" fourth member of the commission was reinforced by van Roden's suggestion that the "Old Timer" make the judge's Media, Pennsylvania, home his "temporary residence" upon the commission's return to the United States in September and prior to its reconvening in Washington to make its report to the Secretary of the Army. Van Roden urged his friend to keep the proposal secret, which Everett appears to have done.[59] But, in fact, competing opportunities to influence those in positions to be of assistance to him and his clients and, perhaps, van Roden's own realization of the impropriety of the invitation prevented the two from meeting privately. Everett had not given up on Supreme Court intervention as the means of freeing the Malmedy case from the army's control, and he could not forget that, had Jackson not abstained, the Malmedy case might have been docketed for review. The fact that Jackson was scheduled to speak in Atlanta on the evening of September 10 presented an opportunity that Everett found irresistible. He did, in fact, engage Jackson in conversation and sought both to flatter the Justice and impress upon him the differences between "Jackson's trial" at Nuremberg, where justice had ostensibly prevailed, and what had transpired at Dachau, where "the foundations and precepts were so different. . . ." Jackson seemed friendly enough, but promised only to try to secure for Everett a copy of the forty-two-volume *Trial of the Major War Criminals before the International Military Tribunal, Nuremberg*, then in the process of publication by the U.S. Government Printing Office (Everett received it in November). The offer may have been precipitated by Everett's effusive praise for Jackson's opening statement in the courtroom in Nuremberg's Palace of Justice ("perfectly cut and polished precious stones of wisdom . . . one of the greatest masterpieces I have ever read").[60] Everett could be shameless in his flattery. Little more productive was a meeting with the Chief Justice of the Supreme Court on September 17, in the context of the opening of Washington & Lee's bicentennial celebration, at which Vinson was the featured speaker. Everett recalled that he and the Chief Justice "were thrown together considerable" [sic] in the course of the festivities and that he had "insisted" to an apparently sympathetic Vinson that Jackson vote on whether the Court could assume appellate jurisdiction in war crimes cases. It is likely that Everett mistook the Chief Justice's sober gentleness (his long, solemn countenance had prompted *Time* to describe him as "a tired sheep with a hangover") for assent.[61] In any event, while Everett was able to meet with the three-man commission in a formal setting in Washington between the two high judicial hobnobbings, the opportunity for a meeting with van Roden "under four eyes" evaporated, to Everett's evident distress. He found at least momentary comfort, however, in van Roden's confidential assurances that he would be "very much gratified by the nature of our report. . . ."[62]

The report of the Simpson Commission was completed on September 14, 1948, and forwarded to Secretary of the Army Royall on October 6.[63] The Department of the Army released a brief statement to the press in which it noted that the report contained unspecified clemency recommendations, although it withheld the full report from the public until early in the following year. Van Roden's views, on the other hand, were not withheld. The *Philadelphia Evening Bulletin* of October 8 published an article based on an interview with van Roden in which the judge made remarks highly critical of the pretrial investigation, citing not only the mock trials but also the alleged beatings of German prisoners and crediting Everett with having provided the necessary impetus for the creation of the Simpson Commission investigation. While he revealed no information on the commission's recommendations to Royall, van Roden revealed a high degree of skepticism in regard to much of the prosecution case. He attached no sinister significance to *Kampfgruppe* Peiper's having been ordered to take no prisoners, as that was standard procedure in panzer units. The responsibility of taking prisoners was normally left to following infantry. In this, van Roden seems to have been reflecting defense testimony and, perhaps, his own battlefield experience, as well. "The Malmedy Massacre was an atrocity," he conceded to the *Bulletin*'s reporter. "Whether it was designed as an intentional atrocity or was the result of itchy fingers on somebody, we'll never know."[64] He was more forthcoming with Everett and confided that the Simpson Commission had recommended the commutation of all of the Malmedy death sentences, in part on the grounds that the case was unlike any of the other Dachau trials in that it involved a "heat of battle" incident, an offense for which an American would have been unlikely to have received a sentence more severe than life imprisonment (as had, in fact, been the case in the court martial of Sergeant West in the Biscari trial). But evidence of investigatory improprieties had also cast sufficient doubt on the proceedings to make the execution of death sentences inadvisable.[65]

Van Roden's enthusiasm for Everett and his acceptance of the Atlanta attorney's perspective on the Malmedy investigation and trial were unabashed. "May I say that my admiration for your integrity and your persistence in unselfishly pursuing your ideals is simply marvelous. I am very happy and proud to be one of your friends."[66] And although he had expressed caution with regard to "going public" with the Simpson Commission's recommendations before the Department of the Army saw fit to do so, in practice he showed little restraint. At the end of October, he proudly revealed to Everett that he was making speeches to Rotary Clubs, veterans' organizations, and church groups concerning the army's war crimes trial program. "I am doing my best to spread the gospel of what was done in these cases. I hope that I do not trespass on the good will of the Department of the Army. I do not believe I shall do so."[67]

If Everett was in receipt of reassuring words from van Roden, he received considerably less from the army, and it was the army, and not van Roden, that had final authority over the fate of the Malmedy defendants. On November 5, he wrote plaintively to General Green, the army's judge advocate general, that he had been unable to carry on with his normal activities during the previous several weeks because of his uncertainty with regard to the Malmedy verdicts.

> Maybe my sense of justice and fairness is a bit old-fashioned, but I cannot help this. . . . [T]he responsibility for human lives weighs down my emotions too much. . . . would you be kind enough to relieve my mind on this matter and let me know at your earliest convenience what decision has been made by the Department of the Army or EUCOM? . . . Each Friday nightmares [sic] my emotions.[68]

Fridays "nightmared" Everett because hangings at Landsberg were normally scheduled for that day, but his *cri de coeur* elicited a distinctly unsympathetic response from Green. No final decisions had been made in the case, he advised, but "action will probably be announced in the press."[69]

The army was growing impatient with Everett, but, then, he had caused it considerable embarrassment over the previous two years. And the Malmedy case was not the only one of the Dachau trials that had created unfavorable publicity for the army. Approximately a year after the Malmedy trial, thirty-one defendants had had been judged for their role in the operation of the Nazi concentration camp at Buchenwald. As in the Malmedy case, all had been found guilty, and twenty-two had been sentenced to hang. Five had been condemned to life imprisonment, one of them a woman. Ilse Koch, the wife of the former camp commandant, Karl Koch, had been alleged to have been implicated in the brutal treatment and murder of camp inmates, some of them killed in order that their tattooed skin might be used in the fabrication of lampshades and other grisly artifacts. Even more than the Malmedy massacre, Ilse Koch and the lampshades of Buchenwald came to symbolize for the American public the essence of the Nazi evil. No Willis M. Everett championed the cause of the Buchenwald defendants, and no critic claimed that the convictions had been based on extorted testimony. The blowzy Ilse Koch was no charismatic Jochen Peiper, and the crimes of Buchenwald, where many thousands had been murdered, could not be passed off as the regretable consequences of modern war. But the Buchenwald trial, like the Malmedy case, had been subjected to review, and, as in the Malmedy case, evidence that had seemed convincing to a panel of line army officers in the dramatic setting of the courtroom seemed less so to a panel of lawyers who soberly analyzed the record. Some death sentences were commuted, and prison terms were shortened. Ilse Koch's life sentence was reduced to four years, and, since her sentence was deemed to have begun with the commencement of her pretrial custody in 1945, she could anticipate freedom before the end of 1949.[70]

News of Koch's likely early release was greeted with a cry of public outrage of sufficient intensity to call forth a full-blown Senate investigation in the fall of 1948, which did not work to Everett's advantage in an election year.[71] Van Roden was convinced that it was the uproar over the Ilse Koch commutation that accounted for the army's decision to keep secret the report of the Simpson Commission, but Everett was not comforted. He wrote in fury to Bishop Muench of the "beautiful job" the army was doing of whitewashing the case and of his dread of the possible imminence of the hangings of his clients. "[M]y mind whirls, my heart pounds, my body trembles and my stomach revolts." The same "evil forces" responsible for the original Malmedy injustices, he was convinced, were still active in Europe. If a single man was hanged on the basis of that "unjust trial," he assured the bishop, "I will be forced into a corner and I will have to draw the sword of public opinion and destroy the enemy. . . ."[72] But Everett was not comfortable with the persona of avenging angel, and he groped desperately and not always with dignity for reassurance. "Ever since our meeting in Washington during September," he wrote to Judge Simpson in mid-November, "I have constantly carried in my mind those honest, sincere, and understanding eyes of yours. It is not often one is priviledged [sic] to sit in the presence of one who has character as yours and has been honored as you have been by your election to the Supreme Court of his State." The army was subjecting him to "torture," he complained, and its attitude "is not one that engenders confidence and friendliness."[73] Simpson was sympathetic and, perhaps, a bit embarrassed. Secretary Royall, he explained, out of deference to General Clay and respect for the grave responsibilities he bore, believed it appropriate for the European commander to make announcements relative to the case, but he assured Everett that Clay was being advised by "most conscientious and kind-hearted American lawyers." Everett's efforts on behalf of the Malmedy defendants were deserving of admiration, Simpson soothed, noting that, in a recent conversation between Simpson and Dr. David Stitt, president of Southwestern Theological Seminary, Everett had been paid "high tribute for the magnificent way you lived up to the traditions of the American bar by defending your clients so conscientiously and so well."[74]

There was, of course, a perspective on the Malmedy controversy quite different from Everett's. Army investigators were also in receipt of testimony from former members of the investigation and prosecution team who indignantly denied the improprieties imputed to them by Everett. Everett's nemesis and opposite number at Dachau, Burton Ellis, had written to Cecil Hubbert of the War Crimes Branch in May, in response to news that Royall was ordering a reinvestigation of the Malmedy case, that "the investigation from my personal point of view is not an unwelcome development, as it has become rather tiresome to every few weeks pick up a paper and read of some more of Everett's accusations."[75] A lengthy affidavit executed by Ellis at the Presidio in San Francisco on October 27, 1948, was a detailed response to allegations contained in Everett's Supreme Court petition, a copy of which, apparently, had been supplied to Ellis by the army. The former chief prosecutor struck back at Everett with thinly concealed anger, implying that Everett was little more than a charlatan who was shamelessly attempting to conceal his clients' guilt and his own incompetence through obfuscation and outright falsehood. That Everett had sometimes played fast and loose with the facts in his petition played into Ellis's hands. Everett, for example, had claimed that the defendants had languished in Schwäbisch Hall "for varying lengths of time but generally in excess of ten months" before being served with charges. In fact, as Ellis was able to point out, no Malmedy suspect had been incarcerated in "Hall" before early December 1945, meaning that the maximum time that any accused had spent there had been somewhat more than five months and, in many cases, no more than a few days.[76] Everett had implied that the "mock trials" had been standard operating procedure, rather than the exceptional stratagems they were, and that they were key instruments in extracting fallacious sworn statements from frightened "18- and 20-year-old" suspects who had been badgered mercilessly and confronted by witnesses who had made false accusations against them. Everett's description of the circumstances surrounding these procedures was not based on personal observation, as he had not seen any of them. Ellis had been present for at least two of the "six or seven" that apparently had been conducted, and he described them as affairs in which suspects were interrogated and confronted only with bona fide witnesses. But none of the "mock trials" had been successful in securing confessions, nor had the suspects all been impressionable adolescents. The suspects grilled in the two procedures that Ellis had attended had been twenty-three and thirty years of age.[77] In his petition, as Ellis pointed out, Everett had misstated the facts surrounding defense testimony offered at the trial on the deaths of Belgian civilians during the Ardennes offensive. An affidavit that Everett attributed to a citizen of Wanne had, in fact, been sworn to by a resident of Büllingen, and not in the presence of his priest but before Miles Rulien, an investigator on Everett's staff.[78] The defense had had not "a few days" to prepare its case after the prosecution had rested, as Everett had claimed, but nine. And Ellis, far from trying to hinder Everett in his preparations for trial, had personally secured for the defense staff accommodations, office space, and equipment, as well as sharing half of his motor transport with Everett's team.[79] In the final analysis, it appeared to Ellis, if Everett had had difficulty preparing an effective defense, that had been the result of the strength of the prosecution case and of Everett's personal shortcomings. Both in court and in his Supreme Court petition, Everett had attributed the failure of most of the defendants to take the stand in their own defense to their residual fear of the prosecution, many of whom, including Ellis, had been involved in the investigation. This was at best a half-truth. As Everett well knew, he himself, after initially supporting the desire of the defendants to testify on their own behalf, had argued vigorously against such a plan when he realized that they were threatening to hang one another by their self-exculpatory testimony. Ellis's pen dripped with sarcasm as he wrote "that the allegations of petitioner . . . may represent the petitioner's state of mind when he made the announcement in court about 'the fear of the Prosecutors lingers on.'" In fact, Ellis averred, Everett had come to him for advice "as a friend and fellow attorney" about the wisdom of continuing to put his clients on the stand. The substance of his avuncular reply, as Ellis recalled it more than two years later, was, "Willis, as far as I know, none of the defense counsel in previous cases have kept the accused off the witness stand. It seems to me that if I were defending one of these cases and felt my accused were guilty, they would only take the witness stand over my dead body. . . ."[80]

In regard to allegations of physical duress, Ellis cited excerpts from his diary, which were contemporaneous with Everett's initial raising of those charges:

> Wiesbaden 28 April 1946
> 2 hour conference today with Col. Straight, Col. Carpenter and Col. Everett. Defendants claim they were beaten. Ordered to make inquiry of my staff and to withdraw all statements gotten under compulsion.

> Dachau 29 April, 1946
> Flew back to Dachau today. Had immediate conference of staff and they assured me none of the defendants were beaten. I so advised Straight, Corbin and Everett.

> Dachau 30 April 1946
> Col. Everett said today that Sprenger, Neve, Hoffman, J. and Jaekel admit fabrication of story of beating.[81]

Everett had, in fact, written to his family on April 30, 1946, that he strongly suspected that "four young kids" among the defendants were lying. About what, tantalizingly, he had said nothing. But, in the margin of a copy of Ellis's affidavit, which he later acquired, he wrote in pencil alongside Ellis's diary entry for April 30, "A lie."[82] Misinterpretation, faulty memory, repression of an awkward truth, or outright fabrication? And on whose part? It would be futile to speculate. But, if Everett, in his zeal to save his clients, was sometimes guilty of conscious or unconscious distortions in addition to carelessness, Ellis exercised great caution in what he said. His denials of specific categories of abuse alleged to have been suffered by the German prisoners but "probably born in the minds of defense counsel"—long periods of solitary

confinement, threats, physical violence, promises of immunity, depri-
vation of food and warmth, and the like—were usually qualified, as
they had to be, by Ellis's "best knowledge and belief." Ellis expressed
"grave concern" in regard to the "aspersions" cast by Everett on the
character and ethics of the members of the investigation-prosecution
team, noting with uncertain relevance that "all the principal investigators and counsel were members of the Bar of some state or Austria."
Harry Thon, a War Department civilian investigator, was noted as an
exception. All, however, were praised by Ellis for their "strong sense of
responsibility and an exhibition of devotion to duty, loyalty and sin-
cerety of purpose never before nor since witnessed by me. . . ." Everett,
it seemed, was guilty of slandering men of the highest character.[83]

Colonel Abraham Rosenfeld, the former law member of the
Malmedy court and subsequent chief of the trial branch of the 7708
War Crimes Group, agreed. In an October interview with the *Stars
and Stripes*, he categorically denied that any forms of duress had been
used and described the "mock trials" as simply means of "outsmart-
ing tough Nazis." "Could you imagine," Rosenfeld asked rhetori-
cally, "beating Piper [*sic*] either physically or mentally into admitting
anything?" The investigators had used the only means they could to
"outsmart those birds."[84]

Rosenfeld's role in the trial had, ostensibly, been that of even-
handed interpreter of law and procedure. His defense of the pretrial investigation, in which he had not participated, could only reinforce
Everett's conviction that Rosenfeld had been derelict in his duty during
the trial and was now working behind the scenes in Germany assisting
the army to "whitewash" the case. But Everett derived comfort from his
knowledge of the recommendations of the Simpson Commission,
which neither he nor van Roden or Simpson thought Royall and Clay
could ignore. This belief was reinforced by press commentary that followed the army's limited release and van Roden's more expansive commentary. The *Chicago Tribune*, a powerful voice of Midwestern conser-
vatism, was most unequivocal in its support, fuming in mid-October
that "never has American justice sank to the degradation depicted by
Judge E. L. van Roden in his summary of the methods used to secure the
conviction of German soldiers accused of killing American prisoners at
Malmedy. . . ." Two weeks later, the *Tribune* commented: "No man who
has talked to soldiers who served in Europe or on the Pacific fronts
believes that only Germans or Japanese were guilty of shooting prison-

ers. . . ." Other newspapers were more cautiously sympathetic. The
Evening Dispatch of Columbus, Ohio, warned that "considerations such
as these do not make innocent the guilty. They do not erase atrocities of
the Malmedy sort. But . . . they raise important questions of the sincerity, honesty and purpose of the Allied prosecution and throw into doubt
the strength of the Allied case. . . ." The *New York Times* was less critical
but urged an open mind: "we are entitled to know . . . what reasoning
was applied by Army officials in reaching their decisions that injustices
had been done. A decent respect for the opinion of others demands that
no final action be taken . . . until a complete and satisfying explanation
is given." Kenneth L. Dixon of the *Denver Post* was frank in his recognition of the brutal realities of war when he mused: "When you think of
the bodies of those kids . . . the fury of such postwar gentleness toward
their executioners gets hot within you. Then you remember the chain
reaction it set off, and how we took mighty few prisoners before the
whole tale was told, and your conclusions become bitterly confused."
Awkward for the army and a likely source of satisfaction to Everett, had
he known of it, was the fact that the Communist *Daily Worker* was one
of the few publications to express unreserved confidence in the rectitude of the investigation and trial.[85]

But the comfort produced for Everett by the revelations of the
Simpson Commission came to an abrupt end in December. Early that
month, Everett had queried Clarence Huebner, Clay's chief of staff, on
whether the arrangement of which he had been informed at the beginning of the year—that the execution of any death sentences confirmed
by Clay would be stayed for sixty days and that he would be personally
notified of such confirmation—still held. He hoped for a more consid-
erate response from Clay's office than he had gotten in November from
the judge advocate general in Washington, who had brusquely advised
him to watch the newspapers. Everett's petition to the Supreme Court
earlier in the year had focused much attention on the Malmedy case. He
now informed Huebner of his intention to appeal to the International
Court of Justice in The Hague, probably in the hope that the threat of
another high-profile legal offensive would encourage Clay to render a
final decision at least in harmony with the recommendations of the
Simpson Commission, if not one producing the outright nullification
and retrial that Everett believed necessary.[86] Everett was understandably desirous of putting Malmedy behind him, remarking to a friend of
his inability to do much to reestablish his law practice since his return

to the United States and the pressing need to "get back to the business of making a living." General Clay, too, had much besides the war crimes trials controversy to deal with. The Soviet blockade of Berlin had begun in June and was to continue until the following May, confirming the long-term estrangement among the wartime allies. But, if Everett hoped that a threatened appeal to The Hague combined with the distraction of an international crisis that might spark World War III would work to his advantage, he was to be brutally disappointed. In his reply, dated December 21, 1948, Huebner coldly acknowledged the concerns expressed by Everett a few weeks earlier and continued:

> I wish to advise you that the Commander-in-Chief, European Command, has approved the sentences of those condemned to death in the Malmedy Case, although the final dates for carrying these sentences into execution have not yet been decided upon. If you still contemplate taking further action in this case by presenting an appeal to the International Court of Justice at The Hague, it would be well to commence this action without undue delay. You are assured, however, that at least sixty days will elapse following the receipt of this letter by you and before any dates are established for the execution of any of the death sentences. In this connection, and unless advised to the contrary by you, it will be assumed that this letter will have reached you not later than twelve days after this date.[87]

Mercifully, Huebner's communication did not reach Everett until after Christmas, and he was able to enjoy a pleasant holiday with his wife, two children, and son-in-law. The "horrible news" arrived on or about December 29. "I am perfectly dumbfounded," he despaired to Leroy van Roden.[88] Bill Denson, his colleague from his Dachau days and the chief prosecutor of the Mauthausen and Dachau concentration camp cases, as well as one of the many reviewers of the Malmedy case, attempted to comfort him by telephone with the opinion that "there would be no Malmedy hangings."[89] But Everett, convinced that the army was determined to protect itself at all costs, even at the price of hanging innocent men, and that the European commander would be difficult to control from Washington in judicial matters, was not reassured. Judge Simpson, too, found Huebner's reply "disturbing," and he did "not know what to think."[90] Everett lamented to van

Roden that it was now necessary for him "to start all over again" by making good on his threat to appeal to the International Court of Justice, which he knew to be a "long shot" as a legal maneuver but at least of value as an instrument for keeping public interest focused on the case and possibly the only means of keeping Peiper and his eleven comrades from the gallows. That the notice to Huebner of his intended approach to The Hague had been a rather hollow bluff was made obvious by his plaintive observation that he knew nothing whatever about procedure in regard to approaching the International Court of Justice, and by a frantic latter to Supreme Court Justice Robert Jackson for bibliographical advice.[91]

Elsie Douglas, Jackson's secretary, was able to send a single volume on the ICJ, the only book on the subject in the Supreme Court's library. Judge Charles Wennerstrum was more helpful. Wennerstrum had presented a paper on the war crimes trials program in September at the convention of the American Bar Association in Seattle, in which he had commented favorably on Everett's fight for "justice" in the Malmedy case as being "of the highest traditions of the American Bar," and he was still convinced of the overall rectitude of Everett's cause, although dubious of some of the charges contained in Everett's Supreme Court petition. As did Everett, he recognized the essential flaw in the plan to attempt an appeal to the International Court of Justice in that states only, not individuals, are permitted to bring cases under the Court's statute. Everett had "bounced off" Wennerstrum the inventive notion of arguing that, in the absence of a German national government since Germany's unconditional surrender, there was no one but Everett to do it.[92] In a letter written on New Year's Eve 1948, Wennerstrum advised that that approach seemed worth a try and suggested buttressing it with the even more adventurous argument that, while the court statute might prohibit individuals from filing cases, "international common law" might be alleged to require it.

> It may be an advanced idea in international relations, but I would at least claim international courts should assume jurisdiction and hear this appeal. I realize that what you are interested in is immediate results but if that court should refuse to entertain jurisdiction it would be a further indictment of the entire procedure which has been followed with these War Crimes Trials.[93]

Wennerstrum had argued in Seattle that the definitive "fix" for the problem of administering even-handed justice in war crimes cases was to be found in the establishment of a permanent system of war crimes courts under the aegis of the United Nations, including an effective mechanism for judicial review.[94] This proposal was of little interest to an Everett concerned, as Wennerstrum correctly noted, with "immediate results." Immediate results in the hopelessly convoluted Malmedy controversy were not to be had, but events were building toward the explosion of the case as a domestic political cause célèbre and as a potentially mortal personal crisis for Willis Everett in the dawning new year.

9

"The Lord Has Given Me Strength to Continue"

THE DEPARTMENT OF the Army released the report of the Simpson Commission, which had been delivered to the Secretary of the Army four months earlier, on January 6, 1949. There was little to be gained by withholding it from the public any longer, in light of Judge van Roden's well-publicized pronouncements. On the contrary, the army might benefit should the report, to which van Roden had affixed his signature, prove to be less damning than the judge's repetitions of Everett's allegations. And, to a degree, it was. The Simpson Commission, it will be recalled, had examined not only the Malmedy case but a total of sixty-five cases involving 139 confirmed but unexecuted death sentences. The report concluded that the trials were "essentially fair" and that "there was no general or systematic use of improper methods to secure prosecution evidence at the trials." On those grounds, the commission, in regard to 110 condemned, saw "no reason . . . why the death sentences under consideration, all of which were imposed for participation in murder, should not be executed." The death sentences of seventeen individuals who had been found guilty in fifteen Dachau trials were recommended for commutation, in most cases to terms of life imprisonment. The Malmedy trial and its twelve remaining death sentences were placed in a separate category. That case, the report noted, "is distinguishable from all other War Crimes cases tried at Dachau." The offenses for which the defendants had been tried and convicted had occurred during one of the most desperate engagements of the war. To be sure, they merited "stern retribution. However, it is extremely doubtful that an American court-martial would fix any punishment more severe than life imprisonment if it were trying members of the American Army who committed like offenses in the heat of battle." The nature of the evidence on which the Malmedy convictions were based also received special comment. Correctly, the report noted that the bulk of the evidence against the accused was in the form of "extrajudicial statements," many of which implicated "to a damaging degree other of the accused." Some of these statements were secured by means of "mock trials," in which the suspects had been led into a room in which had stood a table covered with a black cloth and adorned with burning candles and a crucifix. Investigators dressed as officers of the U.S. Army had acted as prosecutors and defenders, all parts of a process intended "to gain the confidence of the accused in his supposed defense attorney and thus to elicit a statement from him." Mock trials had been the least of the questionable techniques employed by Army investigators, and prosecutors during the trial had admitted their use. But Everett, some of the defendants, and others, both Germans and Americans, had alleged far worse. These supposed abuses were not specified in the Simpson Commission report but hinted at in a reference to "other practices," which had been "reflected" in a preliminary report by the other agency then scrutinizing the Malmedy case, Clay's Administration of Justice Review Board.

The Simpson Commission had drawn two major conclusions from its investigation of the controversy. "Sufficient doubt" had been cast on the Malmedy investigation and trial to make it "unwise" to execute the remaining death sentences. At the same time, however, the record of the trial had sufficiently demonstrated "the guilt of the accused to warrant the findings of guilty." The possible contradiction between the two conclusions was not resolved by the commission's puzzling opinion that any injustice against those defendants who had been sentenced to death would be removed by a commutation of their sentences to terms of life imprisonment.[1]

The release of the Simpson Commission report was widely covered in the press and elicited congratulatory responses from Everett's friends and colleagues. Wilbert Wahler concluded optimistically that the report ensured that none of the Malmedy prisoners would climb the stairs of Landsberg's gallows, apparently assuming that Royall's release of the document would effectively tie Clay's hands.[2] Charles Whiting reached similar conclusions and showered Everett with praise for his achievement:

> You are certainly to be congratulated on the outcome of the single-handed fight that you have made to save the lives of these boys. It seems to me that the greatest satisfaction that can come to a lawyer

is the knowledge that he has been responsible for saving the life of his client and in this instance that satisfaction will be multiplied many times.

Like Wahler, Whiting concluded that the fight to save the lives of the twelve Germans still under sentence of death had been essentially won. Whiting doubted that the new trial that Everett always believed to be the correct course for the army to adopt would ever occur but thought that the sentences of all of the Malmedy convicts still in Landsberg would be further commuted and that in a few years all would be freed. Then, Everett could claim for himself complete victory against what had seemed to be insurmountable odds, having rescued not only his clients from prison and the noose, but "the good name of the [legal] profession from the low estate to which it was dragged in the Dachau trials. . . ."[3]

But neither Wahler nor Whiting had seen Everett's pre-Christmas letter from General Huebner, indicating that Clay had confirmed the Malmedy death sentences. Everett's anxieties, normally at a high level, had been further elevated by news that Clay was proceeding with the hangings of prisoners whose death sentences had been recommended for commutation by the Simpson Commission. None of these were Malmedy convicts, but the Simpson Commission report's conclusion that their guilt had been adequately demonstrated offered little assurance that Clay might not override the commission's recommendations in their case as well.

It appeared to Everett that he had no alternative but to continue with a multipronged campaign of judicial appeal, publicity, and congressional pressure. Congressman Jim Davis and Senator Walter George offered sympathy and the possibility of another visit to the Department of the Army but little else.[4] On the other hand, the release of the Simpson Commission report, in combination with Leroy van Roden's more lurid allegations, secured for Everett the attention of influential national publications. The January 17, 1949, issue of *Time* contained an article in its international section entitled "War Crimes— Clemency," illustrated with a photograph of American dead at the crossroads south of Malmedy and one of "Lawyer Everett," whose gaunt face bore witness to the stress of the months since he had left Atlanta for Germany, holding a volume marked "The Malmedy Case." *Time*'s sympathies were clearly revealed in an italicized statement beneath the two photographs: "*Judges are sometimes conquered by the evil they judge.*" The accompanying article described the "massacre" as "one of the worst atrocities committed by the Germans in combat during the war" and an apparently "open and shut case" until Everett "discovered facts which turned the case into one of the ugliest in the history of the war crimes trials." There followed a list of the most extreme of the brutalities allegedly perpetrated by army investigators, including blows to German testicles and matches driven under fingernails, both charges drawn from lurid German affidavits produced after the trial and given currency by van Roden, although not originally part of Everett's brief.[5]

It was not only "middle-brow" conservative news magazines such as Time that found criticism of the Malmedy investigation worthwhile copy. William Henry Chamberlin, associate editor of the Cold War liberal *The New Leader*, whose editorial board included the likes of John Dewey and Max Eastman, quoted sympathetically and at length from the Simpson Commission report and from Everett's Supreme Court petition before concluding that the Malmedy proceedings "fairly reeked of the odor of a Gestapo or a Soviet state trial" and calling for "severe punishment for the individuals responsible for these methods. . . ." That, Chamberlin opined, "would do more to create confidence in the reality of American justice in Germany than almost any step that could be taken." As had Everett, Chamberlin recognized the moral awkwardness of punishing enemy soldiers for crimes that, when committed by American troops, were punished more leniently or, as was usually the case, not at all. Unlike Everett in his more agitated moments, he was not willing to equate American and Nazi cruelty, although he came perilously close when he argued that the training of Germans in the ways of democracy would be facilitated by demonstrating that it was brutality that the United States opposed, "whether committed by Nazi guards in Buchenwald or by American 'investigators' in Schwäbisch Hall. . . . All honor to Major [*sic*] Everett, to Judge Charles Wennerstrum and to other Americans whose struggle for this kind of justice, if it is known in Germany, will have the best kind of 're-educational' effect."[6]

Contained in February's issue of *The Progressive*, alongside an article on the necessity of national health insurance, was an essay with the provocative title "U.S. Atrocities in Germany," under the byline of none other than Leroy van Roden. The article got immediately to the point, presenting a list of the familiar allegations against army investigators, noting that the foul deeds had been brought to public attention by

Everett, "a very able lawyer, a conscientious and sincere gentleman . . . not a fanatic." In fact, much of the article read as though Everett might have written it. The war crimes trial program had been and continued to be distorted by the desire for vengeance. "We won the war, but some of us want to go on killing. That seems to me wicked." It was particularly wicked, it appeared to the author, in that the vast majority of Germans were innocent of the crimes of the Nazi regime and in most cases had been unaware of them. "I am convinced that the German populace had no idea what diabolical crimes that arch-fiend, Himmler, was committing in the concentration camps. From the atrocities we learned about, he must have been the very prince of devils." The relevance of what "ordinary" Germans might have known or not known to the trials of those who had not only known but probably done *something* was not evident, but logical coherence was not much in evidence throughout an article seemingly written for dramatic effect. And allegations of brutality offered in post-trial German affidavits were offered uncritically as indisputable fact. Kicks to the testicles and testicles damaged "beyond repair" now entered the increasingly lurid discourse of the Malmedy controversy.[7]

While receiving encouragement and support from a wide range of the U.S. political spectrum, Everett pushed ahead with the preparation of his appeal to the International Court of Justice in The Hague. Although he realized the appeal to be the most unlikely of long shots, he persevered both as a means of generating attention and, perhaps more important, because his unforgiving conscience demanded constant activity on behalf of clients who had become his "Malmedy boys." On January 24, Everett mailed to President Harry Truman a copy of his much traveled Supreme Court petition, along with notification of his intention to appeal the case to the ICJ and an invitation to appoint someone to serve as an agent to represent the United States at The Hague. If he saw Everett's letter, it is unlikely that the unpretentious Truman was favorably impressed by Everett's gratuitous and not entirely accurate appeal to pedigree: "All of my ancestors came to the United States prior to the 17th century [sic] and I am confident that my single-handed fight is confined entirely to principles of Justice and Right which coincide with your views."[8] A similar notification of intent went to Attorney General Thomas C. Clark, but neither man saw fit to reply. George Washington, the assistant solicitor general, whose name belied his lowly estate in Truman's administration, tersely noted that Everett had not made a case, "in fact or theory," to demonstrate the jurisdiction of the International Court of Justice and that, consequently, he could not recommend to Attorney General Clark that he appoint counsel to represent the United States or advise the President to do so.[9] Whatever discouragement the reply produced in Everett was likely undone by an argumentative forty-five-minute call to the assistant solicitor general, in which Washington appears to have unwisely attempted to deter the submission of the appeal on the grounds that it would embarrass the United States. This was a perfectly appropriate and salutary result, from Everett's perspective, particularly so, he believed, given the outrage then being expressed by the Truman administration over the trial in Communist Hungary of Cardinal Joszef Mindzenty, who had "confessed" to treason and illegal monetary transactions after what was assumed to have been torture and "brainwashing." Everett agreed with Charles Whiting, with whom he had discussed the matter, that Truman would be well advised to put his own house in order before condemning Hungarian Communists. In any event, he was determined to press on.[10]

By the middle of February, a rough draft of his petition had been completed. Robert Jackson's earlier sympathetic demeanor—he had flattered Everett by addressing him as someone he was "pleased to regard as a friend"—encouraged him to send Jackson the draft for comment. The petition was promptly returned by the Supreme Court Justice with the gentle reproof that his involvement would be "inappropriate."[11] But Everett proceeded to refine the document with limited assistance from friends and associates, including an up-and-coming Jewish attorney, Morris B. Abram, later to be president of Brandeis University and a distinguished figure in public life. In 1949 an associate of the law firm of Heyman, Howell and Heyman, which shared the Connally Building with Everett and Everett, Abram contacted an international lawyer in Paris on Everett's behalf with results that were less than encouraging. Abram concluded that there was no chance of the ICJ's accepting the case on Everett's personal application but suggested the possibility of persuading "some benevolent South American delegate" to bring the matter before the UN General Assembly, which could then approach the court for an advisory opinion.[12] By the time Everett had received this imaginative if somewhat improbable advice, events had moved the controversy to a new venue and reduced Everett to the role of reluctant bystander.

Everett mailed the petition on February 22. In a further extension of an already eccentric effort, he offered himself as representative both of the United States Government, in light of its refusal to appoint an agent to represent it, and of the Germans imprisoned and sentenced to death for the Malmedy complex of war crimes, in the absence of a German government to plead their case. In arguments designed to demonstrate alleged U.S. violations of international law, including The Hague Convention of 1907 and the Geneva Convention of 1929, Everett recited the most extreme version of the catalogue of American investigative atrocities yet presented. All alleged offenses had been "innumerable" in their frequency, including not only the familiar mock trials, beatings, threats, and bribes ostensibly applied to defendants but also threats of violence against members of their families, in order to render the defendants amenable to making the desired sworn statements. Everett called upon the court to immediately notify General Lucius Clay of its assumption of jurisdiction, which would then enjoin the U.S. commander from taking further action against the Malmedy defendants and presumably prevent him from executing the remaining twelve death sentences. That, of course, was the prerequisite to the final resolution of the case: "that judgment be rendered requiring a retrial of Defendants to meet the standards of Justice within the limitations of International Law, Declarations, Conferences and Conventions."[13]

Everett knew there was little chance that the International Court of Justice would accept the case, but the application had been in large measure an expression of conscience and moral principle. "I know full well what is right and wrong," he had written to Wennerstrum, "and I am a bit on the stubborn side when it comes to compromising with evil." The dispatch of the petition provided him with a sense of righteous closure. "I have finished my fight. . . . It would seem that the Lord has given me strength to continue in the name of all Humanity to try to right wrong . . . there is little probability that the . . . Court will assume jurisdiction, but I have given my best from the beginning."[14] The anticipated response from The Hague was dated March 5. E. Hambro, registrar of the International Court of Justice, acknowledged receipt of Everett's petition but expressed regret that there was nothing to be added to Article 34 of the Statute of the Court, which unambiguously stipulated that only states can be parties to cases before the court.[15]

It is not clear when Everett received the notification, for it passed without written comment. He could not have been disappointed by an anticipated result and had, in fact, been given reason for cautious optimism from another and unanticipated source. He had been driven to cobble together his petition to The Hague in large measure by the grim December communique from Huebner, Clay's chief of staff, indicating that Clay had confirmed the Malmedy death sentences and might order them carried out in the near future. As he labored on the petition late in January, Everett sought assurances from Huebner that, at least, none of his "boys" would be hanged before the court had had an opportunity to react to his petition, which he then hoped to have completed by March 1. Included was an implicit and somewhat clumsy offer of a deal. If Clay would see fit to accept the recommendation of the Simpson Commission that the twelve remaining death sentences be commuted, "it would of course then be unnecessary for me take this final action to the International Court of Justice at the Hague."[16] Huebner had replied immediately, but evasively, that the matter was being handled "personally" by General Clay and that he had forwarded Everett's letter to him for response.[17] Clay's reply came a few days later, but routed through the Department of the Army, indicating the increasing involvement of official Washington in the Malmedy tangle. Clay did, in fact, intend to reconsider the death sentences in light of the Simpson Commission recommendations, the recently completed final report of his own Administration of Justice Review Board, and Everett's Supreme Court petition. But, he added ominously, the case had already dragged on too long, and he could not promise that executions would be deferred beyond March 15.[18]

The final report of the Administration of Justice Review Board was more complex than either the Simpson Commission report or Everett's Supreme Court petition. The former had been a hasty overview of numerous cases besides Malmedy, while the latter was a polemic whose sometimes strained allegations the Review Board had been specifically directed to investigate. The trial documentation had been restudied, and evidence, both oral and written, had been received from members of the defense and investigation-prosecution staffs, as well as from Germans who claimed knowledge of conditions at Schwäbisch Hall. Lieutenant Colonel Clio Straight had been subjected to an intense grilling. A certain reluctance to ask hard questions had been evident on the parts of the two military members of the board, Colonel John M. Raymond, Director of the Legal Division, U.S. Military Government, and EUCOM's judge advocate, Colonel James L. Harbaugh, who had been deeply involved in earlier reviews and, perhaps, disinclined to call into question his earlier efforts. Lacking such inhibitions, however, had been the civilian adviser to the military governor for military government affairs, the Harvard University professor of government Dr. Carl J. Friedrich, who reacted to much of the testimony with a healthy skepticism and asked the most significant questions yet posed concerning the investigative techniques employed on the Malmedy suspects, showing a sensitivity to the ease with which young men raised in a totalitarian society and disoriented by defeat and imprisonment might be manipulated by their captors. The report, in general, rejected the more extreme of the claims made by Everett and others, particularly those involving frequent physical brutality and outright dictation of statements, but confirmed the existence of lesser improprieties: mock trials (of course), occasional physical force employed "in the heat of the moment," encouragement of suspects to make statements by suggesting that the investigators were interested primarily in convicting the prisoners' superiors, and threats of reprisals against relatives, specifically, the withdrawal of ration cards if the prisoners did not "talk." Friedrich had left military government and the Malmedy review in the midst of the board's deliberations. Had he been present to the end, the report might have been more adventurous in its conclusions. As matters stood, Raymond and Harbaugh were content with the bland observation "that the conditions obtaining at the prison and the methods employed in the interrogations had a definite psychological effect on the defendants and resulted in their being more amenable to giving statements." Their recommendations offered little guidance and were limited to a suggestion that the report "be considered in connection with any further consideration of the Malmedy case."[19]

It is noteworthy that the army, while rejecting the more extreme of Everett's accusations against the pretrial investigators, was consistently careful to avoid direct criticism of Everett himself and was determined to limit, insofar as was possible, a public confrontation with a man who was clearly driven by conscience to hazard everything in the pursuit of what he believed to be justice. Not all individuals who had been associated with the investigation and trial were similarly restrained. This was, not surprisingly, most evident in the case of members of the investigation-prosecution team, whose reputations had been sullied by Everett's accusations. Ellis made no secret of the fact that he regarded Everett as a knave and a fool, returning to Everett the contempt that

Everett felt for him. But Everett had great affection for Irving and Sally Hayett, the young Jewish court reporters whose nuptial festivities he had organized in Dachau and whose best man he had been. Sally had read the January article in *Time,* which had uncritically espoused Everett's position, and was deeply offended. In a letter to *Time* publisher Henry R. Luce, with copies sent to President Truman, Secretary of Defense Forrestal, Secretary of the Army Royall, and others, she responded with evident anger. She had worked for Ellis during the period of interrogations in Schwäbisch Hall and had, she noted, "firsthand knowledge of exactly what happened." What had occurred, she related, had been very different from what *Time* had reported. Everett had had ample time and assistance to prepare his case, and the German suspects had been well treated. She had been present for "a few" of the mock trials and found them appropriate means of securing confessions from "brutes" and "killers." "Would Colonel Everett have the Prosecution sit down with these killers at tea and say, 'Now, boys, how about giving me the information—please or pretty please?' Colonel Everett forgets that these men were cold-blooded Nazi killers. . . ." If anyone had been conquered by the evil he was judging, she continued, it had been Everett. He had been "hoodwinked" into believing self-serving stories told by "shrewd, calculating liars."[20]

While there is no record of Everett's reaction to Hayett's expression of outrage, it must have caused him considerable pain although, happily, he did not subsume it within the anti-Semitic component of his worldview. But it served to remind him that the warm support and sympathy that had been flowing to Atlanta from van Roden, Wennerstrum, and Whiting was far from universal. For many Americans, and not only Jewish-Americans, the SS men who had become to Everett his "Malmedy boys" were "brutes" and "killers" by ascription of their membership in the SS, and in Adolf Hitler's personal guard division, at that. If unusual interrogation methods had been employed at Schwäbisch Hall, that was hardly a cause for dismay or wonder, given the character of the subjects, who probably deserved much worse, regardless of what they had done in the Ardennes in December 1944. The diametrical opposition between Everett's and Hayett's appraisal of the Malmedy case had been repeated many times in the evidence examined by the Administration of Justice Review Board. Affidavits from members of the investigative staff had denied with varying degrees of eloquence but with great fervor and indignation all charges of improper conduct. On the other hand, affidavits from German citizens who were neither SS men nor war crimes suspects painted a different picture. In addition to dentist Knorr's recollections of mandibular devastation, a young medical student who had worked in the prison hospital at Schwäbisch Hall claimed not only to have seen the results of physical assaults on the suspects but to have been told by an American sergeant assigned to duty at the prison that he could no longer stand to witness such brutality and wanted a transfer.[21] These statements seemed to support affidavits by many of the Malmedy prisoners, which had been sworn in particularly large numbers in January and February 1948 and which, in badly broken English, claimed vicious beatings and inhuman deprivations at the hands of American captors. Many of these affidavits had been sent to General Clay by Josef Cardinal Frings, Archbishop of Cologne, who, like Bishop Neuhäusler, possessed substantial anti-Nazi credentials.[22] In part, the tepid conclusions and recommendations contained in the Administration of Justice Review Board's report reflected simple confusion and an inability, three years after the fact, to reconcile widely differing and largely subjective elements of evidence.

It had long been evident to some of Everett's friends, more sanguine and less conscience stricken than he, that it was highly unlikely that any German would die for his role in the Malmedy massacre. Had the decision been entirely Clay's, the result might have been different. Clay seems to have had no serious doubts that the Malmedy prisoners were guilty and that the twelve sentenced to death deserved to die. He further regarded the case as a political annoyance that he would have preferred to get out of the way with the greatest possible dispatch to avoid complications with German political authorities when military government came to an end. On March 3, he telephoned Assistant Secretary of the Army Tracy Voorhees, who had been helpful to him in the past, in an effort to secure cancellation of the stays of execution that had been ordered by Secretary Royall the previous spring. The refusal of the U.S. Supreme Court and the International Court of Justice to assume jurisdiction in the Malmedy case brought Everett to the morose conclusion that Clay was a figure who, in matters of war crimes justice—in which area he possessed authority to appoint courts, conduct reviews, confirm sentences, and order them into execution—was answerable to no one. That may have been true in the judicial sense, but not in the political, as Royall's earlier interventions had already demonstrated. That Everett's fears were exaggerated was underlined by the prompt response to Clay's appeal for freedom to resort to the gallows: by order of the Secretary of the Army, the execution of all death sentences associated with the Malmedy case was to be postponed until further notice.[23]

Clay's decisions, when reached piecemeal later in the month, were twice compromised. Half of the twelve death sentences were commuted, those that Clay had found to be supported by the most tenuous or questionable evidence. But the six that were confirmed, including Peiper's, could not be scheduled for execution without authorization by the Secretary of the Army, by now a highly improbable eventuality. Clay's first decision, a reaffirmation of the death sentence of Valentin Bersin, was communicated to the Department of the Army on March 12, 1949.[24] Late on the afternoon of the previous day, a Friday, Everett had begun to experience crushing chest pain; early that evening, close to unconsciousness, he was rushed to Atlanta's Piedmont Hospital, where the Everett family's physician, Dr. Carter Smith, diagnosed myocardial infarction, which would hospitalize Everett, in those days of relaxed if also comparatively primitive medical care, until April 25.

Such things cannot be proven, but there is little doubt that the years of stress imposed on Everett by Malmedy had contributed to his heart attack. He had had sharper warnings than the drawn face that had appeared in *Time* at the start of the year. Near the end of June 1946, in the midst of presenting the case for the defense at Dachau, Everett had experienced an episode of chest pain and had received medication from an army physician that had provided relief. About a year and a half later, he had been forced to leave a dinner meeting of the National Sojourners at the Fort McPherson Officers' Club. He lay down on a couch in an anteroom while a doctor among the guests was summoned. The physician found him in great pain, sweating profusely, with weak pulse and shortness of breath. He had no doubt that Everett was suffering from coronary pathology and needed immediate hospitalization. But, on the way to Piedmont Hospital's emergency room in a friend's automobile, Everett stated that his chest pain had subsided, and he insisted on being taken home. Mary phoned Dr. Smith, but Everett took the phone and informed the doctor that his assistance was not needed. Sixteen additional months of neglected heart disease, exacerbated by continued anxiety and heavy smoking, were to bring him close to death at the age of forty-nine.[25]

Everett's long hospitalization and convalescence in the family home on Rivers Road occurred at a crucial point in the Malmedy controversy. In February, General Clay had received a cable from Senator William Langer, an isolationist Republican of North Dakota, informing him of Langer's introduction of Senate Resolution 39, which called for an investigation of U.S. military justice in occupied Europe and urged that Clay suspend all executions until the completion of the review. Langer's cable did not specifically mention the Malmedy case, although Clay assumed that was the prime focus of the senator's concern.[26] Clay was correct. In fact, Langer inserted into the *Congressional Record* the entirety of Everett's Supreme Court petition, with attached exhibits.[27] Several forces within the Senate began to compete with one another for the opportunity to investigate the army's role in the Malmedy affair. Senator Pat McCarran, Democrat of Nevada and chairman of the Senate Judiciary Committee, expressed some interest in conducting such a probe, as did Clyde Hoey, Democrat of North Carolina and chairman of the Special Investigations Subcommittee of the Expenditures Committee. One member in particular of that subcommittee, Joseph McCarthy, the Republican junior senator from Wisconsin, manifested a high degree of interest in the undertaking; he addressed inquiries to the Department of the Army for additional information on the Malmedy affair and received a summary of Malmedy-related events.[28] Everett had contacted McCarthy by phone shortly before the heart attack that, for a time, rendered him hors de combat, but Kil Townsend, his son-in-law and associate in the Everett law firm, temporarily assumed the responsibility of establishing and maintaining links with active and potential supporters of the Cause. He wrote to McCarthy on March 24, explaining his father-in-law's present incapacity and asking the senator's assistance in pressuring the army to abstain from executing the remaining death sentences pending a response from The Hague in regard to Everett's appeal to the International Court of Justice. Everett had either not yet received notification from The Hague by the time he was laid low or had not informed Townsend of it. In any event, Townsend shared with McCarthy the argument that it ill behooved the U.S. government to condemn Communist regimes for conducting trumped-up "show trials" while failing to do justice in the Malmedy case. "I sincerely trust you will bring every resource of the United States Government into action to see that these executions are not carried out and that eventually these men may be retried under such conditions and under such circumstances as to have it later said that they were afforded every opportunity to have a fair hearing."[29] Similar letters went to Senator Hoey and to Senator

Millard Tydings, Democrat of Maryland and chairman of the Armed Services Committee. Hoey and Tydings responded promptly. Hoey simply referred Townsend to Tydings, whose committee "insisted," he said, on conducting the investigation. Tydings made no mention of an investigation but shared with Townsend the information that there would be no executions without Secretary of the Army Royall's permission. "The Department of the Army understands that this procedure is to govern, as does General Clay."[30] McCarthy's reply was delayed until April 16, by which time hearings by an ad hoc subcommittee of the Senate Armed Services Committee were about to begin. The subcommittee was to be chaired by Senator Raymond Baldwin, Republican of Connecticut. McCarthy was not optimistic, he told Townsend, that the Malmedy case would be investigated "in the complete and unbiased detail that it requires."[31]

McCarthy had a point. Tydings, it appears, had seized control of the investigation at the behest of Armed Services Committee member Baldwin. Baldwin had been moved by appeals from constituent and associate in the Bridgeport law firm of Pullman and Comely, Dwight Fanton, who had preceded Burton Ellis as officer in charge of the Malmedy investigation.[32] Although Fanton had left the case prior to Everett's association with it and had not been a focus of Everett's invective, he was offended by the opprobrium that had been heaped upon the investigation and trial and had participated early in March in a press conference called by the anti-German "Society for the Prevention of World War III," in which he and Morris Ellowitz, one of the Malmedy investigators, denied that any improper methods of interrogation had been used at Schwäbisch Hall. The Society had cabled General Clay, urging him to immediately execute the remaining Malmedy death sentences.[33] Also appointed to the subcommittee was Senator Estes Kefauver, Democrat of Tennessee. Kefauver had practiced law with Raphael Shumacker, who had been second to Ellis in prominence on the prosecution team. Kefauver candidly proclaimed Shumacker "a friend of mine for whom I have the highest respect."[34] Rounding out the subcommittee were Senator Lester Hunt, Democrat of Wyoming, who seemed to have little interest in the case, and McCarthy, who, as a courtesy to the Expenditures Committee, was permitted a seat. Armed Services Committee member Chan Gurney of South Dakota, whose support Charles Whiting had attempted to enlist, was not appointed to the subcommittee although, in a "Dear Charlie" letter, he assured Whiting that he would not stand for a "whitewashing" of the case.[35] Senator Richard Russell, Democrat of Georgia, proved a disappointment to Everett. Although appointed to the subcommittee, he withdrew prior to the first session, citing "tremendous pressure of work" on other committees.[36]

It was an irony that, after almost three years of virtually constant involvement in the Malmedy case and its convoluted aftermath, Everett was prevented by his heart attack from participating in what was by far its most public assessment. He was asked to testify but, with the greatest reluctance, declined on instructions from Dr. Smith, who warned of likely dire consequences should he journey to Capitol Hill. Everett could "hardly contain himself" in Atlanta but encouraged his former colleagues on the defense team, Wahler, Dwinell, and Strong, to testify. The army had been successful in getting the investigation switched from the Judiciary Committee to Baldwin's subcommittee, he wrote, and "you can therefore see how the plot thickens." But he was optimistic that "my friend," Senator McCarthy, could prevent a whitewash. "He is in there fighting the old Army gang."[37] Everett outlined the points that should be stressed in testimony, especially the fact that the defendants had told of a seemingly consistent pattern of abuse in early pretrial interviews by the defense staff. Everett's direct role in the hearings would be limited to depositions given in Atlanta, but his perspective would be vigorously and abrasively represented by Joe McCarthy, who had studied not only the reports of the Simpson Commission and the Administration of Justice Review Board but van Roden's article in *The Progressive* and Everett's Supreme Court petition.[38] Van Roden himself was to testify, although in a chastened frame of mind, having come to realize that his career as a reserve officer in the U.S. Army was in jeopardy as a result of his sometimes indiscreet public commentary.[39] Also supporting Everett's critical view in the course of the hearings was James Finucane, Secretary of the National Council for Prevention of War. The Council had begun to take an interest in the Malmedy controversy late in 1948, and Finucane had opened a friendly correspondence with Everett that would last for years. There is irony in this relationship in that the National Council for Prevention of War, a pacifist-isolationist organization established shortly after World War I, had been one of the groups that had been kept under surveillance by Everett in his wartime role as intelligence officer as potentially subversive, and he was less than comfortable with the alliance. But Finucane would assist in keeping the recuperating Everett informed of the course of the hearings and convey to the subcommittee Everett's suggestions for sympathetic witnesses.[40]

Baldwin's subcommittee met sporadically in Room 212 of the Senate Office Building until June 6, then recessed until early September, when it reconvened briefly in Munich. Its published proceedings fill a volume of nearly seventeen hundred pages, including exhibits and the subcommittee's final report. There was a reasonable balance of testimony from witnesses who were supportive of the prosecution and those who supported the defense, although the former had to suffer from the vituperative harassment along with the sometimes perspicacious questioning of Senator McCarthy, prior to his withdrawal from the hearings in theatrical high dudgeon in May. Taken as a whole, the evidence was inconclusive, but critics of the investigation and trial were more cautious in their allegations. Everett was interviewed twice in his Atlanta law office by counsel to the subcommittee, former Marine Corps Colonel (and Congressional Medal of Honor winner) Joseph Chambers. He was questioned gently and responded with unwonted restraint in regard to allegations of duress in the production of pretrial sworn statements by German prisoners in Schwäbisch Hall. Quite apart from whether German posttrial affidavits that claimed both physical and psychological torture were credible, the consistency of the pretrial statements alleging duress that were made by defendants to the defense staff suggested that the prosecution had been engaged in "funny business" at Schwäbisch Hall.

> I couldn't say that I believe that this defendant was lying and that defendant was telling the truth when he made his initial statement, but I do state with certainty that on account of this original pattern without the benefit of collaboration among themselves that there was enough smoke coming out of Schwäbisch Hall to make a reasonable person apprehensive of whether it wasn't possible that all these things could have happened. Whether they did happen or not, I can't say for a certainty, but I believe that they could have happened after what I have seen.[41]

This was a far cry from the unequivocal contentions of torture contained in Everett's Supreme Court petition and may have been the product of a period of reflective calm imposed by his convalescence, but other witnesses confirmed that Everett was not alone in his suspicion of pretrial investigative "funny business." Herbert Strong, the German-Jewish member of the defense team whose fluency in German had been invaluable at Dachau, was less than comfortable in his role as public critic of a trial of seventy-four former SS men, one of whom had been Himmler's adjutant and another the commander of Hitler's personal guard. He had informed McCarthy, who had contacted him, that he was willing to testify but not eager to do so and that he preferred to be subpoened rather than appear to be volunteering.[42] But, although a reluctant witness, he informed the senators and the audience that he had been a participant in several war crimes trials, none of which had stimulated the concerns that the Malmedy trial had done. Strong indicated his suspicion that some truth probably adhered to the defendants' claims of having been subjected to physical violence. Francis Flanigan, who acted as McCarthy's staff assistant, quite reasonably asked why the defense had not attempted to verify the claims of physical abuse through medical examination. Strong answered, as would Everett, that by the time the defense first heard the complaints, the alleged injuries were already at least a month old and were not of a nature to have left long-term evidence. During the trial, Strong asserted, the prosecution had obstructed the calling of defense witnesses and had attempted to intimidate those who were secured. He was convinced, too, that Colonel Rosenfeld had been prejudiced against the defense, having ruled too often against it when the law seemed to be on its side. As Everett was willing to do in his more reflective moments, Strong admitted that he thought some of the Malmedy defendants were guilty as charged but that in many other cases guilt had not been proven beyond a reasonable doubt.[43] The Senate Armed Services Committee had approached Wahler. He, too, asked to be subpoenaed but heard nothing more and did not testify.[44] John Dwinell, Everett's right-hand man during and immediately after the trial, supported Strong's testimony in most particulars. He, too, believed that the Malmedy prisoners had been subjected to some degree of physical duress and that the defense had worked under unnecessary disabilities imposed upon it by the court, so much so that he had developed a "defeatist attitude." He did not doubt that Peiper's troops had committed war crimes during the Ardennes offensive, but he had substantial reservations about the picture that had been painted by the prosecution. Obviously, American prisoners had been killed at the crossroads, but Dwinell was not convinced that the persons whom he had defended were guilty of that crime. Nor was he convinced that American soldiers shot elsewhere had not been killed in combat or that the Belgian civilians killed had not been guerrilla fighters or, at least, mistaken for guerrillas.[45] Former defense counsel Granger Sutton, who testified briefly, agreed with Strong and Dwinell that physical duress had probably been applied to some defendants, although he, like they, had seen no direct physical evidence of it.[46]

Other witnesses offered hints of such evidence. James J. Bailey had been a court reporter employed by the army at Schwäbisch Hall from the end of December 1945 until early March 1946. He testified that he had seen one interrogator, William Perl, slap and "knee" German prisoners but thought the injuries "nothing serious."[47] Kurt Teil, a German refugee from Nazism who had worked for the army as an interpreter-investigator, had had occasion to visit Schwäbisch Hall and had become acquainted with two of the Malmedy investigators, Perl and Harry Thon. Both had spoken approvingly of violent methods of interrogation, and Thon had taken him on a tour of a block of cells occupied by Malmedy suspects. Pausing at a peephole in the door of one cell, Thon invited Teil to have a look. Inside, Teil testified, he saw a prisoner with a hood still over his head, lying crumpled and motionless on the floor of the cell. "He just got out of interrogation," Teil recalled Thon's explaining, "and probably got roughed up a bit." But Teil was confident that instances of physical violence had been few and emphasized that Ellis had repeatedly forbidden it.[48] Dr. Max Karan, a German-speaking American physician who, for about a month, had been in charge of a dispensary at Schwäbisch Hall for the Malmedy defendants, had seen no evidence of physical violence but recalled conversations in which Perl had spoken in admiring tones of methods reputedly employed by the Soviet secret police in extracting confessions. Other interrogators, he remembered, had expressed the view that, since the defendants were "unquestionably" guilty, any methods to encourage talkativeness might be legitimately used.[49] Herbert K. Sloan, employed by the 7708 War Crimes Group as an investigator, although not directly involved with the Malmedy case, testified to the generally decent treatment accorded the prisoners, although he recalled that the belief that things were "a little rough" at Schwäbisch Hall was widespread.[50] But principal figures in the investigation, including, Ellis, Perl, and Thon, categorically denied having used coercive methods, and medical examinations of the Malmedy prisoners in Landsberg failed to produce evidence of physical force alleged to have been inflicted more than three years earlier.[51]

The Baldwin subcommittee's final report reflected the inconclusive nature of the evidence as well as political pusillanimity and the bitterness of a war scarcely four years past. On the basis of the medical examinations, allegations that physical force had been employed to induce confessions were rejected as being without foundation.[52] The issue of "tricks and ruses" was subjected to somewhat greater scrutiny. That mock trials had been employed, albeit in only a handful of cases, could not be denied and was condemned in the report, but less as an illegitimate device than as an unnecessary complication of the investigative process that could be misinterpreted or misrepresented by critics.[53] Odd suppositions lay behind this and other assessments by the subcommittee of the investigative methods employed in 1945 and 1946. The German defendants, in the subcommittee's view, had been abnormal human beings, a condition that had both necessitated and justified the use of creative investigative techniques. The senators conceded that the threat of withholding ration cards from family members had, on occasion, been used against certain suspects; they could hardly have done otherwise, since one of the interrogators questioned by the subcommittee had testified to the use of that tactic. The subcommittee did not condemn the use of the stratagem but expressed doubt that such threats could have had much effect "on the type of individual under interrogation."[54] In general, the subcommittee found little fault with the investigative methods employed at Schwäbisch Hall. The subjects, after all, had been "hardened, experienced members of the SS who had been through many campaigns and were used to worse procedure."[55] Beyond expressing the opinion that the investigation would have been "better handled" if personnel trained for such work had been available and noting, in what might have been a veiled version of Everett's anti-Semitism, that the use of interrogators who were not native-born Americans had aggravated the "natural resentment that exists within a conquered country," the subcommittee found little reason for substantive criticism of the pretrial investigation.[56] Although incorrectly describing Everett as an attorney with considerable courtroom experience, the subcommittee agreed that he had not had adequate time to prepare for the trial, although it did not accept Everett's contention that a request for a continuance would have been futile, and it conceded that the conflicting interests of the seventy-four defendants indicated the desirability of the severance, which the defense had requested but had been denied. Some of Rosenfeld's rulings, while technically correct, had imposed unnecessary constraints on the ability of the defense to develop its case. But the defense, by persuading most of the defendants not to take the stand on their own behalf and to testify to incidences of physical duress, indicated to the subcommittee that it had either not believed the allegations or had "erred grievously."[57]

Finding relatively little about the investigation and trial to condemn, the subcommittee looked askance at those who had reached different conclusions. McCarthy's name was not mentioned, and it was grudgingly conceded that defense counsel and clergy, in their continued efforts on behalf of the Malmedy prisoners, were doing no more than their professional and spiritual duty, but the subcommittee hinted darkly that the long arm of the Kremlin might be manipulating the controversy to discredit U.S. occupation policies and to harness German nationalism to its nefarious purposes.[58] The irony of that allegation in light of Everett's staunch anti-Communism, not to mention McCarthy's later career, was lost on the subcommittee but infuriated Everett as the "final insidious, contemptible and cowardly act."[59]

As the Baldwin subcommittee's investigation dragged to its indecisive conclusion, Everett paced anxiously on the sidelines. He had followed McCarthy's hard-driving assault on the pretrial investigation with satisfaction and offered his support. "I have been informed of your continuing good services," he wrote to McCarthy on May 11, "and the fearless manner in which you have approached this none too popular subject." Assurances of the guilt of Ellis, Perl, and other members of the prosecution staff were accompanied by copies of documents that Everett thought might be of use to McCarthy. These were unidentified but were likely posttrial affidavits by Germans that contained allegations of investigatory brutality at Schwäbisch Hall. McCarthy's withdrawal from the Baldwin subcommittee hearings nine days later, after he accused the subcommittee "of attempting to white wash a shameful episode in the history of our glorious Armed Forces,"[60] was greeted by Everett with dismay. "I cannot help but express my disappointment in the loss of your leadership in the Malmedy fight," he wrote in acknowledging receipt of McCarthy's press release lambasting the Malmedy interrogators and the conduct of the Baldwin subcommittee, and he expressed the hope that the investigation might be reassigned to a Senate committee that would "have the interest of American justice at stake [*sic*] and who are not interested in defending wrong doers, even in the Army."[61] McCarthy explained to Everett that he had withdrawn from the Senate investigation because it had been "too much like trying a case before a jury that was fixed" and that he could do more good working from the outside.[62] Indeed, on July 26, 1949, he carried out a prolonged and slashing attack on the conduct of the Baldwin subcommittee on the floor of the Senate. But, while sporadic correspondence between the two would continue into 1951, the junior senator from Wisconsin soon turned to other matters; in any event, he could not have been encouraged to maintain an active role in the Malmedy controversy by one of Everett's periodic reversions to moderation and even a degree of uncertainty: "There is no person living, including myself, who can positively state that duress of one form or another was used on all of these defendants," he wrote to McCarthy, "but I believe that it is entirely possible, and believing this so strongly, it would seem that any doubt should resolve in favor of a retrial under a real justice system."[63]

In the absence of a mandate from a higher court, retrial of the Malmedy case was never a serious possibility. Not only would a retrial have opened army war crimes justice to further and possibly even more damaging scrutiny, but a precedent would have been set that would have threatened to reopen dozens of other cases at a time when the United States was eager to put war crimes trials behind it. Within that context, the Malmedy case would reach its final resolution, although in a manner less than fully satisfactory to Everett.

10

A Michael Kohlhaas in Atlanta

IT HAD NOT been Everett's ill health alone that had interrupted his compulsive attention to the Malmedy case. Shortly after his heart attack, his wife, Mary, had been struck by a taxi while crossing a street in downtown Atlanta and seriously injured. Three operations to repair cranial damage kept her in Piedmont Hospital after her husband had returned home, and, unable to visit her, he chafed at the lonely circumstances of his own recuperation. "Do what the doctor says," he wrote to her. "I have been doing what they tell me so you do the same and play the game hard so you will be home soon." "I'll be in good shape to wait on you if they decide to let you come home. . . . You have the 'get well' side of the big bed," he assured her. The old doubts about Mary's love for him and his own worthiness were still in evidence. "Love me in 1/100 the way I love you—maybe it's quiet, non-explosive, but still it's deep-rooted. . . ."[1]

Late spring saw Mary's return to the home on Rivers Road; Everett's recovery allowed for a bit of fishing and, in time, a return to his law practice, but his life had changed. His long career in the army reserves, which spanned close to thirty years and which had been the vehicle that had brought him together with Malmedy, was coming to an end. Money seems to have been a matter of some concern, perhaps related to the fact that the cab that had hit Mary had not been insured and certainly linked to the long neglect of his law practice. Everett attempted to make a case for retirement from the reserves with disability pay on the grounds that his health had been undermined by the "tedious and exacting work" of directing security and intelligence for the Fourth Service Command during World War II and later devastated by the terrible stress of organizing the Malmedy defense, which, he now claimed, had resulted in an earlier heart attack at the end of June 1946. The army was not convinced that his incapacity had been incurred while on active duty; however, it followed that determination with a

finding that Everett was now unfit for continued service in the active reserves and transferred him to the honorary reserves, albeit with effusive
praise for his devoted service. Everett's regard for the army was not enhanced by these actions.[2]

Everett had ceased to play the role of defense attorney challenging
the Malmedy verdicts; he had exhausted his juridical options, not to
mention his own physical strength, and had seriously diminished his
economic resources. The magnitude of his financial sacrifice on behalf
of his "Malmedy boys" is not clear but was doubtless substantial. He
would later estimate his out-of-pocket outlay at as much as $50,000,
which, if correct, represents approximately a quarter million end-of-
century dollars, to which must be added the income lost through his
neglect of his law practice. But if no further appeals to higher courts
were to be filed, Malmedy nonetheless refused to loosen its fierce grip
on Everett's conscience.

The Baldwin subcommittee's dark imputation of participation by
Everett in a Soviet scheme to discredit the United States in Germany
was ludicrous. He was becoming a figure well known to the German
public, to be sure, but as an embodiment of American virtue, if understood in a distinctly German sense. As he sought diversion one day during his summer of convalescence, Everett tuned in to an interview of Dr.
Franz Josef Schoeningh on Atlanta radio. Schoeningh, a German jour-
nalist brought to the United States for exposure to American democracy, was being asked the inevitable questions concerning his impressions of the society that he was visiting. What in his responses might
have seized Everett's attention is not known, but, when Schoeningh returned to his Atlanta hotel on a hot July evening, he found Everett's
card, with a suggestion that the two meet the next day. Schoeningh remembered having encountered the name before but did not at first recall its significance. After his return to Germany, he described the man
whom he had met the following morning as middle-aged and slender,
with a face that revealed "none of the . . . comfort of a Mr. Babitt [sic] that
one so often encounters over there. It was, rather, the face of an ascetic
or, if you prefer, that of a fanatic." Everett immediately pulled from his
briefcase newspaper clippings and photographs to accompany an explanation of his impassioned determination to see the outcome of
the Malmedy trial nullified. Here was a man, Schoeningh concluded,
who was "entirely consumed" by his "hunger for justice." The two
repaired to the privacy of Everett's office, where the largely one-sided

conversation continued as Everett shared with his guest correspondence from his domestic supporters. Schoeningh was to report in September to readers of the *Süddeutsche Zeitung* that:

> I recognized at that moment one of the sources of strength of that powerful country, even though sensational reporting in the press sometimes makes it difficult to see clearly. The belief that, in the long run, justice will triumph and must be held sacred, belongs to the almost religious foundations of American public life. This country would not have become as great as it has if this faith were not firm in the broad masses. The letters in Mr. Everett's hands proved to me that he is not alone over there in fighting for the old Roman maxim, "Justice shall triumph even if the world perishes as a consequence," and that he also has arrived in his consuming zeal at that point at which the tragedy of Michael Kohlhaas began. Was not the passionate man next to me a Michael Kohlhaas in a matter not his own? . . .
>
> It had gotten to noon, and Mr. Everett invited me to lunch at his home in the outskirts of the city. In the company of his family, he no longer seemed the same man. He was cheerful, relaxed, a jovial host. We discussed southern Germany, where he had enjoyed living, and Europe, which he loves. As I took my leave, I knew that this strange encounter would be among the most enduring memories of my journey.[3]

While admiring Everett's commitment to justice, Schoeningh had clearly not been fully at ease with this passionate man, a conclusion supported by Schoeningh's comparison of his host to the tragic figure of Michael Kohlhaas. Kohlhaas is a character in a novella of the same name by the nineteenth-century German writer Heinrich von Kleist. The horse trader Kohlhaas believes that he has been denied equity by the courts in a dispute with an arrogant aristocrat and launches a private campaign for rectification. In the end, his tormenter is humbled, but Kohlhaas is sentenced to death for his own excesses. Schoeningh sent Everett a copy of the article, but it is doubtful that the American understood its implications. He did not read German, and materials that he received in that language were only sporadically translated by an unknown party, who would also have had to explain the symbolism of Michael Kohlhaas. But a comforting interpretation was provided Everett by none other than Jochen Peiper, the central defendant in the

Malmedy trial with whom Everett had not communicated in more than three years. Peiper had been a prisoner at Landsberg and under sentence of death since the conclusion of the Malmedy trial, but he was kept aware of its aftershocks by Sigurd, his wife, and by Eugen Leer, his German attorney. A scheme by former Waffen-SS comrades in the spring of 1948 to disguise themselves as U.S. Army officers, overcome the guards, and free Peiper from Landsberg had been discovered by American intelligence agents and had come to naught. On September 6, 1949, Peiper had been interviewed by Senator Lester C. Hunt, representing the Baldwin subcommittee, and had attempted to explain to the unsympathetic Wyoming senator that the psychological effects of defeat and imprisonment had been more relevant to the willingness of defendants to make damaging and possibly false sworn statements than had alleged physical abuse. His recollections of Everett were tepid, perhaps reflecting the dulling effects of three years of solitary confinement:

SENATOR HUNT: What do you think of American counsel?
PEIPER: I have respect for Colonel Everett.
SENATOR HUNT: You think he did a pretty good job in your behalf?
PEIPER: Yes, he was a gentleman; furthermore, I was represented by Dwinell, whom I respected.[4]

But his encounter with Schoeningh's article a short time later brought Everett once more to life in Peiper's consciousness. In a letter written in English sometimes awkward and stilted but rich in imagery, he wrote:

You will no doubt be surprised to hear from me after so long a period of inexcusable silence. However, there are times where silence is the only language possible and, as you certainly will understand, a frontline soldier is not accustomed to bother other peoples [sic] when being confronted by danger. It is a matter of pride and thickheadedness. . . . To cut a long and uninteresting story short: although nothing was farther from me than faithlessness, I did not want to approach you as a doomed petitioner.

The other day, however, as the world goes, a newspaper happened to find its way into my cell, the headline of which struck my eye at once . . . "Michael Kohlhaas of Atlanta" . . . (M.K. is a famous figure of our history and is synonymous with a courageous fighter for justice). . . . I made up my mind to write to that man who for years holds in his clean and unyielding hands the thin avalanche cord of my buried life.

I am not going to turn up an apotheosis now, dear Colonel, don't be afraid. I merely want to state that your gallant struggle for fair play and your unceasing appeal to the [sic] reason have already born fruit abundantly in my shattered fatherland and if ever a foundation stone for democracy was laid in Germany it was by your noble example and chivalrous attitude. However, against stupidity and ill-will even the gods themselves fight in vain and our unsuccessful running against the elastic [sic] wall of prestige, revenge and hybris is nothing but the symptom of the dangerously growing vicious circle.

I trust that our good Dr. Leer has informed you of his troublesome [sic] efforts in our case. . . . Despite the ocean of tendenciously [sic] slanders in the waves of which a certain group is trying to drown the remnants of an old culture, I am well aware that these hyenas of the battlefield are citizens of very recent origin and by far no representatives of your great nation. I cannot help remembering that it takes three generations to make a gentleman and I can therefore well understand their diffi- culties when first meeting a decent society . . . and feel no grudge and hatred against a society that is producing men like you.

The Senate Subcommittee's investigation being over, I wonder what will happen next. Much a do [sic] about nothing, I suppose, and in- stead of the legal way I already see the dark cloud of a so-called way of pardon [sic] at the horizon and expect no clear answer from the lady of easy virtue, that dame Justitia who always serves with the strongest battalions.

But be that as it may, neither the Damoclean sword nor injustice will ever bend our necks. Personally, I keep on the ball and watch with a philosophical smile from my forward observation point the boiling lava round about trying to fill the unforgiving minute. . . . Four stolen years and the incessant sorrow of our impoverished families ought to be enough punishment for the mere losing of a war.

May my children get a better chance and may men of your standard gain ground successfully, that is the closing desire of a decent old crim- inal and indestructible soldier.

Good luck and godspeed, Colonel, thanking you again for all your sac-
rificing efforts and the invaluable moral support.

I am, dear Colonel Everett,

Yours very sincerely,

Jochen Peiper[5]

Peiper's letter might have been a calculated effort to ingratiate himself with the man who had, indeed, held the "thin avalanche cord" of
Peiper's life and to encourage him not to let go of it, but probably not.
Peiper understood that death sentences that had been whittled down in
number from forty-three to six, whose execution had been deferred for
more than three years, and whose circumstances were under senatorial
scrutiny were death sentences not likely to be carried out, and he assumed that at some time in the indeterminate future he and his comrades would be released. The thinly veiled anti-Semitic reference to
"hyenas of the battlefield" was not a calculated effort to play to
Everett's own anti-Semitism. Everett had not had the opportunity to
communicate his negative attitude toward Jews to Peiper; the latter no
doubt simply assumed that an American officer, if also a "gentleman,"
would naturally share that antipathy.

What seems to have been a sincere expression of gratitude, surprisingly, elicited no response from "the Michael Kohlhaas of Atlanta."
Everett's prolific correspondence had been only briefly interrupted by
his heart attack, and the only plausible explanation for his failure to
reply to Peiper is guilt for having, in some sense, let down Peiper and
his comrades, a feeling possibly accentuated by his inability to play a
more active role in the Baldwin subcommittee hearings. A letter dated
October 1, 1949, to his friend and congressman, Jim Davis, is a self-con-
scious diatribe written in a possibly unconscious parody of Peiper's
often pretentious prose and testimony to Everett's sense of having, like
Kohlhaas, suffered martyrdom for the sake of justice:

Initially, the warm impulse of legal brotherhood caused me to open
my arms to these unknown prosecutors. As time continues, the radi-
ance of justice and a fair trial, even to a defeated enemy, urges a clar-
ion call of patriotism to my lips. Words spoken in condemnation of this
prostituted trial are imperishable and will, I hope, set an example of
American fairness and justice for all the years to come. Despite the
babbling denials of these prosecutors and their witnesses, the record

stands as an infamous blot on our American Justice. What else could we expect from a hit dog except a howl of innocence. The guilty men, whom all should despise, are these vengeful ones. . . .

Human brutality thrived during medevial [sic] days on the Continent, just as it thrives in varied forms today among minority groups in New York or Europe. Our American attitude is to scorn and condemn these minority groups. Needless to say, the actions of Perl, Thon and those similarly situated are understandable but not condoned. These "recent arrivals" will no doubt learn during the years ahead what true American justice means.

. . . The fiery ordeal of defending these Malmedy suspects has subjected me to as fierce a storm of abuse and slander as ever assailed a conscience-bound advocate of justice whose consistent attitude has been absolutely patriotic and self-sacrificing.

. . . To dream is one thing—a comparative easy thing; to hold firmly to the Ideals of Justice and Fairness is quite another. It may be well to admit that unless the members of the prosecution have a slight acquaintance with these old and lofty ideals and principles . . . , they naturally would not be abashed. My intolerance of their principles and practices will always remain. There is no drawing back. It has never been my policy to flare up into hot speech and then later refrigerate [sic] the moment passion has passed.

. . . In the final analysis, I have absolutely no fear as to the outcome, because Mr. Secretary Gordon Gray of the United States Army will make a final decision. To my personal knowledge, his hands are clean, capable, strong and just. He will not tolerate injustice. Where doubt hovers as in this Malmedy Case, he will always resolve it in favor of one who he knows as honest and faithful to the precepts of Justice and Fairness.[6]

It was a strange and disturbing letter, which may have caused Davis some alarm. He replied with soothing assurances of his continued interest in "all phases" of the Malmedy investigation and his solicitude for Everett's personal well- being.[7] Everett's eccentric effort at self-justification and expression of confidence that Gordon Gray, Kenneth Royall's short-term successor at the Pentagon, would at last put right the injustice of the Malmedy trial was the cry of a conscience-stricken man who not only had seemingly exhausted his legal options but had been brought face-to-face with his own mortality. His apparent belief that he could depend on Gray to see the rectitude of his cause and to act upon it was based on the slender reed of a wartime association and the conviction that Gray "owed him one." As Everett recalled it, Gray had worked with him as a humble lieutenant on a sensitive case involving a security risk at Fort Benning who had "connections," and Gray had been saved from court martial only by Everett's intervention. It may have been true, but it was probably impolitic of Everett to have reminded Gray of his debt, as he had done in August, and presumptuous to have offered him his appraisal of certain high-ranking army officers along with the prospect of a favorable write-up in *Time* by his friend Bill Howland in the same letter.[8] Everett could be foolish in his attempts to impress others with his importance and connections. In any event, Gray offered no support during his brief service as Secretary of the Army and did not deign to send a personal reply.

Everett spent the last months of 1949 fuming over the "whitewash" of the Malmedy trial by the Baldwin subcommittee. His doctors had forbidden further work on the case, he wrote in the middle of December, but he preferred to "go down fighting to the last" rather than allow "some misguided and unscrupulous Americans" to succeed in "harvesting vengeance and retribution."[9]

Still, what he might be able to accomplish was far from clear, as were the circumstances governing the future of convicted war criminals imprisoned in Germany. The U.S. Army and General Lucius Clay had been superseded at midyear by the State Department and High Commissioner John McCloy as the representatives of United States authority in its zone of occupation, and in September, the Federal Republic of Germany was established under the leadership of Konrad Adenauer. Initially only semisovereign, West Germany was a potentially critical ally in the Cold War confrontation between the United States and the Soviet Union. Moreover, the Simpson Commission had recommended the establishment of a clemency and parole board for convicted German war criminals, and the U.S. Army implemented this recommendation by the end of the year for prisoners convicted by its courts. The new system would eventually include German participants and would preside over the eventual indecisive resolution of the Malmedy conundrum, but, in this process, Everett played no direct role.[10]

His effectiveness as a publicist was limited by his less than dazzling literary talents. The notoriety that had surrounded the Malmedy case since 1946 and that had recently been further stimulated by the Baldwin subcommittee hearings had created a potential market for a book. Early in 1950, Everett was approached by Ed Kuhn, associate editor at Mc-Graw-Hill, with a suggestion that he undertake the project. Kuhn seemed sympathetic to Everett's perspective, noting that his own reaction to allegations of American investigative brutality in the Malmedy case were similar to his feelings when he had read of the crimes of the Germans tried in the Buchenwald concentration camp case: that brutality is part of the human makeup and that Fascism had simply allowed it freer expression.[11] But Everett's response was less than encouraging. Kuhn received copies of Everett's Supreme Court and International Court of Justice petitions, along with a typically rambling and awkwardly written account of his "single-handed fight" for justice, which made his observation that "the writing of a book has never been one of my ambitions and I have no idea that I could master this definite [sic] art" superfluous.[12] Kuhn explored the possibility of engaging a writer for The New Yorker to work with Everett, but, after initial expressions of interest, the man backed out with the cryptic observation that the subject was "destined to remain closed."[13]

The year passed for Everett in a desultory manner. He devoted more time to his law practice than he had done for ten years but seemed to find little satisfaction in it. "As for myself, I am of little value to anyone. . . . My hours are long (18), my work is much slower, but I can't seem to find a graceful ending to the countless details of an old-fashioned law office," he mourned to Wennerstrum in April.[14] His own health remained worrisome, and Mary's emotional equilibrium had suffered as a result of her violent encounter with the taxi the previous spring. "My wife is looking fine, feeling fair and extremely emotionally upset as a final result of the accident."[15] He may have welcomed the occasional alarms, which recalled the imperative of Malmedy, to his consciousness. Early in the spring, Jim Davis alerted him to efforts from a "left-wing congressman from New York" who was urging the execution of the death penalties still pending against German war criminals, leading Everett to lament that "Jewish pressure from New York City is again demanding blood and death penalties" and that no help could be expected from New York newspapers because they would not publish "all that stuff against the Jews."[16] Rumors that reached him from Eugen Leer in Germany at the end of the year that the U.S. Army was planning suddenly to hang the remaining condemned Malmedy prisoners or, perhaps, Peiper alone as a sacrificial "victim" elicited telegrams to Mc-Cloy and to Clay's successor as EUCOM commander, General Thomas T. Handy, but these representations were somewhat perfunctory and self-exculpatory in tone. "General George Washington and General Robert E. Lee left my university the heritage of honor and honesty. Fidelity was also a prerequisite. I have kept the faith."[17]

Everett's telegram to Handy was answered by Lieutenant Colonel T. L. Borom, chief of the war crimes section in the office of EUCOM's judge advocate. Borom had been on the job only since the middle of 1950 but was thoroughly familiar with the large file of correspondence that Everett had generated since 1946, and he was openly sympathetic to Everett's effort. Borom was then in the process of reviewing all army war crimes cases and making recommendations to the new War Crimes Modification Board, almost always for greatly reduced sentences, if not outright remission, and his advice was being generally adopted. "I might say I practiced law in a country town for ten years prior to entering the army and a large portion of it was criminal defense. Need I say more about my personal opinion of the trials of a large number of the cases I am reviewing?" The suspended death sentences, including those of the six remaining Malmedy convicts awaiting execution, were then in the final stages of review, but Borom was optimistic about the outcome. And he was delighted to convey good news to a man who, in 1946, had longed to return to his native South as Borom did in 1951. "I would like very much to be home. Hope to retire in about '53 and return to Ozark, Alabama. Practiced there from 1929 to 1940."[18]

Borom's folksy letter, dated January 23, 1951, fell afoul of the postal service and did not reach Everett until April, but he read it with pleasure and responded as if to an old friend. "You were grand and as I have always said 'if we tell a nigger in Ga. or Ala. that we will give him a fair trial' you can always count on us going all the way to see that he gets one." If Nazis had metaphorically become "niggers" in discourse with another son of the deep South, Everett's army antagonists had assumed a uniformly Jewish identity. "To have seen the intrigue of 'Red' Straight, Bert Ellis, Dwight Fanton and the other recent Jewish arrivals is most revolting to a decent person. . . . How you could witness such rottenness and stay on the job is stamina [sic]. Maybe some of the old days of the 'Rosenfeld' heirarchy had passed on when you arrived."[19]

There was more than cultural affinity behind Everett's good spirits.

The optimism contained in Borom's long-delayed January letter had proved to be well founded. On the last day of January, a Wednesday, General Handy announced his decision on the cases of thirteen German prisoners being held under death sentences in Landsberg. Eleven of these sentences were commuted to life imprisonment. The two death sentences confirmed were assigned to former concentration camp functionaries plausibly connected to the deaths of huge numbers of prisoners; George Schallermair, roll call leader at Muehldorf, a satellite camp of Dachau, had personally administered beatings from which hundreds of inmates had died, and Hans Schmidt had served as adjutant in Buchenwald for three years, near the end of which inmates had expired at the rate of about five thousand per month. Handy declared himself satisfied that there was "no doubt whatsoever" that the six Malmedy prisoners were guilty as charged and that Peiper's "forceful" and "inspiring" leadership had made it impossible to dissociate him from the crimes committed by his battlegroup; in fact, he had been the "motivating spirit" behind them. But they had been perpetrated in the context of "a confused, fluid and desperate action," which made them "definitely distinguishable from the more deliberate killings in concentration camps." Although not mentioned by name, Everett came in for implicit censure. Although the evidence was, according to Handy, convincing to "everyone who has read it objectively," the execution of the sentences had been delayed for more than four years "by a continuous and organized flood of accusations and statements made to discredit the trial. . . ."[20]

As Peiper had foreseen more than a year earlier, "dame Justitia" had given "no clear answer." In fact, through General Handy, she had given a contradictory answer, for if the commutation of the Malmedy death sentences was justified because the offenses were "definitely distinguishable" from the mass murders committed in the concentration camps, then had not efforts to discredit the trial served the cause of justice? But the Malmedy prisoners were not, at the time, inclined to cavil. On February 6, Peiper dispatched a letter to Everett that reflected both euphoria and an improved command of the English language:

> We have received a great victory and next to God, it is you [from] whom our blessings flow. In all the long and dark years you have been the beacon flame for the forlorn souls of the Malmedy boys, the voice and the conscience of the good America, and yours is the present suc-

cess against all the well-known overwhelming odds. May I therefore, Colonel, express the everlasting gratitude of the red-jacket [worn by pisoners sentenced to death] team (retired) as well as of all the families concerned.[21]

Less eloquent expressions of gratitude from other defendants were to trickle into Atlanta during the succeeding months and would assume metallic substance in the form of a brass table lamp, handmade in a Landsberg prison workshop and emblazoned with the LAH (Leibstandarte Adolf Hitler) monogram the craftsmen had worn on their epaulets in palmier days. One German prisoner explained that Everett had showed him and his comrades that "real Americans believe in a correct international justice [sic], without any regard to nationality, color or religion. . . . Take this brass lamp as token of our deep thankfulness and be assured that your name is engraved in golden letters in our mind."[22]

Congratulations flowed in from those who had provided advice and encouragement during Everett's long struggle. Fellow war crimes trials critic Judge Charles Wennerstrum mixed compliments on Everett's tenacity and "high conception of the duty of an American lawyer" with regret that the army had not based its commutations on the recognition that justice had miscarried in the Malmedy case.[23] Leroy van Roden was "a little proud and very pleased" that he had had a part in saving the lives of the Malmedy condemned but revealed to Everett that he was being made to pay a price for his sometimes imprudent conduct. Strong circumstantial evidence indicated, he was convinced, that he had been blacklisted by the judge advocate general's office and denied further active duty in the army reserves, with likely adverse effects on his retirement prospects.[24] Judge Gordon Simpson, van Roden's more circumspect colleague, expressed satisfaction with the commutations but combined regret that the army had not implemented his commission's recommendations in 1948 with praise for Everett's determination to uphold the best traditions of the American bar.[25] Perhaps most valued by Everett was a brief letter received from Supreme Court Justice and Nuremberg prosecutor Robert Jackson, who succinctly observed, "It must be a relief to you that at last the end of the road has been reached. You have made a valiant fight for your clients and you have my best wishes."[26] Jackson's expression of approbation earned for him a shipment of tree-ripened Georgia peaches, which Everett claimed to have been grown on his farm south of Atlanta, but which had probably been purchased from another source.

In his hour of triumph, Everett did not forget Joe McCarthy. By now, McCarthy had emerged as the scourge of Communists in high places and through his reckless accusations and bullying tactics had greatly enlarged his army of detractors, among whom Bert Ellis was a charter member. Everett read in the *Atlanta Journal* an anti-McCarthy editorial by the nationally syndicated columnist Drew Pearson. The two men had recently scuffled in the cloakroom of Washington's posh Sulgrave Club, and Pearson had been kneed twice in the groin (ironic, given the outrage that McCarthy had expressed during the Senate hearings over alleged damage done to German testicles by army interrogators!).[27] Pearson attempted to knee McCarthy figuratively with a distorted account of the Malmedy massacre and the senator's controversial role in the Senate investigation of 1949, branding him a dupe of the National Council for the Prevention of War and "other outfits with close German connections."[28] Everett sensed an opportunity to reinvolve McCarthy in the Malmedy controversy, which, although it had been deprived of its mortal urgency by the commutation of the remaining death sentences, had lost none of its ability to infuriate him. Indeed, van Roden's recent letter had served to sharpen his conviction that the sinister forces within the Judge Advocate General's Corps that had been responsible for the judicial travesty of Malmedy were still at work. "I would like, irrespective of my physical condition," he wrote McCarthy on February 13, 1951, "to verify, amplify or explain any part of the terrible injustice meted out at the hands of these Jewish refugees . . . ," and he added an expression of outrage at the "sadistic attitude" allegedly evinced toward van Roden.[29] But McCarthy had other interests and did not reply.

Malmedy remained a "hot" issue in a West Germany on the path to sovereignty and courted by a West struggling to contain Communism. From January to June 1951, U.S., British and French high commissioners engaged in negotiations with German representatives regarding a future German military contribution to European security. Many Germans who had tended to regard Allied war crimes trials of German soldiers as little more than "victors' justice" demanded a halt to executions and the release of prisoners as a necessary precondition to rearmament.[30] These pressures had likely encouraged the decision to commute the remaining Malmedy death sentences and would continue to work in favor of the eventual release of Peiper and his comrades from Landsberg. As Allied-West German conversations were getting under way, the popular illustrated magazine *Die Strasse* (The Street), published in Hamburg, ran a series of sensational articles on the Malmedy investigation and trial. Under headlines such as "Justice for the Red Jackets" and "Millions Plead for Peiper," readers were treated to lurid renditions of the alleged brutalities inflicted on the prisoners in Schwäbisch Hall, as well as wrenching photographs of Peiper's wife and three blond children, gloating American prosecutors, and an apparently sneering William Perl.[31] The bathos of the piece was enhanced by the recollection of a woman who claimed to have worked as a secretary in Dachau that Everett had informed her of the verdicts "with tears in his eyes," and that he had been the indomitable hero in the long struggle for justice was left in little doubt.[32] Eric Verg, editor of *Die Strasse,* mailed copies of the magazine to Everett with the information that his office had been flooded with letters from readers in praise of Everett's devotion to his clients and assurances that "your name is not forgotten in Germany."[33]

Everett's name remained in the minds of Germans opposed to the hanging of seven other prisoners in Landsberg who still wore the red jacket. Two of these were the concentration camp functionaries whose sentences had been confirmed by Handy; the remaining five had been convicted in Nuremberg proceedings subsequent to the trial of the major war criminals and were subject to the authority of the U.S. High Commissioner, John J. McCloy. McCloy could find no reason to commute the sentences of four officers of the *SS-Einsatzgruppen,* mobile killing formations that, along with police units, had murdered more than one million Jews in the Soviet Union, or of Oswald Pohl, a former SS administrative chief who had presided over the brutal exploitation of concentration camp slave labor.[34] German lobbying organizations attempted to enlist Everett's support in a campaign to commute the seven remaining death sentences. These Germans did not always draw distinctions between genocide and simple battlefield excesses, but some expressed themselves with considerable sophistication. Werner Rietz, first secretary of the "Working Group for Truth and Justice," wrote to Everett in March of his admiration for the Atlantan's crusade and added:

In doing so, you have served the American people in maintaining their esteem and authority in the world much more than you could have done by winning a war. As a former Nazi, I confess quite openly and frankly that your behavior and the fact that you have been entirely free to act and discuss matters as you liked, have persuaded me of democratic principles more than all measures of the alleged re-education.[35]

Rietz's appraisal had been paralleled six weeks earlier in an awkward but eloquent letter signed by several of the Malmedy defendants in which they expressed profound gratitude for Everett's efforts, pains, and sacrifices on their behalf over the previous five years:

> We do not harbor any doubts that most of us had not been spared a disgraceful death [sic] if you had not defended us and . . . the dignity of law at a time when you must have been aware that this decision would cost you much of what people cherish . . . the name Everett has become a conception [sic] in Germany—a conception representing justice, decency and fairness that has done more towards an understanding of our peoples than many a conference.[36]

Five German judges brought to the United States by the State Department in the fall of 1951 to study U.S. judicial procedure would likely have agreed, as they separated from fourteen of their colleagues to pay Everett a reverential visit in Atlanta. One of these jurists, *Landesgerichtpräsident* Dr. Hans Meuschel, would later join the Mixed Parole and Clemency Board, activated in 1955 and composed of three Germans and one representative each from Great Britain, France, and the United States. As Meuschel later remarked to Everett on the occasion of his appointment to the Board, he would be considering the cases of the men on whom he had received firsthand reports while in Atlanta.[37]

The Mixed Parole and Clemency Board would free the last of the Landsberg prisoners within the space of several years, but Everett showed little interest in doing battle for prisoners other than his "Malmedy boys." That this could sometimes assume impractical forms was reflected in a recommendation to the office of the Secretary of the Army that Peiper and Fritz Kraemer, former chief of staff of the Sixth Panzer Army, be released from prison and brought to the United States as advisers to the U.S. Army on means of combating the Red Army. Peiper had had more than one hundred tanks and armored personnel carriers disabled under him during his years in combat, Everett informed Lieutenant Colonel J. R. Deane, of the Department of the Army, "and was considered by American authorities in Germany in 1945 and 1946 as the outstanding German tank commander on Russian warfare," while Kraemer "as I was informed is considered as one [sic] of the outstanding historical authorities among the Germans insofar as general staff, operation and strategy is concerned [sic]." Peiper should be brought to Fort Knox as an instructor on armored warfare, argued Everett, who was willing to guarantee that he would do nothing inimical to United States interests while living in this country. "I firmly believe that Col. Peiper, and many others [sic] of these defendants, are honorable soldiers. . . ."[38]

Everett's proposal was implausible on a number of grounds. Neither Peiper nor Kraemer could be considered major authorities on armored warfare or operational staff work, although both had been interviewed on the Ardennes offensive by U.S. Army historians while in captivity. And, although the United States armed forces had been eager to avail themselves of German expertise in a wide variety of fields and had not been squeamish about the sometimes unsavory aspects of what Germans who possessed valuable knowledge or skills might have done while in the service of the Third Reich, those relationships had lacked the explosive political potential that was implicit in the proposal to employ men convicted in a widely publicized case of murdering surrendered GIs. Nothing came of the proposal, of course, but the desire of the U.S. government to put the awkward matter of war crimes trials behind it slowly rendered Everett's inventiveness increasingly redundant. Near the end of January 1952, seven months after his approach to the Department of the Army, Everett received a warm letter from Fritz Kraemer, revealing that he had been freed from Landsberg shortly before Christmas. "Colonel, no one will forget you. Your name has entered our hearts and those of our families. . . . I press your hand in spirit. . . . Maybe we will become soldiers again. Who will condemn us then?"[39]

Everett had become, for many West Germans, the embodiment of impartial justice who, by holding the alleged misdeeds of American investigators and prosecutors up to censure, seemed to mitigate however slightly the immense burden of German wartime guilt. Americans reacted to him in manners more diffuse. His friends and associates were virtually unanimous in their conviction that Everett's prolonged assault on the Malmedy verdicts had been the consequence of a rigorous code of ethics and of a higher form of patriotism than that which had been demonstrated by the defenders of the investigation and trial. Inevitably, given the embarrassment he had caused the U.S. Army and government, he had been subjected to a "very discreet" special inquiry conducted by the Federal Bureau of Investigation in the fall of 1949, the primary purpose of which was to determine whether Everett was in the pay of sinister alien forces. Those who knew him well found the idea preposterous. Typical was the response of the informant who "stated that he knows of no person that he could recommend more highly as to loyalty, personal integrity, courage of conviction and general reputation" and that "Everett felt it his duty to defend American legal principles which he felt had been violated, as well as the defendants . . . , and that he had great respect for the stand which Everett took in the matter."[40] The FBI agent in charge of the investigation found no evidence to substantiate an allegation of unknown origin that Everett was in contact with a resident of Boston who was married to the daughter of one of the defendants, an allegation for which no support is provided by Everett's correspondence. On the other hand, the Bureau's conclusion that Everett was not in communication with Malmedy defendants is contradicted by that same correspondence. What is remarkable about the investigation is the complete absence of a sense of offended patriotism on the part of those interviewed, most if not all of whom were either members of the Atlanta area's business, professional, and political elite or persons who had worked with Everett in military intelligence during the war. Several informants alluded to Everett's preoccupation with the alleged misdeeds of Jewish members of the investigation-prosecution team, and one was willing to call it "anti-Semitism," although he attributed it to the determination of Jews "to gain their revenge on the Nazis."[41] That anti-Semitic element attracted some Americans, who saw in Everett's crusade a confirmation of their own prejudices. A Salt Lake City woman wrote to Everett in August 1952 in praise of his "courageous fight against a power of greatest temporary strength. . . . A man of your ability and righteousness ought to be president of your country! But the dark powers that be would prevent it! I have no use for any of the candidates, least of all for General Eisenhower."[42] The writer would have been disillusioned had she known that Everett had been active in organizing support in Georgia for Eisenhower's presidential bid, activity that came as no surprise to those close to him, who were aware of his estrangement from the Democratic Party and its northern liberalism.[43] Another admirer wrote that she and a number of her acquaintances shared deep appreciation for Everett's "valiant fight in behalf of those luckless victims of Jewish wrath."[44]

Everett's association with Joseph McCarthy had blossomed prior to the Wisconsin senator's campaign against Communism in high places in the United States, but other anti-Communist activists found the Malmedy controversy and Everett relevant to their purposes. Freda Utley, a former British Communist who had shown some sympathy for Nazism early in the war and had emerged in the postwar years as an ardent anti-Communist, seized upon the mistakes and abuses of the western Allies in occupied Germany as acts likely to throw West Germans into the arms of the Soviet Union. In *The High Cost of Vengeance*, published by the Henry Regnery Company in 1949, Utley reproduced the most extreme of the allegations of abuse lodged against the Malmedy investigators and implied that the extraction of confessions under torture had been characteristic of the Dachau trials in general. Everett and van Roden were singled out by Utley as points of light in an otherwise somber picture of American "crimes against humanity," a contention she repeated in October 1953 in an article in *The American Legion Magazine* and again a year later in *The American Mercury*.[45] Her "Malmedy and McCarthy" of November 1954 was written as the Wisconsin senator lurched toward censure on the floor of the Senate in the wake of the lurid "Army-McCarthy hearings" of that year. Some of McCarthy's critics had recalled his controversial role in the Senate's 1949 investigation of the Malmedy trial; Senator Ralph Flanders of Vermont used it to suggest a more than passing resemblance between Joe McCarthy and Adolf Hitler. Utley raged: "Now that an ignorant old man from Vermont has smeared McCarthy on the Senate floor with the same false accusation as Drew Pearson, Elmer Davis [both prominent news commentators of the period] and other Pharisees, it is more than ever necessary to publish the facts." Everett, with whom she had entered into correspondence, was again cited as the authoritative source for what had happened at Schwäbisch Hall and Dachau; to his assessment Utley added the implication, which had never occurred to Everett even in his most imaginative moments, that some of the army's investigators at Dachau had been Soviet agents.[46]

Everett still occasionally felt compelled to wield his pen against those for whom Malmedy remained a synonym for Nazi barbarity rather than for twisted American justice. A letter to the editors of the

Atlanta Journal in the autumn of 1954 aroused his ire when its author offered the argument that the United States should invest in Germany rather than France as the chief bulwark in the defense of western Europe because Germans were as savage as Russians. Nazi concentration camps, the genocidal murder of seven million human beings, and the Malmedy massacre were cited as evidence in support of the contention that German fire was best suited to combat the Soviet version. Everett objected petulantly to the author's "excessive and sensational statements" and responded in kind. While not denying German atrocities, Everett rejected the contention that seven million had been murdered as "a gross exaggeration," while foolishly passing off concentration camps and genocide as the by-products of war "which have always existed."[47] The release on parole of Sepp Dietrich in October 1955 called forth additional expressions of anti-German feeling to which Everett felt obligated to respond. In a letter to the *New York Times,* Judge William Clark decried the freeing of "a monstrous SS General who ordered the massacre of our unarmed boys at Malmedy," although, incongruously, Clark also found "outrageous" the hanging of Wehrmacht high command chief Wilhelm Keitel, who "was only doing his duty." Everett collaborated with Herbert Strong in framing a response that reflected the moderating influence of the Jewish member of the Malmedy defense team. Following a review of the flaws in the Malmedy investigation and trial, which called into question the guilt of the accused, Everett and Strong argued that, except for the horrors of the concentration camps, it would be best to forget the terrible things that had happened during the war.[48]

Everett was subjected to surprisingly little criticism for his indefatigable efforts on behalf of men who, in the eyes of most Americans, were the butchers of unarmed American boys. But then, Everett could be seen simply as a soldier who had performed his duty with a remarkable degree of fidelity. The diplomat Edwin Plitt, U.S. representative to the Mixed Parole and Clemency Board, on the other hand, was condemned for his ongoing role in approving freedom for the Malmedy convicts. Near the end of 1955, Timothy J. Murphy, commander of the Veterans of Foreign Wars, demanded Plitt's removal from the Board. One of Everett's staunchest supporters from the desperate days of the late 1940s, now Apostolic Nuncio to Germany Bishop Muench, wrote on Christmas day to Secretary of State John Foster Dulles in defense of Plitt, noting that those who called for his removal should read Everett's legal briefs as he had done and give no credence to "that handful of naturalized Americans who, not imbued with the spirit of Anglo-Saxon traditions of jurisprudence, unwittingly, I am sure, dishonored due process of law in essential points."[49] Muench sent a copy of the letter with its thinly veiled anti-Semitic allusion to Everett with a request that he use his contacts in Washington in support of Plitt, lest he become the victim "of certain pressure groups that still have an axe of vengeance to grind in Germany."[50] Everett drafted a letter to Dulles in which he, following Muench's lead, decried attacks on Plitt based on false information secured by "un-American methods" employed by "pseudo-Americans" and "certain minority pressure groups who are still seeking revenge."[51]

Expressions of outrage over alleged leniency shown to the Malmedy defendants flared up again less than a year later with the release of Peiper, the last of the Malmedy prisoners to walk free from Landsberg. That event prompted Dan Daniel, National Commander of the American Legion, to comment bitterly that what *The American Legion Magazine* termed "the merry Christmas of Joachim Peiper" was "the most sordid travesty on justice in the history of international law."[52] Everett did not record his own undoubtedly very different thoughts on that climactic event but had written in anticipation of it about six months earlier to Josef Diefenthal, one of Peiper's battalion commanders in the Ardennes, whose own death sentence had been commuted and who had recently been released from Landsberg. Addressing Diefenthal as "Dear Friend," he observed that "Ten years ago we were nearing the end of a great injustice filled with intense feeling guided by the invisible hands of vengeance and prompted by a diabolical scheme to obtain retribution." That prolix observation, the sense of which would have been readily understood by a former SS officer, was followed by Everett's projection of a future in which all of his "Malmedy boys" would have returned home. Then, he confided to Diefenthal, "I hope to open a real campaign and tirade against the inequities of our prosecutors. . . . It is my dream to once again return to Germany when we have Colonel Peiper . . . released, and it would seem very fitting that Dr. Lear [*sic*] and the 70 odd fine German soldiers who sat day after day at Dachau have a reunion."[53]

What "a real campaign and tirade" might have been, given Everett's exertions of the previous decade, is difficult to imagine. In any event, neither the all-out punitive expedition nor the reunion in

Germany took place following Peiper's parole. Once all of his clients were free, Everett was content to live out his final years in a degree of tranquility he had not known since 1940. To be sure, he worked long hours in his law office often well into the evening; Mary, perhaps still the distrustful wife, often sat with him until he was ready to return to their home on Rivers Road following a bite to eat. He seemed determined to compensate for the years of neglect he had visited upon Everett and Everett, probably as much in veneration of his revered father as out of economic necessity. He and Mary were comfortable. They acquired a vacation retreat at Lakemont on Lake Rabun in the mountains of north Georgia, and Everett enjoyed polishing the family Cadillac on weekends until its chrome sparkled. His son, Willis III, had grown to young manhood during the elder Everett's preoccupation with the Malmedy trial and had entered the University of Georgia in 1952. Everett might have experienced a twinge of disappointment when young Willis decided to pledge Phi Delta Gamma rather than his beloved Beta Theta Pi, whose chapter adviser he was at Georgia Tech, but he followed his son's progress with close attention and copious infusions of paternal advice:

> You are learning the value of money. As time goes on, you will see the advantages it can bring you. Be thrifty, not mizerly [sic]. Spend wisely, not foolishly. . . . I have never tried to make lots of money so as to 'buy' my way in life. . . . By serving my fellow man I have made lots of lasting friendships which will not fade away. I can really recommend the same . . . the real job is to gain a good, well-rounded education in books . . . and having the respect of everyone around you for your high ideals and principles.[54]

A four-month stint at the navy's officers' candidate school at Newport, Rhode Island, which followed his graduation from the University of Georgia was initially difficult for the son, who suffered from a combination of homesickness, the pangs of separation from his sweetheart, and the arcana of navigation, but Everett was ready with uncomplicated advice both practical and spiritual:

> [G]o direct to your commanding officer and tell him in a pleasing (not despondent) manner that you need some counselling advice because you can't seem to get into the grove [sic]. . . . Put on a front. Life is noth-

ing but an acting game. . . . It is my idea that things will open up for you if you will open the door and let your commanding officer, the counseling officer and the chaplain inside. Don't forget to open up and talk to God in a big way.[55]

Everett was often infelicitous in his use of language and did himself a disservice by his careless reference to life as "an acting game." His struggle against the Malmedy verdicts had been no act, although he had been sometimes willing to dissimulate to achieve his ends. His long service as trustee and legal counsel to Clark College and Gammon Theological Seminary, which continued until his death, and the unabashed delight he took in his role of guiding spirit or "Wooglin" of the Gamma Eta chapter of Beta Theta Pi at Georgia Tech were evidence of a man with a sincere and simple desire to do good.

As the decade of the fifties neared its end, Malmedy had, not surprisingly, lost its dominant position in Everett's consciousness, although it resurfaced from time to time. He was invited to speak on the trial by law students at Emory University and at the University of Georgia and, in February 1958, he was contacted by John Toland as the writer struggled with the Malmedy puzzle in writing his book on the Battle of the Bulge. While doing research in Germany, Toland had met "quite a few" people who insisted that he get Everett's views on Malmedy, which he was eager to do, as he did not want to repeat "old fallacies."[56] Toland's approach revived old passions and elicited an invitation to Toland to visit Atlanta to examine Everett's archive of documents and correspondence on Malmedy. Everett was willing to give the writer "as much time as possible," although he was at pains to impress upon Toland that the "fight" had cost him $40,000 over a period of eleven years.[57] Toland refused the offer, explaining that he was "long overdue on the book . . . and now it's a race between time and my advance."[58] Perhaps he realized that, once in face-to-face contact with Everett, escape would be no easy matter. Nevertheless, Everett's influence on Toland's appraisal of the investigation and trial is evident.[59] Everett continued to be a minor hero in the Federal Republic of Germany and, as "Colonel Evans of Atlanta," a figure in a serialized, semifictional account of the Malmedy affair by Will Berthold that appeared in the popular magazine *Revue* during the summer and fall of 1957, was characterized as "a lawyer of the truth. Justice meant more to him than the flag of his nation."[60] More tangible recognition came in the summer of 1958 when Dr. Karl H. Schoenbach, the West German consul in Atlanta, presented Everett with a check for $5,000 from the government of the Federal Republic as a gesture of appreciation for his inexhaustible efforts on behalf of the Malmedy defendants. Everett accepted the money with more than a touch of ill grace. He had fought to free his German clients as a matter of conscience, he told Schoenbach, and rectitude was its own reward. Yet, he was clearly offended by the niggardliness of the compensation offered by the German government. His efforts had cost him two heart attacks, he noted, while $5,000 was but a small fraction of the estimated $40,000 he had spent fighting the verdicts and sentences.[61]

Communication between Everett and the Malmedy prisoners had ceased following Peiper's release. But, in October 1959, Everett received a letter from a German physician, Dr. Benno Mueller of Kirchhofen in Baden, who had served with the Fifth SS Panzer Division "Wiking" during the war. Mueller told Everett that he had met Peiper a few months earlier and had taken some photographs of the chief defendant in the Malmedy trial, prints of which were enclosed. In the course of their conversation, Peiper had spoken of Everett with great admiration and had made of Mueller an admirer as well.[62] Everett promptly responded with thanks for the letter "together with the four enclosures of a gallant soldier" and a request for Peiper's address, which he promptly received along with Mueller's comment that Everett's letter, which he had read to Peiper over the phone, had been to him "the greatest pleasure of the last ten years."[63]

With that began a series of exchanges between Everett and Peiper that punctuated the last few months of Everett's life. Shortly before Thanksgiving, Everett composed a long and rambling letter that reflected the weight with which Malmedy still lay upon his conscience. Peiper's smile in one of Mueller's photographs had brought "great joy to my heart. I had never seen that smile and never thought to see it. Frankly, I never smiled inwardly during that time. . . ." There followed a lengthy effort to justify the manner in which he had conducted the defense during the trial. He had not wanted the assignment because he lacked courtroom experience, he told Peiper, but he found that weakness to be irrelevant before a court controlled by "Colonel Abraham Rosenthal" [sic], whose rulings had violated the promise made to him by the president of the court, "General Darby" [sic], that Peiper and his comrades would get a fair trial. Everett's spelling, always problematical, perhaps had taken on a punitive significance with his anomalous rendering of the names of two officers who, he believed, had contributed mightily to the injustice that had been sealed in the Dachau courtroom. His decision to persuade most of the defendants not to take the witness stand in their own defense continued to trouble him. Had they done so, he still believed, "the majority would have been hung [sic]," a conclusion not easy to support, unless any testimony that alleged duress would have been unconvincing or decisively undermined during cross-examination.[64]

Between Everett's exchange of letters with Dr. Mueller and his conscience-stricken letter to Peiper, he had been contacted by a figure from the new world that Peiper had entered following his release from Landsberg. This was a very different world from that in which the Peiper of Everett's memory was located. William J. Sholar was the executive secretary of the Porsche Club of America and had come to know Peiper and his "charming family" in the course of International Porsche Club meetings in Europe. Peiper, as Mueller had already explained to Everett, had found employment at the Porsche factory at Stuttgart-Zuffenhausen. He had worked initially as a car washer but rose quickly to manager for sales to Americans traveling in Europe, a position for which his command of English, much improved during his last years in Landsberg, well suited him. His past, of course, was another matter, and Mueller had characterized Peiper's position with Porsche as "a slight parody of fate." Sholar seemed intent upon enlarging the parody by extending an invitation to Peiper and Sigurd ("Sigi"), his wife, to attend the American Porsche Club's national meeting in Aspen, Colorado, scheduled for July 1960. But there was an obvious problem. As a convicted war criminal, Peiper would have difficulty securing a visa for the anticipated three-week visit, although Sholar had learned that there was a chance that a visa might be gotten by "special request." He turned to Everett for help.[65] Everett advised Peiper to simply submit his application along with those of other Germans who intended to visit Aspen and to hope that his name would not be recognized. If it was, Everett would pull strings with his senators and congressmen for a dispensation.[66]

It was a patently silly, not to say dangerous, suggestion and is best explained by the intensely emotional nature of Everett's involvement in the Malmedy affair, which, as in the past, could still overwhelm his critical faculties. Peiper's perspective was different. He had, he told Everett, received his letter with "deep joy and sincere appreciation." He continued:

> When there is not the slightest vestige of resentment or revengefulness [sic] in my heart towards the nation that robbed me of the 12 best years of my life and put my family to endless hardship and trouble, this solely is up to you [sic], to your upright and unfailing example and the unsurpassed way in which you represented your country. You have been America's best ambassador to Germany, setting an example that was respected and recognized far beyond the defendants of the Malmedy case.[67]

It was clear that, unlike Everett, Peiper was trying to forget the past. He correctly judged Everett's stratagem for obtaining a visa for entry to the United States to be "more than improbable" and reacted with less than enthusiasm to Everett's revelation of plans for a trip to Europe in the spring. Business and a scheduled skiing trip would prevent him from accompanying Everett on his anticipated tour, although Sigi might prove available for the purpose, and he looked forward to "the many stories we will have to tell each other." Everett's bitterness remained unabated. He was unable to share Peiper's "patient understanding since 1946," he replied. "My temperament will not allow me to forget the past," he wrote, and he looked forward to sharing with Peiper "many things that I cannot write in connection with the ten fighting years to keep you alive."[68]

The reunion would not take place, for Everett was a dying man. In a final letter early in February 1960, he advised Peiper that his physician, Carter Smith, hoped to attend an international medical convention on cardiac disorders in Paris that summer and wanted to take delivery of a Porsche 1600 (white, with red upholstery, sliding steel roof, and seat belts) upon his arrival. Everett still hoped to visit Stuttgart in the spring, perhaps in April, and asked Peiper to "pick me off a four passenger convertible, either new or used. . . ." His departure from the United States would probably have to be postponed a bit, he added, because he had been receiving treatment for two months "for the uncommon malady of lymphoma. . . ."[69]

By March, Everett's condition had become grave. His son's tour of duty with the navy had ended, and he, Mary Campbell, and Mary were in close attendance. So were the young men of Georgia Tech's Beta house, some of whom stood vigil outside his hospital room as he slipped away. A letter posted on the tenth of the month expressed deep affection for a man whose need to assist others had not been limited to his "Malmedy boys."

> There's never been a tougher scrapper than Willis Everett. . . . Down through the years . . . you've seen us through with no complaint, with equal vigor, and, with God's help, equal ease. . . . Wooglin, we feel that same God who has answered your prayers and ours before will be answering all of ours for you now. . . . We love you, Wooglin; there's a whole chapter pulling and praying for you over here on the Tech campus. . . .[70]

As death neared and he ceased eating, four fraternity brothers brought him some vegetable soup, carried in the chapter's loving cup, and persuaded him to swallow several spoonfuls. A few days later, on April 4, 1960, Everett died.[71]

Epilogue

Expressions of sympathy poured into 2510 Rivers Road NW. Although Everett's obituary in the *Atlanta Journal*, based on information provided by his son-in-law, Kil Townsend, stressed his role in the Malmedy controversy,[1] it was a matter ignored by the friends and acquaintances who offered condolences to Mary. But the traits of character they chose to remember—a deeply ingrained selflessness and a need to serve those who needed him—were not inconsistent with his epic struggle to save his Malmedy boys. Everett's long pro bono efforts on behalf of Christian higher education for African Americans was recognized by the Methodist bishop Arthur J. Moore, who remembered him as "God's good man," an assessment shared by the small Presbyterian congregations in the mountains of northern Georgia, where he and Mary had built a vacation retreat in their later years together:

> Mr. Everett was vitally interested in the extension of the Kingdom of God in these beautiful mountains, which he loved so well. He was directly responsible for the lovely electric lamps which adorn both sanctuaries of the Hemphill Memorial and Wiley Churches. The pews in the Clayton church are there because of his efforts. Large contributions of cash which he secured from different sources were received by the Wiley church. . . . He loved God and had a great heart. He was a free, indomitable spirit—full of conviction, love and fellowship.[2]

He had, of course, cultivated powerful men, too, a practice that had served him well in his confrontation with army justice. Jim Davis, who had likely come to regard Everett as a bothersome presence and who may have resented his conversion to Eisenhower Republicanism, reacted to his death with a perfunctory telegram of sympathy, but a moving handwritten letter came from the "Swamp Fox," Georgia Congressman Carl Vinson, and his wife, Kate:

We loved Willis and know full well that we will never again have the
joy of such a friend as he. He was truly one of the sweetest, gentlest,
kindest, best men it has ever been our privilege to know, and we have
known fine men all over the world. He was the soul of chivalry in an
age when many do not even know what that is, the very heart of good-
ness and generosity.[3]

Gratitude from those who had the most reason to express it is not
reflected in the many letters of sympathy preserved by the family.
Peiper outlived Everett by fifteen years, but they were not the tranquil
years of the gallant soldier *ausser Dienst*. His notorious past destroyed
his brief career with Porsche and, later, with Volkswagen, and it drove
him into bitter self-imposed exile in France. In December 1975, he addressed a letter to Mary in which he outlined his plan to write a book
on the Malmedy incident and requested assistance in the form of relevant papers and photographs.[4] But, in July 1976, he was killed in a fire-
bomb attack on his home by persons unknown, overcome by smoke
while attempting to salvage personal possessions and papers, some of
which were likely related to the book, which he planned to dedicate
to Everett.[5]

It would have been a dedication amply deserved. Without Everett,
Peiper would probably have died on the gallows at Landsberg thirty
years earlier, and so would many of his comrades. It is this that lends to
Everett's persona an element of the tragic. Had he dedicated ten years
of his life to the rescue of United States citizens convicted of a street
gang mass murder under circumstances comparable to those surrounding the Malmedy case, he might have become a figure of popular
veneration in his own country, as he was, for a time, in West Germany.
Hollywood might have seen fit to produce "One Angry Man," starring
Henry Fonda or, perhaps, Jimmy Stewart.[6] But he had worked for the
freedom of former members of the Nazi SS who had been found guilty
(as some of them undoubtedly were) of killing defenseless GIs. Those
GIs had been murdered by men who, for most Americans, embodied
the evil that the United States had fought and sacrificed to destroy.
Everett's crusade was tainted by the associations of those he saved.

And it was tainted, too, by his own anti-Semitism. Yet, that anti-
Semitism had been tangential to the primary forces that motivated
Everett's assault on the Malmedy verdicts: the conviction that even a
despised and defeated enemy deserved due process and had the right

to have his offenses punished according to standards no more stringent than those applied to the victor for similar misdeeds. Everett's ethnic prejudices were not incompatible with a deeply internalized sense of obligation to assist flesh-and-blood human beings in need and, perhaps, sharpened by doubts of his own worthiness.

Everett had not achieved his quasi-victory unaided. He had secured numerous allies in his campaign against the Malmedy verdicts within a broader current of skepticism in the United States regarding the legitimacy and wisdom of the war crimes trials program, a phenomenon that Everett's fearless persistence had done much to encourage. The motives of these allies had included Everett's own conviction that former Axis personnel suspected of war crimes had not always been tried according to American ideals of justice, while the anti-Semitism that darkened Everett's idealism had been present in the minds of others, too. To these were often added partisan politics and Cold War pressures, the latter resulting in the transmutation of Germans from hated enemies to indispensable allies.[7]

Not everyone, of course, viewed Everett as a selfless fighter for justice. Burton Ellis, who had led the prosecution team before and during the Malmedy trial, repaid Everett's sometimes overwrought accusations of malfeasance with a loathing whose intensity did not diminish with the passage of time or with Everett's death. More than forty years after the conclusion of the trial, Ellis observed in the course of an interview:

> The chief counsel Everett, why it was a travesty of justice to put a guy like that as the chief defense counsel of anything. Now, he was a social lawyer as far as I know, allegedly a wealthy man. He was not happy to be a defense counsel. He came over there with the idea of being a big shot and going after these people, but he couldn't have done it. He did not know how to. The only thing he could do, you know, [sic] the things that he alleged that we did were conclusively proven to be wrong, like kicking the balls and testicles [sic] off these people. . . . Well, a guy that would say something like that is wrong someplace mentally.[8]

Ellis's antipathy towards Everett, which the latter had reciprocated, was in large part the consequence of the antagonistic roles, intertwined with issues of ego and self-esteem, in which circumstances had cast them.

But, in playing his part in the drama of Malmedy, Everett had heaped a volume of opprobrium on Ellis that the prosecutor could not forgive.

Everett's condemnation of U.S. Army war crimes justice and his oft-repeated claim that German battlefield atrocities had been no worse than those committed by Americans gave support and comfort to Germans eager to shrug off the enormous burden of Nazi guilt. But it is clear, too, that some Germans, including Peiper, found in Everett's determination and freedom to fight for the nullification of the Malmedy trial a validation of American democracy. Ironically, therefore, Everett's assault on Army justice, which some critics had incorrectly linked to Soviet efforts to discredit U.S. occupation policy in Germany, may have contributed to the democratization of German society, one of the chief objectives of the American occupation.

Whatever contribution Everett may have made to the democratic reform of Germany was fortuitous. There was no calculation in what he did beyond that necessary to achieve what he believed to be justice for his Malmedy boys. He acted on a personal ethical imperative, which, as far as he was concerned, removed ameliorative action from the realm of choice.[9] Everett thereby endowed an otherwise depressing slice of history with moral value. That is not a bad epitaph.

Notes

NOTES TO CHAPTER I

1. Miscellaneous biographical clippings and undated biographical sketch in Willis M. Everett Jr.'s hand in papers of Willis M. Everett Jr. (hereafter Everett papers).

2. Undated biographical sketch, Everett papers.

3. James Michael Russell, *Atlanta 1847–1890: City Building in the Old South and the New* (Baton Rouge: Louisiana State University Press, 1988), 147.

4. Ibid., 233; miscellaneous biographical material, Everett papers.

5. "Atlanta Girl Killed by Lightning Bolt," undated clipping, Everett papers.

6. "Miss Wooldridge Introduced at Elaborate Dancing Party," undated clipping, Everett papers.

7. Washington and Lee University, "Traditions of Honor" (pamphlet published by Washington and Lee, n.d.).

8. *Calyx* (Lexington: Washington and Lee University, 1921), 78.

9. Chronological Statement of Service, n.d., Everett file, National Personnel Records Center, Overland, Mo. (hereafter "NPR"); *Calyx*, 178.

10. Record of Everett, Willis Mead, Jr., Washington and Lee University; Personal History Statement, n.d., Everett file, NPR.

11. Officer's and Warrant Officer's Qualification Card Copy, n.d., Everett file, NPR.

12. Willis M. Everett to Willis M. Everett Jr., January 25, 1925, Everett papers.

13. Presbyterian Church in the U.S.A., *A Digest of the Acts and Proceedings of the General Assembly of the Presbyterian Church in the United States, 1861–1965* (Atlanta: Office of the General Assembly, 1966), 137–40.

14. Chronological Statement, NPR. Record of Everett, Willis Mead, Jr.

15. Russell F. Weigley, *History of the United States Army* (Bloomington: Indiana University Press, 1984), 400–401.

16. Franklin S. Chalmers to the Adjutant General, March 23, 1923, NPR.

17. Earl Lamspech to Reserve Officer Corps, March 28, 1923; William R. Hoyt to Reserve Officer Corps, March 24, 1923, NPR.

18. Report of an Examining Board, April 19, 1923; certificate of appointment to second lieutenant May 25, 1923, NPR.

19. Interview of Willis M. Everett III, June 6, 1997; Personal History Statement, n.d., NPR.

20. Everett interview, June 6, 1997; interview of Kiliaean Townsend, August 8, 1996; Willis M. Everett Jr. to Mary Everett, November 1, 1945, Everett papers.

21. Lieutenant Colonel P. M. Stevens to Commanding Officer, 326th Infantry, October 8, 1925; certificate of appointment to first lieutenant, December 22, 1925, NPR.

22. Army Correspondence Courses: Cancellation of Enrollment, June 25, 1929; certificate of appointment to captain, January 14, 1930, NPR.

23. "U.S. Scared to Death, Liberty Editor Thinks," *Sunday American*, January 30, 1938.

24. Roy Talbert Jr., *Negative Intelligence: The Army and the American Left, 1917–1941* (Jackson: University Press of Mississippi,1991), 235–36; Joan M. Jensen, *Army Surveillance in America, 1775–1980* (New Haven: Yale University Press, 1991), 178 –203; Anthony J. Badger, *The New Deal: The Depression Years, 1933–1940* (New York: Hill and Wang, 1989), 38–39.

25. Talbert, *Negative Intelligence*, 237.

26. Everett to instructor, 326th Infantry, October 24, 1932, NPR; certificate of appointment to captain of military intelligence, December 19, 1932, NPR. The appointment was made retroactive to January 14, 1930.

27. Reserve Officer's Qualification Card for period 1923–1937, NPR.

28. Van Horn to Commanding General, Fourth Corps Area, May 27, 1935, NPR; Moseley to Everett, October 30, 1937, NPR.

29. Proceedings of Board of Officers, November 4, 1935, NPR.

30. Curt Gentry, *J. Edgar Hoover: The Man and the Secrets* (New York: Plume, 1992), 110.

31. Talbert, *Negative Intelligence*, 250; Active Duty Report of Reserve Officer, August 13, 1938, NPR.

32. Report of Military Intelligence Reserve Officer for Fiscal Year July 1, 1939, to June 30, 1940, NPR.

33. Special Orders No. 195, September 9, 1940, NPR.

NOTES TO CHAPTER 2

1. Weigley, *History of the United States Army*, 428.

2. Talbert, *Negative Intelligence*, 258; Jensen, *Army Surveillance*, 214; Ian Sayer and Douglas Botting, *America's Secret Army: The Untold Story of the Counter Intelligence Corps* (New York: Franklin Watts, 1989), 21.

3. Interview of William Hartman, Tom Forkner, and Kiliaen Townsend, June 4, 1997.

4. Number of Installations and Activities by Class, March 1945, records of Security and Intelligence Division, Fourth Service Command, Box 72, Record Group 338, National Archives and Record Service (hereafter "NARS, SID, 4SC").

5. Hartman, Forkner, Townsend interview.

6. Court Martial under the 96th Article of War for Making Disloyal Statements, June 21, 1943, Box 67, NARS, SID, 4SC.

7. Disposition of Potentially Subversive Personnel, July 31, 1942, ibid.; War Department Special Organization, July 17, 1944; Everett to District Intelligence Officer, Camp Forrest, Box 68, NARS, SID, 4SC; Hartman, Forkner, Townsend interview.

8. War Department Special Organization, July 17, 1944; Brady to Knopf, May 6, 1944, Box 68, NARS, SID, 4SC. Michio Nishida to Tsugio, November 20, 1944, Box 69, NARS, SID, 4SC.

9. Jensen, *Army Surveillance,* 215; Hartman, Forkner, Townsend interview.

10. "Reports of Fires, Explosions, and Other Serious Occurrences," July 4, 1942, Box 67, NARS, SID, 4SC; David Kahn, *Hitler's Spies: German Military Intelligence in World War II* (New York: Macmillan, 1978), 327–33; I. C. B. Dear and M. R. D. Foot (eds.), *The Oxford Companion to World War II* (New York: Oxford University Press, 1995), 1202.

11. Security Education; Security Notes No. 10, April 1, 1945, Box 70, NARS, SID, 4SC.

12. Talbert, *Negative Intelligence,* 268–69, n. 3; Sayer and Botting, America's Secret Army, 26.

13. "Report of Special Communist Cases in America," a presentation made to an "anti-subversive seminar" of the Georgia American Legion, January 11–12, 1948, Everett papers.

14. Harvey Klehr et al., *The Secret World of American Communism* (New Haven: Yale University Press, 1995), 205, 210.

15. "Report of Special Communist Cases," n.d., Everett papers.

16. Leonard Dinnerstein, *Antisemitism in America* (New York: Oxford University Press, 1994), 128ff.

17. Communist and German Activities among the Negroes, June 21, 1941, Box 69, NARS, SID, 4SC; First Service Command, Domestic Intelligence Memorandum No. 33, March 13, 1945, Box 72, NARS, SID, 4SC.

18. Sixth Service Command, Domestic Intelligence Memorandum No. 12, February 13, 1945, ibid.

19. Eighth Service Command to Fourth Service Command, April 29, 1945, Box 73, NARS, SID, 4SC.

20. Everett to Commanding General, Camp Shelby, May 1, 1945, ibid.

21. Talbert, *Negative Intelligence,* 268; Hartman, Forkner, Townsend interview.

22. Conclusions—Negro Activities, June 20, 1942, Box 69, NARS, SID, 4SC; First Service Command, Domestic Intelligence Memorandum No. 32, Box 72, NARS, SID, 4SC.

23. Everett to Director of Intelligence, Army Service Forces, July 13, 1945, Box 73, NARS, SID, 4SC.

24. See File 452.4, General (Japanese Balloons), ibid.

25. Transcript of telephone conversation, April ?, 1945, ibid.

26. Officer's and Warrant Officer's Qualification Card Copy, Everett File, NPR; interview of Willis M. Everett III, June 6, 1997.

27. Hartman, Forkner, Townsend interview; "Everett Nuptials Set," undated clipping, Everett papers.

NOTES TO CHAPTER 3

1. Miscellaneous material in Box 72, NARS, SID, 4SC; Officer's and Warrant Officer's Qualification Card, Everett File, NPR; Hartman, Forkner, Townsend interview

2. Willis M. Everett Jr. to Mary Everett, n.d. and November 1, 1945, Everett papers.

3. James H. Critchfield to author, June 20, 1997.

4. Willis M. Everett Jr. to Mary Everett, November 20, 1945, Everett papers.

5. Digest of Everett's correspondence with family, fall 1945, Everett papers.

6. Willis M. Everett Jr. to Mary Everett, November 13, 1945; January 14, 1946, Everett papers.

7. Willis M. Everett Jr. to Mary Everett, November 15, 1945; November 19, 1945; December 11, 1945; January 10, 1946; January 27, 1946, Everett papers.

8. Willis M. Everett Jr. to Mary Everett, November 18, 1945, Everett papers; Randall Balmer and John Fitzmier, *The Presbyterians* (Westport, Conn.: Greenwood Press, 1993), 158–59.

9. Willis M. Everett, Jr. to Mary Everett, November 27, 28, 29, 1945; January 14, 25, 1946, Everett papers.

10. Record in the Graduate Faculties of Political Science, Philosophy and Pure Science, Columbia University in the City of New York; The Adjutant General's Office. Subject: Movement Orders, January 29, 1946, Everett file, NPR.

11. Everett to Family, March 24, 1946; Willis M. Everett to Mary Everett, May 12, 1946, Everett papers.

12. Everett to Family, n.d., Everett papers.

13. Everett to Family, March 24, 26, 1946, Everett papers.

14. Everett to Family, March 27, 28, 1946, Everett papers.

15. Ibid.

16. Everett to Family, March 29, 1946, Everett papers.

17. Everett to Family, March 30, April 1, 3, 1946, Everett papers.

18. Everett to Family, March 31, 1946, Everett papers.

19. Everett to Family, March 29, 1946, Everett papers.

20. Everett to Family, April 2, 5, 1946, Everett papers.

21. Everett to Family, April 8, 10, 1946, Everett papers.

22. Trevor N. Dupuy, *Hitler's Last Gamble: The Battle of the Bulge, December 1944–January 1945* (New York: HarperCollins, 1994), 9–10; Charles B. MacDonald, *A Time for Trumpets: The Untold Story of the Battle of the Bulge* (New York: William Morrow, 1985), 618.

23. James J. Weingartner, *Crossroads of Death: The Story of the Malmedy Massacre and Trial* (Berkeley: University of California Press, 1979), 67–71.

24. Frank M. Buscher, *The U.S. War Crimes Trial Program in Germany, 1946–1955* (Westport, Conn.: Greenwood Press, 1989), 1–2, 9.

25. Everett to Family, April 10, 1946, Everett papers.

26. Konnilyn G. Feig, *Hitler's Death Camps: The Sanity of Madness* (New York: Holmes and Meier, 1979), 48; James J. Weingartner, "Early War Crimes Trials" in Susan D. Bachrach (ed.), *Liberation 1945* (Washington, D.C.: United States Holocaust Memorial Museum, 1995), 83–84.

27. Everett to Family, April 15, 16, 1946, Everett papers; *Malmedy Massacre Investigation Hearings before a Subcommittee of the Committee on Armed Services, United States Senate, Eighty- first Congress, First Session, Pursuant to S. Res. 42* (Washington, D.C.: U.S. Government Printing Office, 1949), hereafter "MMIH," 34.

28. Everett to Herbert Strong, n.d., Everett papers.

29. Everett to Family, April 16, 1946, Everett papers; Diary of Colonel Burton Ellis, entry for April 20, 1946; MMIH, 571–72.

30. Everett to Family, April 23, 1946, Everett papers.

31. Peiper to Everett, April 19, 1946, Everett papers.

32. Everett to Family, April 23, 1946, Everett papers; "Testimony of Colonel Willis M. Everett, Jr. Taken before Colonel J. M. Chambers, Professional Staff Member by Direction of the Senate Subcommittee on the Malmedy Matters, for Inclusion in the Record of the Investigation on Senate Resolution 42, October 10, 1949," MMIH, 1560–61.

33. MMIH, 883–85.

34. MMIH, 890–91; Testimony of Colonel Willis M. Everett Jr., MMIH, 1561; Ellis Diary, entries of April 28 and 29, 1946.

35. MMIH, 923.

36. Testimony of Colonel Willis M. Everett Jr., MMIH, 1556–57.

37. Everett to Family, May 12, 1946, Everett papers.

38. Everett to Family, April 30, 1946, Everett papers.

39. Ellis Diary, entry of April 30, 1946.
40. Everett to Family, May 1, 1946, Everett papers.
41. Everett to Family, May 12, 1946, Everett papers.

NOTES TO CHAPTER 4

1. Charge Sheet, MMIH, 1191–92; Maximilian Koessler, "American War Crimes Trials in Europe," *Georgetown Law Journal* 39 (November 1950): 56.
2. Ibid., 47, 69–71.
3. MMIH, 1382–83; Box 73, NARS, SID, 4SC.
4. Charge Sheet, MMIH, 1192.
5. W. Michael Reisman and Chris T. Antoniou (eds.), *The Laws of War: A Comprehensive Collection of Primary Documents on International Laws Governing Armed Conflict* (New York: Vintage Books, 1994), 233; *U.S. vs. Valentin Bersin, et al.* (hereafter *U.S. v. Bersin*), U.S. National Archives Record Group No. 153, Roll 4, Frames 000487–88, transcript pages 3003–4, hereafter cited in the following form: 153/4/000487–88 (3003–4).
6. *U.S. v. Bersin,* 153/1/000008–75 (3–70).
7. Ibid., 000078–80 (73–75).
8. Ibid., 000081 (76).
9. Ibid., 000082–84 (77–79).
10. Everett to Family, May 16, 1946, Everett papers.
11. *U.S. v. Bersin,* 153/1/000097–102 (92–97).
12. Ibid.
13. Ibid., 000106–07 (101–2).
14. Ibid., 000191–226 (186–221).
15. Ibid., 000233 (228).
16. Ibid., 000287–88 (274–75).
17. Ibid., 000296, 000298–99 (283, 285–86).
18. Ibid., 000335 (322).
19. Ibid., 000131 (126), 000168 (163), 000245 (240).
20. Ibid., 000419–36 (406–23).
21. Ibid., 000526 (513).
22. Ibid., 000531 (518).
23. Ibid., 000569–74 (550–55).
24. Everett to Family, May 20, 23, Everett papers.
25. *U.S. v. Bersin,* 153/1/000923–25, 000934–35 (896–98, 907–8).
26. Ibid., 000977–79 (950–52).
27. Ibid., 000980 (953).
28. Everett to Family, May 27, 1946, Everett papers.
29. Everett to Family, May 26, 1946, Everett papers.
30. Everett to Family, May 28, 1946, Everett papers.

31. *U.S. v. Bersin*, 153/1/001046–52, 001058–64, 001067–87 (1015–21, 1027–33, 1036–56).

32. Ibid., 001107–17 (1076–86).

33. Ibid., 001022–27 (9919–6).

34. Ibid., 001128–29 (1097–98).

35. Ibid., 000718 (699).

36. Ibid., 000118–24 (113–190); Koessler, "American War Crimes Trials," 65–66.

37. Ibid., 2/000364–69 (1474–79).

38. Ibid., 000388–94 (1498–1504).

39. See, for example, ibid., 1/000151–55 (146–50).

40. Ibid., 2/000469 (1579).

NOTES TO CHAPTER 5

1. Everett to Family, May 29, 1946, Everett papers.

2. Everett to Son, June 3, 1946; Everett to "Dearest Kids," June 4, 1946, Everett papers.

3. Everett to Family, June 7, 1946, Everett papers.

4. Ibid.

5. Everett to Family, June 7, 1946, Everett papers.

6. Everett to Family, June 11, 1946, Everett papers.

7. Brigadier General William K. Harrison to Adjutant General, May 27, 1946, Records of the Adjutant General's Office, NARS, RG 407, AG 000.5.

8. Everett to Family, June 14, 1946, Everett papers.

9. *U.S. v. Bersin*, 153/2/000473–77 (1580–84).

10. Ibid., 000495–97 (1602–4), 000500–000505 (1607–12).

11. Internal Route Slip, Headquarters, U.S. Forces, European Theater. Subject: Discharge of German Prisoners of War, April 26, 1946, ibid., 6/000705.

12. Ibid., 2/000509–15 (1616–22).

13. Ibid., 000517 (1624).

14. Ibid., 000519 (1626).

15. Ibid., 000519–20 (1626–27).

16. Ibid., 000524–42 (1631–49), 000543–83 (1650–90).

17. Everett to Family, June 19, 1946, Everett papers.

18. *U.S. v. Bersin*, 153/3/000035–44 (1815–23).

19. Ibid., 000050–51 (1829–30).

20. "Behind the German Lines, Annexe I to Part C of Intelligence Notes No. 43 dated 6 January 1945," p. 3, ibid., 6/000709; MMIH, 1429.

21. *U.S. v. Bersin*, 153/3/000054 (1833).

22. Ibid., 000054–55 (1833–34).

23. Ibid., 000057–61 (1836–40).

24. Ibid., 000067–73 (1846–52).

25. Everett to Family, June 20, 1946, Everett papers.

26. "Statements by Prisoner SS Standf. Joachim Peiper," Sept. 15, 1945, Records of the Adjutant General's Office, NARS, RG 407, 333.9, McCown, Hal D. "Joachim" was Peiper's given name. He preferred "Jochen." By war's end. He had attained the rank of *Standartenführer*, or Colonel.

27. *U.S. v. Bersin*, 153/3/000107 (1886).

28. Ibid., 000107–08 (1886–87).

29. Ibid., 000109–12 (1888–91).

30. Ibid., 000112, 000120–22, 000129–33 (1891, 1899–1901, 1908–11).

31. Ibid., 000115–16, 000138–60 (1894–95, 1917–39).

32. Ibid., 000177–86 (1956–65); Everett to Family, June 21 & 22, 1946, Everett papers.

33. Ibid., 000200 (1979).

34. Ibid., 000208 (1987).

35. Ibid., 000209–10 (1988–90).

36. Ibid., 000214–38 (1993–2017).

37. Everett to Family, June 22, 1946, Everett papers.

38. U.S. vs. Bersin, 153/3/000266–67 (2041–42).

39. Ibid., 000267 (2042).

40. Everett to Family, June 24, 1946, Everett papers.

41. U.S. vs. Bersin, 153/3/000521–24 (2291–92), 000563–70 (2333–40), 4/000269–73 (2788–91).

42. Ibid., 3/000496–504 (2271–79).

43. Ibid., 000578–85 (2348–55), 000609 (2379).

44. Ibid., 000610–12 (2380–82), 000432 (2207).

45. Ibid., 000621–26 (2391–96); Everett to Family, June 25–29, 1946, Everett papers.

46. Peiper to Everett, July 4, 1946, Everett papers.

47. *U.S. v. Bersin*, 153/4/000034–39 (2558–62).

48. Ibid., 000300 (2819), 000306–8 (2825–27), 000403 (2923).

49. Ibid., 000412–13 (2932–33), 000422–27 (2938–43).

50. Exhibit P-132, ibid., 000466 [4,33]70 (2982–86); 000471–82 (2987–98).

51. Ibid., 000486–552 (3002–68).

52. Everett to Family, July 4, 1946, Everett papers.

53. Weingartner, *Crossroads of Death*, 155–58.

54. *U.S. v. Bersin*, 153/4/000693–94 (3206–7).

55. Ibid., 000694–95 (3207–8).

56. Ibid., 000695 (3208); Everett to Family, July 11, 1946, Everett papers.

57. Ibid., 000695 (3208); Everett to Family, July 11, 1946, Everett papers.

58. *U.S. v. Bersin*, 153/4/000696 (3209).

59. Ibid., 0006967–37 (3209–50)

60. Ibid., 000737 (3209–50); Peiper to Everett, July 4, 1946, Everett papers.

NOTES TO CHAPTER 6

1. Everett to Family, July 13, 1946, Everett papers.
2. Ibid.
3. Everett to Family, July 14, 1946, Everett papers.
4. *U.S. v. Bersin*, 153/4/000737–57 (3751–3720).
5. Everett to Family, July 17, 1946, Everett papers.
6. Ibid.
7. Everett to Family, July 23, August 5, 1946, Everett papers.
8. Everett to Family, August 3, 6, 1946, Everett papers.
9. Everett to Family, August 2, 1946, Everett papers.
10. Everett to Mary, August 9, 1946; Everett to Mary Campbell and Kil, August 11, 1946, Everett papers.
11. Ibid.
12. Everett to Family, August 16, 17, 18, 1946, Everett papers.
13. Everett to Family, August 19, 20, September 4, 1946, Everett papers.
14. Everett to Family, September 7, 1946, Everett papers.
15. MMIH, 925.
16. Deputy Theater Judge Advocate's Office, War Crimes Group, United States Forces, European Theater, "War Crimes Group Conference," Records of the Judge Advocate General's Office, RG 407, NARS.
17. Everett to Family, September 6–7, 1946, Everett papers.
18. Headquarters, U.S. Forces, European Theater, to Everett, November 4, 1946, Everett papers; Everett interview, June 6, 1997.
19. Ibid.; "What Democracy Are We Demonstrating to Europe and the World?" undated handwritten manuscript, Everett papers.
20. Ibid.
21. Deputy Theater Judge Advocate's Office, 7708 War Crimes Group, USFET, December 19, 1946; Headquarters, Third United States Army, Letter Orders No. 1344, December 27, 1947; Headquarters, Fort McPherson, Special Orders No. 87, April 16, 1947, Everett File, NPR.

NOTES TO CHAPTER 7

1. "Christmas 1946 War Crimes," Everett papers.
2. On the Biscari incident, see James J. Weingartner, "Massacre at Biscari: Patton and an American War Crime," *Historian* 52 (November 1989): 24–39.
3. See, for example: Stephen E. Ambrose, *Citizen Soldiers: The U.S. Army from the Normandy Beaches to the Bulge to the Surrender of Germany, June 7,*

1944–May 7, 1945 (New York: Simon and Schuster, 1997), 352–53; Gerald F. Linderman, *The World within War: America's Combat Experience in World War II* (New York: Free Press, 1997), 127–31; John C. McManus, *The Deadly Brotherhood: The American Combat Soldier in World War II* (Novato: Presidio Press, 1998), 192–96; Peter Schrijvers, *The Crash of Ruin: American Combat Soldiers in Europe during World War II* (New York: New York University Press, 1998), 78–80. Reports of the Malmedy massacre circulating among U.S. troops provided motivation for the killing of German prisoners and would-be prisoners during the winter of 1944–45. Ibid., 79.

4. Bailey to Judge Advocate General, June 5, 1946; Bailey to Everett, March 24, July 11, 1947, Everett papers.

5. Memorandum for Judge Patterson, February 1, 1944, Records of the U.S. Army Judiciary (Biscari Case).

6. "Testimony of Colonel Homer W. Jones," February 17, 1944, pp. 24, 29, Records of the Office of the Inspector General, NARS, Record Group 159, File 333.9.

7. "Army Justice in Europe," *St. Louis Globe-Democrat,* September 17, 1946.

8. "Charge by SS of GI Beatings Is Kept Secret," *New York Times,* January 23, 1947.

9. "Malmedy Plea Stirs Capital," *Stars and Stripes,* January 27, 1947.

10. Everett to Mickelwaite, January 28, 1947, Everett papers.

11. "Army Reveals Defense Brief in Trial of Nazis: 'Malmedy Massacre' Case Is Called Parody on Justice; Confessions Are Impugned," *New York Times,* January 29, 1947.

12. Everett to Mickelwaite, February 28, 1947, Everett papers.

13. Report of the Deputy Judge Advocate for War Crimes, European Command, June 1944–July 1948, p. 34, NARS, RG 338.

14. Everett to Mickelwaite, February 28, 1947, Everett papers.

15. MMIH, 1338–44, 1351, 1355, 1365–66.

16. Ibid., 1047.

17. Resume of William Dowdell Denson, Everett papers.

18. James J. Weingartner, "Comprehending Mass Murder: The Buchenwald Trial of 1947," *Midwest Quarterly* 30 (Winter 1989): 249.

19. MMIH, 1063.

20. Huebner to Everett, March 27, 1947, Everett papers.

21. Richard L. Merritt, *Democracy Imposed: U.S. Occupation Policy and the German Public, 1945–1949* (New Haven: Yale University Press, 1995), 159–62.

22. *U.S. v. Bersin,* 153/2/000668–3/000033 (1775–1813).

23. Ziemssen to Everett, April 9, 1947, Everett papers.

24. Everett to Hubbert, June 17, 1947, Everett papers.

25. Ibid.

26. Young to Everett, July 10, 1947, Everett papers.

27. Everett to Reid, July 26, 1947, Everett papers.

28. Reedy to Everett, August ?, 1947, Everett papers.

29. Colonel T. Sakia (?)-Bosch to Everett, August 13, 1947, and February 27, 1948, Everett papers.

30. MMIH, 927; Weingartner, *Crossroads of Death*, 175–79.

31. MMIH, 1063.

32. Dwinell to Everett, June 18, 1947, Everett papers.

33. Rosenfeld to Everett, October 8, 1947, Everett papers.

34. Weingartner, *Crossroads of Death*, 133.

35. James J. Weingartner, "Otto Skorzeny and the Laws of War," *Journal of Military History* 55 (April 1991): 217–21.

36. Koerner to Everett, April 5, 1947; Everett to Koerner, May 28, 1947, Everett papers.

37. Peiper to Everett, July 14, 1946, Everett papers.

38. Sigurd Peiper to Everett, July 14, 1946, Everett papers.

39. Sigurd Peiper to Everett, June 10, 1947, Everett papers.

40. Everett to Sigurd Peiper, November 6, 1947; Sigurd Peiper to Everett, November 16, 1947, Everett papers.

41. Everett to Clay, January 10, 1948, Everett papers.

42. Everett to Wallens, January 12, 1948, Everett papers.

43. MMIH, 1145–46, 1164.

44. Weingartner, *Crossroads of Death*, 180–83.

45. MMIH, 1165.

46. Ibid., 447.

47. Weingartner, *Crossroads of Death*, 184–85.

NOTES TO CHAPTER 8

1. Everett to Wahler, February 24, 1948; Wahler to Everett, February 27, 1948, Everett papers.

2. "Nazi Trial Judge Rips Injustice," *Chicago Tribune*, February 23, 1948; "Judge Stands on Criticism of U.S. Trial," *Chicago Tribune*, February 24, 1948.

3. Everett to Wennerstrum, March 8, 1948, Everett papers.

4. White to Everett, May 21, 1948, Everett papers.

5. White to Wennerstrum, June 1, 1948, Everett papers.

6. Everett to Wahler, March 11, 1948, Everett papers.

7. Everett to Sally and Irving Hayett, March 8, 1948, Everett papers.

8. Everett to Leer, March 17, 1948, Everett papers.

9. Everett to Dwinell, March 16, 1948, Everett papers.

10. Everett to Young, March 15, 1948, Everett papers.

11. Dwinell to Everett, February 13, 1948, Everett papers.

12. War Crimes Branch to Everett, April 12, 1948, Everett papers.

13. Sigurd Peiper to Everett, March 26, 1948, Everett papers.

14. Huebner to Everett, January 30, 1948, Everett papers.

15. John A. Appleman, *Military Tribunals and International Crimes* (Westport, Conn.: Greenwood Press, 1971), 345–56; Frank Reel, *The Case of General Yamashita* (Chicago: University of Chicago Press, 1949), 239.

16. Murphy to Everett, April 22, 1948, Everett papers.

17. Everett to Charles E. Cropley, May 12, 1948, Everett papers.

18. E. P. Cullinan (for Cropley) to Everett, May 14, 1948, Everett papers.

19. *In the Supreme Court of the United States, Willis M. Everett, Jr., on behalf of Valentin Bersin, et al., Petitioner, vs. Harry S. Truman, James V. Forrestal, Kenneth C. Royall, General Omar N. Bradley, Thomas C. Clark, Respondents* (hereafter *Everett v. Truman*), i.

20. *United States Supreme Court, Law. ed. Advance Opinions, 1947–1948,* Vol. 92, No. 17 (Rochester: Lawyers Cooperative Publishing Co., 1948), 1051–52.

21. Koessler, "American War Crimes Trials," 102–3.

22. *Everett v. Truman,* "Petition," 5, 9–11, 13–14, 16, 64ff.

23. Ibid., "General Statement," 3.

24. Ibid., "Petition," 5–7.

25. Ibid., p. 16; Everett to Wahler, March 11, 1948, Everett papers.

26. Strong to Everett, May 19, 1948, Everett papers.

27. Gary M. Pomerantz, *Where Peachtree Meets Sweet Auburn: The Saga of Two Families and the Making of Atlanta* (New York: Scribner, 1996), 153.

28. Everett to Clay, January 10, 1948, with enclosure, Everett papers; Dinnerstein, *Antisemitism in America,* 136.

29. Davis to Everett, May 19, 1948, Everett papers.

30. Everett to Davis, May 20, 1948, Everett papers.

31. George to Everett, May 22, 1948, Everett papers.

32. MMIH, 4.

33. Ibid.; Young to Everett, May 25, 1948, Everett papers.

34. MMIH, 4; Weingartner, *Crossroads of Death,* 191.

35. Dwinell to Everett, June 17, 1948, Everett papers.

36. Lucius D. Clay, *Decision in Germany* (New York: Doubleday, 195), 236–37.

37. Neuhäusler to Case et al., March 24, 1948, Everett papers.

38. Whiting to Everett, May 1, 1948, Everett papers.

39. Everett to Whiting, May 10, 1948, Everett papers.

40. Whiting to Case, May 18, 1948, Everett papers.

41. Whiting to Everett, May 18, 1948, Everett papers.

42. Whiting to Everett, May 22, 1948, Everett papers.

43. Case to Eberle, n.d. but in response to a letter of May 20, 1948, Everett papers.

44. Whiting to Everett, May 26, 1948, Everett papers.

45. Muench to Everett, May 26, 1948, Everett papers.

46. Everett to Reedy, May 14, 1948, Everett papers.

47. Leer to War Crimes Group, Post–Trial Section, April 2, 1948, Everett papers.

48. Huebler affidavit, May 6, 1948, Everett papers.

49. Knorr affidavit, May 29, 1948, Everett papers.

50. Von Chamier affidavit, April 11, 1948, Everett papers.

51. Bartels affidavit, March 15, 1948, Everett papers.

52. Reiser affidavit, April 8, 1948, Everett papers.

53. Jirasek affidavit, April 29, 1948, Everett papers.

54. Everett to Wahler, June 8, 1948, Everett papers.

55. McClure to House of Delegates, American Bar Association, July 22, 1948, Everett papers.

56. MMIH, 231–32; "Van Roden Criticises Tactics Used to Make Nazis Confess," *Evening Bulletin,* October 8, 1948.

57. Everett to Mrs. van Roden, August 4, 1948, Everett papers; Iris Gorsuch to Everett, August 6, 1948, Everett papers.

58. Van Roden to Everett, August 16, 1948, Everett papers.

59. Van Roden to Everett, August 18, 1948, Everett papers.

60. Everett to Jackson, November 16 and 30, Everett papers.

61. Everett to Owen Cunningham, December 7, 1948, Everett papers; Clark Clifford (with Richard Holbrooke), *Counsel to the President: A Memoir* (New York: Random House, 1991), 72.

62. Van Roden to Everett, October 4, 1948, Everett papers.

63. Weingartner, *Crossroads of Death,* 191; MMIH, 4.

64. "Van Roden Criticises Tactics," *Evening Bulletin,* October 8, 1948.

65. Van Roden to Everett, October 18, 1949, Everett papers.

66. Ibid.

67. Van Roden to Everett, October 28, 1948, Everett papers.

68. Everett to Green, November 5, 1948, Everett papers.

69. Green to Everett, November 10, 1948, Everett papers.

70. Weingartner, "Comprehending Mass Murder," 251.

71. See *Conduct of Ilse Koch War Crimes Trials: Hearings before the Investigation Subcommittee of the Committee on Expenditures in the Executive Departments, United States Senate, Eightieth Congress, Second Session, Part 5, September 28, December 8 and 9, 1948* (Washington: U.S. Government Printing Office, 1948).

72. Van Roden to Everett, October 4, 1948, Everett papers; Everett to Muench, October 25, 1948, Everett papers.

73. Everett to Simpson, November 15, 1948, Everett papers.

74. Simpson to Everett, November 26, 1948, Everett papers.

75. Ellis to Hubbert, May 25, 1948, NARS, RG 338, Box B.

76. Ellis affidavit, October 27, 1948, 5.

77. Ibid., 7–9.

78. Ibid., 12.

79. Ibid., 4, 12, 14.

80. Ibid., 13–14.

81. Ibid., 7.

82. Ellis's affidavit was reproduced in MMIH, 1217–1223. Everett's penciled comment is on page 1220 of his copy.

83. Ellis affidavit, 14–15.

84. "Officer Denies Duress at Dachau," *Stars and Stripes,* October 13, 1948.

85. "The Judicial Processes Concerning the Malmedy War Criminals: Digest of Editorial and Column Opinion, 22 May 1946–27 January 1949," Department of the Army, Public Information Division, Analysis Branch, January 27, 1949, p. 2.

86. Everett to Huebner, December 2, 1948, Everett papers.

87. Huebner to Everett, December 21, 1948, Everett papers.

88. Everett to van Roden, December 29, 1948, Everett papers.

89. Ibid.

90. Simpson to Everett, December 31, 1948, Everett papers.

91. Everett to Jackson, January 31, 1949, Everett papers; Jackson to Everett, February 3, 1949, Everett papers.

92. Everett to Wennerstrum, December 29, 1948, Everett papers.

93. Wennerstrum to Everett, December 31, 1948, Everett papers.

94. "Paper by Charles F. Wennerstrum Presented at a Joint Luncheon Meeting of Section of International and Comparative Law and Junior Bar Conference at the Annual Meeting of the American Bar Association," September 7, 1948, pp. 5–6. Copy in Everett papers.

NOTES TO CHAPTER 9

1. Simpson Commission Report, September 14, 1948, Appendix III, pp. 1–2, NARS, RG 338.

2. Wahler to Everett, Jan. 7, 1949, Everett papers.

3. Whiting to Everett, January 10, 1949, Everett papers.

4. George to Everett, January 29, 1949, Everett papers; Everett to George, February 7, 1949, Everett papers.

5. *Time* 81 (January 17, 1949): 19.

6. William Henry Chamberlin, "A Scandal Exposed," *New Leader* 32 (January 15, 1949): 16.

7. Judge Edward L. van Roden, "American Atrocities in Germany," *Progressive* (February 1949): 21–22. The article had actually been written by James Finucane from a speech by van Roden. MMIH, 202–3

8. Everett to Truman, January 24, 1949, Everett papers.

9. Everett to Clark, January 24, 1949, Everett papers; Washington to Everett, February 4, 1949, Everett papers.

10. Everett to Whiting, February 16, 1949, Everett papers; Whiting to Everett, February 18, 1949, Everett papers; Everett to Whiting, February 25, 1949, Everett papers.

11. Jackson to Everett, February 3, 18, 1949, Everett papers.

12. Abram to Everett, April 21, 1949, Everett papers.

13. "To the International Court of Justice at The Hague, Holland and to the Honorable Judges Thereof Through the Registrar," n.d., Everett papers.

14. Everett to Wennerstrum, February 25, 1949, Everett papers.

15. Hambro to Everett, March 5, 1949, Everett papers.

16. Everett to Huebner, January 31, 1949, Everett papers.

17. Huebner to Everett, February 10, 1949, Everett papers.

18. Young to Everett, February 15, 1949, Everett papers.

19. Weingartner, *Crossroads of Death*, 191–94.

20. Hayett to Luce, January 14, 1949, Papers of Harry S. Truman, Official File, Harry S. Truman Library.

21. Weingartner, *Crossroads of Death*, 194.

22. Ibid., 195.

23. Jean E. Smith, ed., *The Papers of General Lucius D. Clay, Germany, 1945–49* (Bloomington: Indiana University Press, 1974), II, 1041.

24. Clay to Department of the Army for CSAD, March 12, 1949, NARS, RG 338.

25. Everett affidavit, June 23, 1949, NPR.

26. *Papers of General Lucius D. Clay*, II, 1012–13.

27. *Congressional Record, Proceedings and Debates of the 81st Congress, First Session*, Vol. 95, No. 37 (March 10, 1949), 2203–9.

28. Royall to Truman, March 14, 1949, Truman Library; Royall to McCarthy, March 14, 1949, Truman Library.

29. Townsend to McCarthy, March 24, 1949, Everett papers.

30. Hoey to Townsend, March 28, 1949, Everett papers; Tydings to Townsend, March 31, 1949, Everett papers.

31. McCarthy to Townsend, April 16, 1949, Everett papers.

32. Thomas C. Reeves, *The Life and Times of Joe McCarthy: A Biography* (New York: Stein and Day, 1982), 167.

33. Record of press conference, March 3, 1949, Everett papers.

34. MMIH, 803.

35. Gurney to Whiting, April 28, 1949, Everett papers.

36. MMIH, 1.

37. Everett to Wahler, April 22, 1949, Everett papers.

38. Reeves, *McCarthy*, 168–69.

39. MMIH, 303–19; Finucane to Everett, December 31, 1948, Everett papers; van Roden to Everett, February 18, 1949, Everett papers.

40. Finucane to Everett, May 2, 10, 1949, Everett papers.

41. MMIH, 1556.

42. Strong to McCarthy, April 25, 1949, Everett papers.

43. MMIH, 572, 576–78, 580–84, 595–96.

44. Wahler to Everett, May 13, 1949, Everett papers.

45. MMIH, 434–36.

46. Ibid., 1169–80.

47. Ibid., 161.

48. Ibid., 546–49.

49. Ibid., 844–47, 854, 857.

50. Ibid., 902.

51. Weingartner, *Crossroads of Death*, 215–16, 218; "Summary Report on the Medical Examination of the Malmedy Prisoners," MMIH, 1616–18.

52. *Malmedy Massacre Investigation, Report of Subcommittee on Armed Services, United States Senate* (Washington, D.C.: U.S. Government Printing Office, 1949), 16.

53. Ibid., 7–8.

54. Ibid., 17–18.

55. Ibid., 19.

56. Ibid.

57. Ibid., 22–26.

58. Ibid., 32–35.

59. Everett to Finucane, n.d., Everett papers.

60. Everett to McCarthy, May 11, 1949, Everett papers.

61. Everett to McCarthy, June 2, 1949, Everett papers.

62. McCarthy to Everett, June 2, 1949, Everett papers.

63. Everett to McCarthy, June 2, 1949, Everett papers.

NOTES TO CHAPTER 10

1. Undated notes from Everett to his wife during her hospitalization, Everett papers.

2. Everett affidavit, June 23, 1949, NPR; Brigadier General George H. Weems to Everett, October 17, 1950, NPR.

3. Franz Josef Schoeningh, "Ein Michael Kohlhaas in Atlanta," *Süddeutsche Zeitung*, September 9, 1949.

4. MMIH, 1637.

5. Peiper to Everett, September 21, 1949, Everett papers.

6. Everett to Davis, October 1, 1949, Everett papers.

7. Davis to Everett, October 4, 1949, Everett papers.

8. Everett to Gray, August 17, 1949, Everett papers.

9. Everett to George T. Washington, December 14, 1949, Everett papers.

10. John Mendelsohn, "War Crimes Trials and Clemency in Germany and Japan," in Robert Wolfe (ed.), *Americans as Proconsuls: American Military Government in Germany and Japan, 1944–1952* (Carbondale and Edwardsville: Southern Illinois University Press), 249–52.

11. Kuhn to Everett, January 10, 1950, Everett papers.

12. Everett to Kuhn, January 14, 1950, Everett papers.

13. Kuhn to Everett, January 24 & April 12, 1950, Everett papers.

14. Everett to Wennerstrum, April 16, 1950, Everett papers.

15. Ibid.

16. Davis to Everett, March 24, 1950, Everett papers; Everett to Davis, April 20, 1950, Everett papers.

17. Leer to Everett, December 16, 1950, Everett papers; Everett to McCloy, January 7, 1951, Everett papers.

18. Borom to Everett, January 23, 1951, Everett papers.

19. Everett to Borom, April 24, 1951, Everett papers.

20. "Text of Headquarters European Command Press Release 31 January 1951," Everett papers.

21. Peiper to Everett, February 6, 1951, Everett papers.

22. Willi Schaefer to Everett, June 6, 1951, Everett papers.

23. Wennerstrum to Everett, February 14, 1951, Everett papers.

24. Van Roden to Everett, February 5, 1951, Everett papers.

25. Simpson to Everett, February 8, 1951, Everett papers.

26. Jackson to Everett, February 13, 1951, Everett papers.

27. Reeves, *McCarthy*, 348–49.

28. "Pearson Accuses McCarthy of Giving Boost to Communistic Propaganda," *Atlanta Journal,* January 15, 1951.

29. Everett to McCarthy, February 13, 1951, Everett papers.

30. Buscher, *U.S. War Crimes Trial Program,* 71.

31. *Die Strasse* 4 (January 11, 1951): 8; ibid. (January 28, 1951): 1; ibid. (February 4, 1951): 9.

32. Ibid., 1.

33. Verg to Everett, February 3, 1951, Everett papers.

34. Buscher, *U.S. War Crimes Trial Program,* 63.

35. Rietz to Everett, March 12, 1951, Everett papers.

36. Unidentified Landsberg prisoners to Everett, January 30, 1951, Everett papers.

37. Meuschel to Everett, December 14, 1953, Everett papers.

38. Everett to Deane, June 29, 1951, Everett papers.

39. Kraemer to Everett, January 25, 1952, Everett papers.

40. Federal Bureau of Investigation, File # 77-44545 (Willis Mead Everett Jr.), 5.

41. Ibid., 14.

42. Smiley to Everett, August 22, 1952, Everett papers.

43. Interview of Kiliaen Townsend, August 18, 1996.

44. Signature illegible to Everett, November 8, 1952, Everett papers.

45. Freda Utley, *The High Cost of Vengeance: How Our German Policy Is Leading Us to Bankruptcy and War* (Chicago: Henry Regnery, 1949), 185–88; Freda Utley, "Second Chance in Germany," *American Legion Magazine* (October 1953): 49; Freda Utley, "Malmedy and McCarthy," *American Mercury* (November 1954): 55.

46. Utley, "Malmedy and McCarthy."

47. Everett to Editor, *Atlanta Journal,* October 6, 1954.

48. "Letters to the Times," *New York Times,* January 19, 1956.

49. Muench to Dulles, December 25, 1955, Everett papers.

50. Muench to Everett, December 29, 1955, Everett papers.

51. Undated draft of letter to Dulles, Everett papers.

52. "Malmedy Massacre: Second Butcher Free," *American Legion Magazine* (February 1957): 37.

53. Everett to Diefenthal, June 28, 1956, Everett papers.

54. Everett to son, October 15, 1952, Everett papers.

55. Everett to son, October 23, 1956, Everett papers.

56. Toland to Everett, February 18, 1958, Everett papers.

57. Everett to Toland, February 27, 1958, Everett papers.

58. Toland to Everett, March 3, 1958, Everett papers.

59. John Toland, *Battle: The Story of the Bulge* (New York: Random House, 1959), 382.

60. Will Berthold, "Mitgefangen, Mitgehangen, Malmedy," *Revue* 30 (July 27, 1957): 16.

61. Everett to Schoenbach, July 30, 1958, Everett papers.

62. Mueller to Everett, October 9, 1959, Everett papers.

63. Everett to Mueller, October 19, 1959, Everett papers.

64. Everett to Peiper, November 24, 1959, Everett papers.

65. Sholar to Everett, November 2, 1959, Everett papers.

66. Everett to Peiper, November 24, 1959, Everett papers.

67. Peiper to Everett, December 13, 1959, Everett papers.

68. Everett to Peiper, December 22, 1959, Everett papers.

69. Everett to Peiper, February 5, 1960, Everett papers.

70. The Men of Gamma Eta to "Dear Wooglin," March 10, 1960, Everett papers.

71. Interview of Dave McKenney, June 5, 1997.

NOTES TO THE EPILOGUE

1. *Atlanta Journal,* April 5, 1960.

2. *Presbyterian Newsletter,* April 25, 1960.

3. Davis to Mary Everett, April 6, 1960, Everett papers; Congressman and Mrs. Carl Vinson to Mary Everett, April 5, 1960, Everett papers.

4. Peiper to Mary Everett, December (?), 1975, Everett papers.

5. Jens Westemeier, *Joachim Peiper: Eine Biographie* (Osnabrück: Biblio Verlag, 1996), 150.

6. Members of Everett's family believe that a film studio gave consideration in the late fifties to producing a motion picture with Henry Fonda in the role of Everett but can supply no documentation.

7. Buscher, *U.S. War Crimes Trial Program,* 29–44.

8. "Senior Officer Oral History Program: Colonel Burton Ellis, USA, Retired," Interview with Stephen F. Lancaster, 1988, U.S. Army Military History Institute, Carlisle, Pa. 73–74.

9. See Kristen Renwick Monroe's "How Identity and Perspective Constrain Choice," paper presented at the 1998 meeting of the American Political Science Association, Boston, September 3–6, 1998.

Index

Abram, Morris B., 182
Achille, Andre, testimony of, 69
Adenauer, Konrad, 205
Administration of Justice Review Board, 178, 184, 186, 187, 191
African American "army," 23
African Americans, and wartime fear of subversion, 20
Aisemont, recapture of, 70
Allegheny College, and Willis Everett Sr., 1
American Bar Association, and war crimes trials, 162, 163, 175
American Legion: Everett and, 12, 21; "Red scare" and, 11
American Legion, on Malmedy trial, 215, 217
American Mercury, on Malmedy trial, 215
Anti-Semitism, 129, 203; Everett and, 31, 206, 214, 217; McCarthy and, 210; Bishop Muench and, 159; Senate Malmedy investigation and, 195; wartime U.S. and, 22–23
Antwerp, 132
Ardennes offensive, 139, 162, 170. *See also* Battle of the Bulge
Army, Department of the, 148, 166, 167, 177, 184, 189, 212
Army, Secretary of the, 177, 188
Associated Press, 121
Athanason, Colonel, 35
Atlanta: early growth of, 1–2; openness to Northerners, 2; General Sherman and, 2
Atlanta Journal, 210, 216, 224
Atlanta Law School, 5

Ba'hai, and wartime fears of subversion, 23
Bailey, James J., on beating of German prisoners, 194
Bailey, Theodore L., on killing of German WWI prisoners, 119

Baldwin, Senator Raymond, and Malmedy investigation, 190–92
Bartels, Bernhard, and killing of American prisoners, 161–62
Battle of the Bulge, 38. *See also* Ardennes offensive
Baugnez crossroads, 54, 83
Belfor, Sophie, 29, 31, 32
Belgium, and Malmedy trial jurisdiction, 52
Bersin, Valentin, 149, 188; sentenced to death, 109
Berthold, Will, article by, on Malmedy affair, 219
Beta Theta Pi: Everett adviser for, 218; Everett's death and, 222–23
Biscari, murder of Axis prisoners near, 118, 119
Blockian, Father Louis, and alleged murders in La Gleize, 99
Boltz, Marcel, release of, by U.S. Army, 103, 128
Borom, Lieutenant Colonel T. L., and review of Malmedy trial, 207, 208
Bradley, General Omar N., 149
Brady, Colonel Johnson, and 1800th Engineer General Service Battalion, 18
Bresee, Colonel Howard, 111, 143, 158; and Everett, 77–78; Christmas greetings of, 117; review of Malmedy case, 138, 140, 147
Buchenwald, 118, 180, 206, 208; trial, 167–68. *See also* Koch, Ilse
Budik, Johann, testimony of, 57
Bull, General Harold, 111
Büllingen, 96, 170; alleged murders in, 54, 66–67, 98

Camp Croft, 17
Camp Forrest, 1800th Engineers and, 17

Camp McClellan, 9
Camp Shelby, 23; 1800th Engineers and, 19
Capitol City Club, 17
Carpenter, Lieutenant Colonel Edwin, 171; allegations of duress, 44
Carroll, Captain Earl J., on U.S. military justice in Europe, 119–20
Case, Senator Francis, 155, 157, 158, 159, 164
Chalmers, Franklin S., 7–8
Chamberlain Institute and Female College, and Willis M. Everett Sr., 1
Chamberlin, William Henry, 180
Chambers, Joseph, and Senate Malmedy investigation, 192
Chamier, Willi von, sworn statements of, 161
Cheneux, 105
Chicago Tribune, 143, 145, 150, 172
Chrisenger, Captain, at La Gleize, 86
Christ, Friedrich, 162
Civilian Security Education Committees, 20
Clark, Attorney General Thomas C., 181–82
Clark, Judge William, and release of Sepp Dietrich, 216
Clark University, Everett family's service to, 2, 9, 219
Clay, General Lucius D., 128, 136, 141, 143, 147, 152, 154, 155, 163, 164, 169, 173, 174, 178, 179, 183, 184, 187, 190, 205, 207; Everett's letter to, 137; Harbaugh's recommendations, 142; review of Malmedy case, 125; Senator William Langer and, 189
Cold War, 226
Colinet, Antoine, testimony of, 70
Columbia University, Everett arrives at, 27–28
Columbus Evening Dispatch, 173
Communism: post-World War I perceived threat of, 11–12; World War II fear of, 20
Congressional Record, Langer inserts Everett's Supreme Court petition in, 189
Conyers, Everett farm at, 31
Corbin, Colonel, 171; allegations of duress and, 44; assists Everett in securing German confessions, 46; and Everett, 77–78

Counter Intelligence Corps (CIC), 115; domestic intelligence role of, 15
Crawford, Lieutenant Colonel Homer B., examines witness, 67
Cullinan, E. P., 149
Curry, Dr., 112

Dachau, 150, 160; concentration camp at, 39–40, 75, 117, 208; German defendants transferred to, 42; town of, 47, 112; trial of operators of, 124, 174; war crimes trials at, 49–50, 79, 113, 143, 157, 163, 165, 166, 167, 177, 215
Daily Worker, 173
Dalbey, Brigadier General Josiah T., 52, 54, 56, 81, 88, 94–95, 104, 110, 119, 129; Everett's opinion of, 68; nervousness of, 53; opens trial, 51; president of Malmedy court, 50; pronounces sentences, 108–9
Daniel, Dan, 217
Davis, Elmer, 215
Davis, Congressman James, 179, 206; Everett and, 153–54, 155, 203–4, 224; Ku Klux Klan and, 151
Deane, Lieutenant Colonel J. R., 212
Deck, Major Lucius, 27
Delcourt, Henri, testimony of, 69
Democratic Party, Everett and, 214
Denson, Colonel William, 108, 131, 174; Buchenwald trial and, 124; Dachau trial and, 124; review of Malmedy case, 124, 126, 129, 130; Mauthausen trial and, 124
Detroit, race riots in, 20
Dewey, John, 180
Diefenthal, Josef, 43, 159; Everett and, 217
Diefenthal, Magda, 159
Dietrich, "Sepp," 54, 90, 103, 117; life sentence of, 109; pre-attack conference and, 83; release of, 216; review of conviction, 139; sworn statement of, 58
Dixon, Kenneth L., 173
Dluski, John M., deposition of, 66
Dobyns, Samuel, testimony of, 63
Douglas, Elsie, 175
Douglas, Joseph A., and African Americans in the U.S. Army, 24
Drew Field, suspected sabotage at, 19
Dulles, John Foster, 216
Durst, Colonel Robert, and Skorzeny trial, 132

Dwinell, Lieutenant Colonel John, 41, 101, 107, 120, 122, 155; Bresee board and, 140–41; cooperation of German defendants, 47; cross-examination of Kirschbaum, 73–74; desire to leave Dachau, 131; defense effort, 77, 79; Everett and, 147, 154; moves to strike depositions, 66; objects to sworn statements, 72; Senate Malmedy investigation and, 148

Elias, Jean, testimony of, 70–71
Ellowitz, Morris, and sworn statements, 160
Ellis, Lieutenant Colonel Burton F.: and allegations of duress, 44, 71; cross-examination of Peiper, 91–94; delivery of sworn statements to defense, 42, 46; Everett and, 40, 171, 185, 226; presents charges, 51; sworn statements and, 81
Engel, Gerhard, testimony of, 83
Everett, Mary Campbell, 8, 26, 148
Everett, Mary Louise, 3
Everett, Mary Wooldridge, 9, 29–30, 33, 198, 206, 218
Everett, Willis M., Jr.: African Americans and, 30–31, 207, 219; anti-Semitism of, 53–54, 68, 69, 110, 115, 186, 206, 210, 214, 217, 225–26; Army intelligence, entry into, 12–13; and corruption in Germany, 110–11; death of, 223; Ellis and, 41, 171, 186, 226–27; father and, 5–6; FBI investigation of, 214; Germans and, 34, 36–37, 75, 115, 133–34, 199, 200–203, 211–12, 227; heart attack of, 188; Senator McCarthy and, 196–97, 210; Peiper and, 43, 47, 134–35, 208–9, 212–13, 221, 222; Senate Malmedy investigation, 191–96; social and political outlook of, 10; son and, 8, 9, 29, 218–19; Supreme Court and, 120, 123, 144, 147, 148, 149–51; Kiliaen Townsend and, 26, 29, 76; U.S. occupation forces and, 36–37; Washington and Lee University and, 3–4; wife and, 29–30, 33, 198
Everett, Willis M., Sr., 1, 5–6, 26

Fanton, Dwight, 190
FBI: domestic intelligence during World War II, 15; German espionage and, 19–20; investigation of Everett, 214
Finucane, James, 191
Flanders, Senator Ralph, 215
Flanigan, Francis, 193
Fleps, Georg, 62
Flyers' cases, 42; Everett observes, 37
Forkner, Tom, 19
Forrestal, Secretary of Defense James V., 149; James Davis and, 154
Fort Benning, 19, 22, 205; Everett's discharge at, 116
Fort Jackson, 32
Fort McPherson, 9, 188
Fosdick, Harry Emerson, 30
Frankfurt, Everett's reaction to, 33–34
Freimuth, Arvid: interrogation of, 73; suicide of, 43, 151; sworn statement, 72
Friedrich, Carl, and Malmedy case, 155, 185
Frings, Josef Cardinal, 187

Gammon Theological Seminary: service to, of Willis Everett Sr., 2; service to, of Willis Everett Jr., 9, 219
Geneva Convention, 51, 54, 84, 87, 93, 118, 150, 183; sworn statements and, 80–81
George, Senator Walter F., 154; Everett and, 155
German military units: Sixth Panzer Army, 54, 139; First SS Panzer Division, 117, 125; Fifth SS Panzer Division, 220; 150th Panzer Brigade, 132; Kampfgruppe Peiper, 54, 56, 57, 63, 69, 78, 82, 84–87, 89–90, 96, 98, 117, 162, 166
German prisoners of war, killing of, 118–19, 237–38n. 3
Germany: Everett's image in, 219–20; sympathy for Malmedy prisoners in, 210–11
Gray, Secretary of the Army Gordon, 204–5
Green, General Thomas H., 154
Gregoire, Regina, testimony of, 69–70
Gurney, Senator Chan, 190

Habeas corpus, writ of, Everett's petition for, 148–51
Hague Convention, 51, 54, 118
Hambro, E., 183

Harbaugh, Colonel James, 127, 128, 129, 137, 141, 147, 155, 163; background of, 138; receives trial review, 130; recommendations to Clay, 142

Harrison, Brigadier General William K., and alleged murders in La Gleize, 78

Hartman, William, Fourth Service Command and, 17, 27

Hartrich, Edwin, 120; on Malmedy case, 121–22

Hayes, Major Ellen V., 113

Hayett, Irving, wedding of, 114

Hayett, Sally, view of Everett during Malmedy case, 186

Hennecke, Hans, sworn statement of, 58

High Cost of Vengeance, The (Utley), 215

Hilliard, Sergeant, 107, 114

Himmler, Heinrich, 40, 117; Peiper and, 92, 134

Hitler, Adolf, 54, 81, 117; Peiper's loyalty to, 135

Hitler's Typhoid Marys, Rosenfeld mentioned in, 50

Hoey, Senator Clyde, 189, 190

Hofmann, Joachim, and alleged beatings, 46, 171

Honsfeld, 66, 162; alleged murders at, 54

Howland, Bill, 110, 205

Hubbert, Cecil, 169; Everett's letter to, 127, 128

Huebler, Hans Georg, and alleged beatings, 160

Huebner, Lieutenant General Clarence, 125, 127, 173, 174, 175, 179

Hunt, Senator Lester, 190; and Peiper, 201

International Court of Justice: Everett plans appeal to, 175–76; petition filed and rejected, 181–83

International Military Tribunal, 39

Jackson, Supreme Court Justice Robert, 149, 150, 175; commutation of the Malmedy death sentences, 209; Everett and, 165; Everett's petition to the International Court of Justice, 182

Jaekel, Siegfried, and alleged beatings, 46

Japan, balloon attack on the U.S., 24–25

Jirasek, Friedmar, affidavit of, 162

Jones, Colonel Homer, and Biscari massacre, 119

Jonsten, Anton, affidavit of, 99

Judge Advocate General's Corps, 163

Judge Advocate General's Department, 119, 154

Karan, Dr. Max, and allegations of duress, 194

Kefauver, Senator Estes, 190

Kirk, Grayson, 28, 31

Kirschbaum, Joseph: and alleged beatings, 160; on mock trials, 73

Kleist, Heinrich von, 200

Knopf, Colonel Stacy, 16, 27

Knorr, Dr. Edward, and alleged beatings, 160–61

Koch, Ilse, 167, 168. *See also* Buchenwald, trial

Koessler, Maximilian, and Malmedy trial review, 123–24, 129

Kohlhaas, Michael, Everett compared to, 200–203

Kraemer, Fritz: and alleged orders to kill prisoners, 83; Everett and, 213; Harbaugh and sentence of, 142; recommended as adviser to U.S. Army, 212–13; review of verdict and sentence of, 139; sentence of, 109

Kramm, Kurt, testimony of, 56–57

Kremser, *Obersturmführer*, testimony on actions of, 57

Kuhn, Ed, 206

Ku Klux Klan, Congressman James Davis and, 151–52

La Gleize: alleged murders in, 55, 78, 85, 90, 92–94, 99, 100; *Kampfgruppe* Peiper's escape from, 87

Lakemont, Everett vacation home at, 218

Lamp, made by prisoners for Everett, 209

Landsberg: Malmedy prisoners incarcerated at, 109; medical examinations of prisoners, 194

Langer, Senator William, 189

Lary, Virgil P., testimony of, 59–63

Lawrence, Colonel Charles W., 163

Leer, Eugen, and Everett and, 146, 217

Leiling, Otto: cross-examination of Budik, 57–58; cross-examination of Elias, 70–71; cross-examination of Gregoire, 70; Everett and, 146
Liberty, 10
Ligneauville, alleged murders at, 54
Luce, Henry, 186
Lutre Bois, alleged murders at, 55
Lymphoma, Everett ill with, 222–23

Maertz, Homer, and anti-Semitism, 23
Malmedy massacre, 38; investigation of, 42–43
Manhattan Project, 16
Mauthausen trial, 42, 124, 174; Rosenfeld and, 50
McCarthy, Senator Joseph: Everett and, 196–97, 210, 215; Senate Malmedy investigation and, 190–92, 196–97; Kiliaen Townsend and, 189–90
McCloy, John, 205, 207
McClure, Lieutenant Colonel Donald, 162–63
McCown, Major Harold D.: Everett and, 78–79; Peiper and, 85–86, 88–89, 135; testimony of, 84–88
McNarney, Lieutenant General Joseph, 108, 111, 120, 121; Biscari massacre and, 118; Marcel Boltz and, 10
Mickelwaite, Colonel Claude B., 111, 112, 113, 121, 127, 143; allegations of duress and, 44, 45; Everett and, 35, 42, 104, 137; War Crimes Branch and, 35
Mindzenty, Cardinal Joszef, 182
Mitchell, Margaret, 9
Mixed Parole and Clemency Board, 212, 216
"Mock trials," 74, 138, 157, 161, 172, 178, 183; Administration of Justice Review Board and, 185; Sally Hayett and, 186; Senate Malmedy investigation and, 195
Moore, Bishop Arthur J., 224
Morgenschweiz, Karl, 162
Moscow Declaration, 39, 51
Motzheim, Anton, claims to have been beaten, 43
Mueller, Dr. Benno, 220
Muench, Bishop Aloisius J., 168, 216, 217; anti-Semitism and, 159; Magda Diefenthal and, 159

Murphy, Supreme Court Justice Frank, 148
Mussolini, Benito, 132

Narvid, Captain Benjamin, 41; defense effort, 77; motion for severance, 52
Nashville Banner, 19
National Council for Prevention of War, 191, 210
National Defense Act of 1920, 7
National Negro Congress, 22
Negro Worker, 24
Neuhäusler, Bishop Johannes, 156, 157, 164, 187
Neumann, Franz, 28
Neve, Gustav, alleged beatings and, 46
New Leader, 180
New Yorker, 206
New York Times, 120, 121, 173, 216
Nuremberg Trial: German public support for, 156; legal novelties of, 50

Patton, General George S., and Biscari massacre, 118
Pearson, Drew, 215; and McCarthy, 210
Peiper, Jochen (Joachim): Battle of the Bulge and, 83; death of, 225; death sentence, 109; death sentence commuted, 208; death sentence confirmed by Clay, 188; employed by Porsche, 221, 225; employed by Volkswagen, 225; fellow defendants and, 98; Everett and, 43, 47, 134, 200–202, 208–9, 212–13, 220, 222; Himmler and, 92, 134; Hitler and, 135; "Jochen" or "Joachim," 236n. 26; La Gleize and, 92–94; Landsberg and, 201, 217; last years of, 225; McCown and, 84, 85–86, 88–89, 135; Perl and, 89–90, 100; requests death by firing squad, 106; sentence sustained, 139, 140; sworn statement of, 58; testimony of, 89–95; Leroy Vogel and, 88; Zuffenhausen confinement, 92, 100
Peiper, Sigurd, 109, 136, 146, 147, 201, 221, 222
Perl, Lieutenant William, 194, 196, 204, 211; alleged beatings and, 97, 194; Freimuth and, 72–73; Peiper and, 89–91, 100
Petit Thiers, alleged murder at, 55, 139

Philadelphia Evening Bulletin, 166
Piedmont Driving Club, 8
Plitt, Edwin, and parole of Malmedy prisoners, 216–17
Poetschke, Werner, 56, 64
Pohl, Oswald, 211
Porsche Club of America, 221
Post Hostilities School, Everett assigned to, 27
Presbyterian Church: death of Everett, 224; Everett and, 144; Willis Everett Sr. Moderator of General Assembly, 2;
Priess, Hermann, sentence of, 109
Prisoners of war, killing of in World War II, 118–19
Progressive, 180, 191

Rankin, Congressman John, speech to House of Representatives, 152–53
Rau, Dr., 52
Raymond, Colonel John M., and Malmedy trial review, 155, 184, 185
Reedy, Tom: Everett and, 121, 129, 138, 160; Rosenfeld and, 131
Reid, Judge Charles S., 128
Reiser, Rolf, affidavit of, 162
Republican Party, Everett and, 224
Revue, 219
Reynolds, Richard, and review of Malmedy trial, 130
Rietz, Werner, Everett's impact on Germany and, 211–12
Rosenfeld, Colonel Abraham H., 57, 58, 66, 69, 94–95, 193; career of, 50; Everett and, 131; Everett's anti-Semitism, 53–54, 88; *Hitler's Typhoid Marys,* 50; McCown and, 86; Peiper and, 131; ruling on court's jurisdiction, 52; ruling on severance, 53; Senate Malmedy investigation and, 196; Skorzeny trial, 131–32; sworn statements, 81
Royall, Secretary of the Army Kenneth, 150, 163, 186, 187, 190, 204; Senator George and, 154; stay of execution, 154
Rulien, Miles, 98
Russell, Senator Richard, 191

Schallermair, George, 208
Schmidt, Hans, 208
Schoenbach, Dr. Karl H., 220

Schoeningh, Dr. Franz Josef, assessment of Everett, 199–200
Schwäbisch Hall: alleged beatings in, 43, 160–61; death of Freimuth in, 72; Everett ordered to, 38, 40; Sally Hayett and, 186; hoods used in, 72; Peiper's confinement in, 92; prison hospital at, 187; Senate Malmedy investigation and, 195
Senate, U.S., 168; Malmedy investigation and, 189, 190, 191–96
Severance: motion for, 52; Senate Malmedy investigation and, 195–96
Sholar, William, and Porsche Club of America, 221
Shumacker, Captain Raphael: Budik and, 58; conspiracy theory, 52–53; Kefauver and, 190; summation of prosecution case, 100–101
Simpson, Judge Gordon: commutation of death sentences, 209; Everett and, 168–69
Simpson Commission, 163, 164, 172, 173, 179, 184, 191, 205; report of, 177–78
Skorzeny trial, 131–32
Slaton, Governor John, 148
Sloan, Herbert K., on conditions at Schwäbisch Hall, 194
Smith, Dr. Carter, 188, 191, 222
Society for the Prevention of World War III, 190
Soldatensender Calais, 83
Southwestern Theological Seminary, 169
Sprenger, Axel, and alleged beatings, 46, 171
Stars and Stripes, 121, 172
State Department, U.S., 205, 212
Stavelot, alleged murders at, 55
Stegle, "Johnie," murder of, 66
Stengel, Hans, 65, 114
Stern, Curt, 164
Stitt, David, 169
St. Louis Globe-Democrat, 119
Stoumont, alleged murders at, 55
Straight, Lieutenant Colonel Clio: Administration of Justice Review Board, 184; Denson's trial review, 124; duress and, 44; Everett and, 77–78; Koessler's trial review, 124; trial reviews and, 127, 130–31, 141
Strasse, Die, 211

Strong, Herbert, 53, 57; cross-examines witness, 68; Everett and, 216; Everett's anti-Semitism, 69; habeas corpus petition, 151; key member of Everett's staff, 42, 47; Senate Malmedy investigation, 193, 194

St. Simons Island, 3, 29

Süddeutsche Zeitung, story on Everett in, 200

Sulgrave Club, 210

Supreme Court, U.S., 148, 165, 173; Everett's appeal to, 120, 144; Everett's petition to, 169, 170, 175, 180, 181, 184, 191, 192, 206

Sutherland, William A., 148

Sutton, Granger, 77, 194

Taylor, General Maxwell, and killing of prisoners, 119

Taylor, Brigadier General Telford, and Judge Wennerstrum, 144

Teil, Kurt, testifies on Perl and Thon, 194

Thon, Harry, 172, 194, 204

Time, 165, 188, 205; article on Malmedy in, 179–80

Toland, John, Everett and, 219

Townsend, Kiliaen: Everett and, 76; Everett's death, 224; McCarthy and, 189; marriage to Mary Campbell Everett, 26

Trois Ponts, 70, 91

Truman, President Harry S, 149, 181, 186

Tuttle, Judge Elbert P., 76

Tydings, Senator Millard, 190

United Nations General Assembly, 182

United Nations Relief and Rehabilitation Administration, and Everett's anti-Semitism, 110

U.S. Army Service Commands (initially "Corps Areas"): First, 20, 24; Third, 20; Fourth, 6, 12–14, 16, 17–19, 25, 27; Sixth, 20, 23; Eighth, 16, 23

U.S. Army units: Third Army, 49; Seventh Army, 118–19; Thirtieth Infantry Division, 78; Forty-fifth Infantry Division, 40, 118; 101st Airborne Division, 119; 1800th Engineer General Service Battalion, 17–19; 7708 War Crimes Group, 113, 116, 117, 131, 172, 194

USFET (U.S. Forces, European Theater): Everett's reaction to, 143; Frankfurt headquarters of, 33;

Utley, Freda, and Everett, 215

van Horn, Brigadier General R. O., 12

van Roden, Judge Leroy, 177, 186, 191, 210; Everett and, 163–64, 165, 166, 209; article in *The Progressive*, 180–81, 242n. 7

Verg, Eric, 211

Veterans of Foreign Wars, 216

Vinson, Congressman and Mrs. Carl, sympathy note of, 224–25

Vinson, U.S. Supreme Court Chief Justice Fred M., 149

Vogel, Captain Leroy, interrogation of Peiper, 88

Volkswagen, and Peiper, 225

Volunteer Ordnance Works, 25

Voorhees, Assistant Secretary of the Army Tracy, 187

Wahler, Lieutenant Wilbert J., 40, 41, 53, 143, 151, 178, 179, 191, 193; cross-examination of Dobyns, 64; and defense effort, 77; and Everett, 162; jurisdiction of court, 51

Walker, DeLoss, 10

Wallens, "Red," 138

Walters, Frank, 45, 65

Wanne, alleged murders at, 55, 170

War Crimes Branch, 41, 125, 127, 128, 136, 147, 154, 169; Ellis assigned to, 40; allegations of duress, 44; Col. Straight and, 131

War Crimes Modification Board, 207

War crimes trials program, 39

Washington, Booker T., 24

Washington, George (Assistant Solicitor General), 181–82

Washington and Lee University, 165, 207; Everett's career at, 3–5

Washington Seminary, 3

Wennerstrum, Judge Charles F., 163, 164, 175–76, 180, 183, 186, 206; attacks war crimes trials, 143–44; commutation of Malmedy death sentences, 209

Werbomont, 84

West, Sergeant Horace T., and Biscari trial, 166

Westernhagen, Hein von, 91
White, H. Beatty, 145
Whiting, Charles, 156, 164, 178, 179, 182, 186; Everett and, 158; Gurney and, 190
Wilson, Captain Lloyd A., 161
Wooldridge, Mary, Everett married to, 3

Yamashita, Tomoyuki, 103, 148
Young, Colonel Edward H., 128, 147

Ziemmsen, Dietrich, 125–26
Zuffenhausen, Peiper imprisoned at, 89, 100

About the Author

JAMES WEINGARTNER is Professor of History at Southern Illinois University and author of *Crossroads of Death* and *Hitler's Guard*.